Men who are good for you

and men who are bad

Men who are good for you

and men who are bad

LEARNING TO TELL THE DIFFERENCE

Susanna Hoffman, Ph.D.

1⊖ Ten Speed Press

1©
TEN SPEED PRESS
Post Office Box 7123
Berkeley, California 94707

First Printing, 1987

Cover, book design and typography by
Fifth Street Design, Berkeley, California

Library of Congress Cataloging-in-Publication Data

Hoffman, Susanna M.
  Men Who Are Good for You and Men Who Are Bad

  Rev., updated ed. of The Classified Man. c1980.
  1. Men–Physiology.   2 Mate selection.
I. Hoffman, Sussannah M. Classified Man.   II. Title.
HQ1090.H63 1987   646.7'7   87-7082
ISBN 0-89815-212-7

Manufactured in the United States of America

2 3 4 5 – 91 90 89 88

For
Florence, Deborah, Gabriella, Elaine,
Rebekah, Natalie, Victoria, Lisa,
Marida, May, Nancy P., Barbara,
Gail, Cielo, Sandy, Margaret, Gerta,
Etta, Gale, Nancy S., Susan,
Marti, Eleanor,
and all the others too numerous to mention
❧

Acknowledgments

For the second version of this book I would again like to thank Milton Stern, Nancy Podbielniak, Robert Mandel, William Chambers, Victoria and Rick Wise, Karin and Tim Knowles, Gail Stempler and Stuart Lake, Robbie Greenberg and Lisa Rich, J. David Wyles, and Richard Cowan. I would also like to thank Toby Rafelson whom, regretfully, I forgot to thank before, and to thank again all the many women I watched, talked to, or interviewed, and all the men who asked, and still ask, "Which kind of man am I?"

In addition, I would also like to express my gratitude to Drs. Marida Hollos and Nancy Sheper-Hughes and my other anthropologist colleagues and friends, D. Michael Hughes, Dr. Tessa Warschaw, Susan Mitchell, Martha Casselman, Gale Hayman, my "L.A." agent and friend Bernie Weintraub, Phil Wood, Patti Breitman, and Kim Knutson, along with all the other people at Ten Speed Press.

As before, I can never completely express how grateful I am to Abe and Florence Hoffman, Levi, Deborah, Lee, Rebekah and Mark Bendele, Elaine Fahlstrom, and especially Jesse and Gabriella Aratow who continue to sacrifice the most so that I can write. Added to them, there is one more special person to thank, Stephen Hettenbach, without whose care, comfort, and help life would be a lot more difficult and a lot less wonderful.

Contents

Here's to women, all women,
God's gift, so divine,
Who blossom every month
And bear every nine.
The only little creature,
This side of Hell,
Who can get juice from a nut
Without cracking the shell.

— A Sunday School Teacher
in Estes Park, Colorado

Learning To Tell The Difference
Between Good Men and Bad

Men.

A man may seem wonderful at first, only to turn into a criticizing woman-hater once a woman is truly committed to him. Other times a man who comes on with a rush of loving care only means to spend a quick six weeks enjoying a woman's companionship and body. He never intends a further commitment. Other men choose particular women to control them. Others charm a woman with a portrait of the exciting life they have to offer, obscuring how they will always think they are more important. Perhaps under his beguiling smile a man really wants support, financial and otherwise. He remains a perpetual child, or he turns a woman into an angry shrew with his relentless, saccharine kindness.

Other times a man who seems wonderful, turns out wonderful. He's a loving caretaker who stays forever. He shares with you on every level. Maybe he has a great devotion to something other than you, his work or a hobby, but beyond it, he's an adoring, romantic, and committed partner.

The trouble is, how do we tell?

How do we know when we have allied ourselves with a caring supporter, or with a man so driven for power and achievement he will always ignore us? How can we tell when we are with a man who will constantly endanger himself and maybe us, or who will perpetually father us? What are the early signs of a man who hates women or one who respects them? Should we leave a man who drains our energy with his compelling intensity? Or should we stay?

I believe there are ways a woman can tell. We can learn to decipher the difference between a man who is good for us and a man who is bad. We can identify relationships that will work and those that will prove detrimental. There are even clues to how we attract the men who choose us and how we play into the unions we form.

That's what *Men Who Are Good For You and Men Who Are Bad* is all about. This is a book about men for women. In it my intention is to give women the information and tools they need to learn about the different kinds of men and what alliances with those men are like.

In *Men Who Are Good For You and Men Who Are Bad* I describe many sorts of men, and tell how relationships with those men proceed. I talk about men we love and shouldn't, men we should love and often don't, and I explain why. I detail alliances that blossom and those that go sour, those that enrich and those that might even become physically harmful.

In order to be a truly helpful learning device, one that each of you can put into effect in your life, this book is specific. It outlines the types of men in detail. It describes the early warning signs a man gives off about his character. It tells what his behavior will be like, what clothes he might wear, what car he might drive, what his motivations are. It details how he behaves in bed, uses money, and treats his relatives. It goes into what his assets are and why a woman might want him or like him, along with his drawbacks.

Having described the man, the book goes on to chart how a relationship with that kind of man generally progresses. It details the stages the relationship goes through, the telltale signs of trouble, the signals when things are going well or badly. It also discusses – right away – whether a man is likely to change or not. It gives a summary of what a woman's chances are in the relationship, outlining options and giving advice on whether she should stay with that type of man or not. Most importantly it outlines the kind of women different men go for, so each of us can begin to look at how, wittingly or not, we might attract certain kinds of men and encourage certain kinds of relationships.

This book can help at any stage of a relationship. It offers aid for a woman who is looking for a union. It helps women who are already in a union. And – for most of us – it also gives reassurance and understanding about what happened with a man or in a relationship we already experienced.

I wrote this book for several reasons. The first was to provide women with knowledge. Actually, it isn't so much knowledge as acumen; quickness and accuracy of judgment, keenness of insight. As a social scientist, adviser, and friend to many women, and a woman myself, I realized that far, far too often we go into our unions blindly. For whatever reason, we don't use acumen. We don't decipher the signs men give off about their nature or what they will be like as partners. Yet *there are signs,* and with more knowledge of those signs clearly at hand, we can better decide what kind of man we want, what kind is best for us and whether a relationship is one we care to stay in. We can tell when a relationship we thought would unfold happily turns into something different. We can tell when a man reveals himself to be something other than what we expected.

This gives us options. Choice comes into play. Knowing the possible outcomes, the chances for changes, we can weight them. We can decide whether an alliance is "worth it." We can choose to remain or not. And, if we decide to stay with particular men or relationships despite their drawbacks, we aren't surprised. We don't have to mourn the decisions we made. We also get confirmation that we are not the only ones who encounter certain kinds of men, or endure certain kinds of unions. There are others like us.

I wrote this book also to give us ballast. Lately women have found themselves on the receiving end of a great deal of advice. We have been chastised for loving too much, warned about men who hate us, but whom we still love, and told we are fools in our choices. That all may well be true. Absolutely I believe that each of the books telling us these things is beneficial. But the recent books of advice also tend to perpetuate certain fallacies. They fuel the notion long foist upon women and that women too often accept, that we are the erring parties. Perhaps they do so unconsciously and with the best intentions, but they do so anyway. If a choice is bad, we made it. If anything goes amiss in our romances, it is our fault. We allowed it, didn't see it, or it happened because we have a problem. These books also charge us to "correct" the situation. We alone, once again, are to take on the role of "love" fixers, largely by "fixing" ourselves.

I believe, as Robin Norell so aptly pointed out, that women *can* love too much and that it is a destructive syndrome. I also agree with Susan Forman that some men hate women and many women love them anyway. I admit that many times our choices in men are foolish. Yet none of these works clarifies the point that sometimes we don't choose men, *they choose us*. We don't necessarily pick the types of men we meet or are with; we are often on the receiving end. Sometimes men overwhelm or pressure us into relationships with them. We also do not love men "too much" in a vacuum, some of them *compel* us to love them that way. Many men know exactly how to hold a woman in an emotional vortex and succeed very well. Nor can we necessarily alter our choices in men or unions, especially merely by changing ourselves. We often don't have the opportunity. Moreover, we make some of our choices on *purpose*, knowing full well the problems we are getting into, and are content with them.

The recent books also do not tell us all we need to know. They don't tell us the early warning signals of a man who hates us or a man who would be a foolish choice. They don't describe how the men act and what they do. They also clump the men and problems together. There are, for example, several types of men who hate women, not just one. Also some men who aren't woman haters still aren't the best men for us. On the surface some men are very supportive mates, but furtively manipulate us for the next forty years. Others crush us under the burden of their irresponsibility, or choose us because we are young, or passive, or foreign, so that they can dominate.

Nor do the books chart the progress of relationships so we can know when we are in a bad one. They don't tell us the signals in a courtship that indicate that trouble lies ahead. They don't describe turning points, nor what to do when those points appear. Without a doubt these books have helped us greatly. They analyze. They clarify. But they aren't pragmatic guides. They are good books, very good. But we need more.

I believe also that the recent rash of advice aimed at women perpetuates yet another notion that we have long carried: that to have a good union a woman must be perfect. She must choose perfectly, and after choosing, she must handle everything absolutely right. She must, furthermore, constantly improve. Much of the advice also implies that every woman wants a man. Not only a man, but a permanent, life-long alliance with one. And that is not so.

Men Who Are Good For You and Men Who Are Bad describes how a woman fits into the relationship she forms. It tells what she might be doing to attract a bad situation, compound it, or beckon repetition in her relationships. Such insights aid us tremendously. We want and need them. But mostly this book *focuses on men*. I may be wrong, but I think we need to know about men as much as about ourselves. We need to know which men are harmful to a woman, and which ones are good. In addition we need to know that not all men – even good ones – suit all women. The best relationships don't go completely smoothly. And, we should consider enjoying some men only for a short while, not forever.

This book results not only from my perceptions as a woman, but also from my work as an anthropologist. As an anthro-pologist I am trained to see and sort out people's cultural behavior. The analysis of the types of men involved here, in fact, derives from the anthropological theory that there are patterns to the behavior of people in any culture. The patterns in a culture aren't many. They are limited. Neither are they rare. Quite the opposite. Many people within a society learn and share the same patterns. People reflect their cultural patterns in many ways. They show them in their use of time and space, in adornment and actions, even in the "plot" they might follow in life. An anthropologist, then, looks at "group" personality, rather than individual personality. And that is what I have done here. I have analyzed syndromes shared by many men. The analysis is also based on that kind of scientific explanation that involves identification – that is, learning what something is – rather than deciphering how it got that way. Knowing what something is, after all, is a primary step to learning what caused it's formation.

Identification alone can also be enlightening. From knowing what something is, you can predict its likely traits. You can tell how something will act, calculate what it will do, and determine whether it might change.

I have studied gender and behavior in our society for many years, written books and articles and made films of the subject. The patterns of men I write about here are those of today's men. They won't be exactly the same patterns as those of men in the past, but they won't be all that different either. They will quite probably also be with us for at least a while into the future. As women we will meet the men depicted in this book in many ways. Mostly I have structured the book to deal with romantic alliances – dating, courtship, unions – since that is usually women's primary concern. But the men described will also be our bosses, employees, colleagues, politicians. They will be among the lawyers, bankers, salespeople, artists, craftspeople, friends, and enemies we deal with daily.

Of course, I also write from experience. As a woman who made her way through graduate school alone, married, had children, divorced, and became single again, I have had my share of relationships. I know two or three of the types of men from my own involvements with them. Others I know as associates and friends. Some I recognize as relatives, officials, students, and the mates of friends. I made my share of romantic mistakes. Almost every woman of our times has. The "relationship business" has not been easy for us. Rarely nowadays do we find a perfect mate and union the first time around. We go with more men and have more complex lives than any generation before us. We don't necessarily get our partnerships right even the second or third time. Many of us have numerous broken unions behind us. Others have made only a single error, but one that has lasted twenty to thirty years. On the other hand, some of us have found relationships in which we thrived quickly, or relationships that were formed after only a few missteps. We should learn about those as well.

This book is for the wary but generous-spirited woman, who *likes* men. It is written from the point of view of women who want one of those "things" loosely termed a "relationship with a man." The relationship may be short or long, temporary or permanent, but I do not deal with anonymous "one night stands." I do not condemn those, but I find that most women want more. They want an interaction, a friendship, a pairing. Most women are, in fact, looking for something lasting, and I try to give the odds for that with each type of man. I am also writing for those women who, while they don't fall into bed with a man at first meeting, believe sex comes before a full commitment. Lovemaking is part of courtship and the act of sex tells something about what a man is like, what a union will be like, and how valuable it will be to have. How a man uses money, treats his family, deals with the issue of children and companionship also tell. I write for women who want to think highly of themselves and want to treat themselves well.

Obviously every man is a complex individual, and no man will exactly fit any of the portraits. So, while the book gives many specifics, no man is going to match every one. You may know, for example, a Short Affair and Quick Escape Artist whose last affair lasted months, not weeks. You may meet a Father Knows Best who is generous with money, not tight. Also be aware that few men are precisely one kind of man. Most overlap several types. They bear a combination of traits, although one set usually predominates. I note the more likely overlappings at the end of each chapter, but there may be others. Some men also change. With stage of life, age, monetary success, or failure, they shift from one sort of man to another. A Sugar Pie Honey, for instance, often turns into a Secret Manipulator. A Man Who Would Be Mogul sometimes becomes a Woman Hater or Baby Chaser. Others never change at all. I have listed the more common changes.

Occasionally I might seem to imply that the men I describe are conscious of and purposeful about their actions toward women. This may be so sometimes, but not usually. Mostly I am writing about deeply learned and unconscious patterns of behavior. The men who show these patterns may well regret their actions as much as the women they know. The book is not at all against men! On the contrary, it is a book for women who are for and are concerned about men. It is for women who believe men generally want the same thing we want, but who realize different sorts of male and female personalities exist, some not as suited for each of us as others. So while I mean to be accurate in my descriptions I never mean to be acrimonious. And although I do not describe the different types of women for men, nor the pain and despair men sometimes feel, I very much empathize with men. My hope is to improve everyone's relationships – men's and women's alike. Clearly a book such as this could be written about women. Maybe one day I will write it.

This book is updated and revised from an earlier version that was out before we recognized women haters and bad choices as much as we do now. I have tried to write it, then as now, with a good deal of humor. Much of the advice aimed at helping women treats the whole matter of our mistakes and problems with men so *soberly*. Yes, our relationships with men can be painful. True, changing our own patterns and unions takes a lot of work. Often we need professional help. But it's not all doom and gloom. Sometimes laughter gives us some distance. It cuts through the hurt and helps us see ourselves objectively. It can help us reassure ourselves that while we got ourselves in a pickle, we are not alone and not entirely to blame. Whatever experiences we have, even if they wind up involving many years, three kids, two dogs, and financial ruin, are merely experiences, often common ones. We can keep going, especially if we can look at, laugh at, and learn from our foibles.

The chapters in this book are organized so they begin with men who are the worst for a woman. They go on to men who are somewhat better, arriving finally at those who are the best. Those who constitute the worst for women are a mixed group. Some of them are physically harmful, others controlling. Some demean women, others are behaviorally deceitful. Still, we might choose to be with one of these men for a number of reasons. A Short Affair and Quick Escape Artist, for example, can be fine for those of us who don't desire lengthy unions. Even a Disaster Broker or Idle Lord might be fine for an adventurous stage. However, some of the men are downright dangerous, and I recommend all women definitely avoid them. Of those men who are better for us, through not perhaps the best, some could still be highly detrimental to specific women. For instance, The Father Knows Best and The Kid would be devastating men for me. Generally, though, the men closer to the end and the "best" group, have more potential for change. Each of the three best types offers a wonderful relationship. Still, they might not be right for every one of us. Some of us would wither with a Loving Traditional Man, but flourish with a Many-Faceted Man, or vice versa. Others would find both the Traditional and Many-Faceted Man too involving and would prefer the more distant caring of a Loving Limited Partner.

True, *Men Who Are Good For You and Men Who Are Bad* depicts only three types of men who are the very best for women, while it outlines far more types of men who are bad. There are two reasons for this. In the first place, there simply are more types of men who are bad for us. The other reason is that the most caring men and those who form the best unions with us really only fall into three types. It seems the basic elements of love and good treatment, respect and value, don't vary all that much. Mistreatment, meanwhile, can take many forms. Even those three "good ones" are closely related to one another and often overlap.

It is important to read the whole book. The men outlined are very different from one another. Many options are presented. Skip around to check out the men you recognize most, if you want. But come back. The men you don't recognize yet may show up later in your life. They may appear as your brother, your baker, your sister's husband, or your next date. You will still have a relationship with them and they will treat you and other women the same way, whether you are their lover or their client. Also, don't get depressed if the book seems heavily weighted toward men who are less than wonderful. Skip ahead to some of the better ones, but come back. You will learn the most about men, relationships, and yourself if you read the entire book, especially in order.

There is a lot to learn. How unions proceed, where we fit in, and what the signs are of a detrimental pairing are complex matters. Once you have the information, I don't promise that you will never make another mistake. I do promise that you will know more about what you are doing. You will be able to shun the bad steps if you want. You will be more aware of what's right for you. You will have more freedom.

When you learn the difference between men who are good for you and men who are bad, you still may not make the right choice or the right decision about a union. You may even make the wrong one *on purpose.* But at least you will know the consequences and be prepared. You could well make the very best decision – about a relationship, about a man, and about yourself. ❦

The Short Affair and Quick Escape Artist

The Man Who Has a Thousand Walls and a Million Reasons Why "It Will Never Work"

The first kind of man I describe is one women meet a lot nowadays. He's become very common. I call him the Short Affair and Quick Escape Artist. To be ready for him, go to the blackboard and write "Hello. Good-bye." one hundred times. That's what you'll be saying when you meet the Short Affair and Quick Escape Artist, "Hello. Good-bye."

Magicians practice sleight of hand, but the Escape Artist practices sleight of relationships. He's a master of disappearance, a king of escape. One day he's around, full of life, and you two seem to have something going. Next day he's nowhere in sight, and your something isn't going anywhere any more. All that's left is a puff of smoke in your bedroom.

If he seems so available when you meet him, it's because he is. His attachments don't last long enough to keep him out of circulation long. He's available all right, but he's not for the keeping. You can have him on thirty-day loan, then you must return him.

Unfortunately, the Escape Artist tends to head exactly for the woman who doesn't need him at the moment. If you're temporarily a little shaky on your pegs, alone and lonely of late, a little too detached in an isolated job or journey, recovering from wounds or perhaps nervously, maybe bleakly, looking to settle down, that's when the Escape Artist finds you. Women who need exactly what he hasn't got to give – namely permanence and stability – appeal to him. They give him a built-in reason for getting out. You'll probably meet a dozen Short Affair and Quick Escape Artists while trying to get over a deep, defunct union with someone else.

Story

I've watched my former student Sally fall many times for the Short Affair and Quick Escape Artist. One after another, it was always the same song, just a different verse.

Sally came from a small, self-contained, loving family. But for whatever reason, she had never felt very popular or special. Her one long relationship hadn't worked out. She had good friends and all, but she was a bit of a loner. Sally got tired of her small bed, her alienating job, and her solitary dinners. She was anxious to stop being Single Sally.

As a television producer, she was set apart by her work. She met a lot of people at home and on the road who wanted something from her – her stamp of approval. When she started to go out with Patrick, one of the footloose men she met, a repetitive refrain seemed to haunt her. Right away the man treated Sally as if she were the greatest discovery of his life. He really *liked* her, was attracted by her, enamored of her. In no time he moved in. He shelved his razor in her bathroom, hung shirts in her closet, stocked her larder with his favorite canned chili.

Every now and then he'd mention some drawback. Soon he would have to get back to work. Or he hadn't quite recovered from some woman in the past. Or he really wasn't the domestic sort (though he certainly seemed to be). Over at his digs, a strangely large number of women telephoned him. He was very friendly to them all. He talked about their problems and jobs, occasionally took one to dinner. And still Sally's head was spinning. Patrick was warm and affectionate, concerned and considerate. His lovemaking was stupendous, though he took a very long time and didn't always climax.

Then, before you could say Patrick Robinson, he panicked. After all, a woman might make him eat meals at normal hours, borrow his undershirts, or (God forbid) expect to see him on Sunday. A symphony of excuses poured forth. He said he couldn't write if he made love. His future was too tenuous for an involvement. He was busy. He was sick. He had company. His cat had leukemia. A strange black void just ate up all his finances. While building a mighty fence of unbreakable appointments and insoluble worries, he removed himself part by part. Out went his dandruff shampoo and his bottle of barbecue sauce. He brushed it off on Sally, saying she was *too dependent* on him or *too desperate* for attention.

Patrick Robinson rode off into the sunset before she'd even learned his middle name. But he had left a calling card with his telephone number. Now she was one of the women who dialed it. He would talk to her from afar like an old friend. When she had a crisis, he would take her to lunch.

That's the Short Affair and Quick Escape Artist. He appears on the scene as an unexpected *is* and immediately turns into a *was*, in and out the door before you can bake a cake. One part of him wants a woman body and soul, but another part of him is truly terrified. At some time someone told him that women are an encumbrance, not a joy. And it really sank in. Now, despite all contrary evidence and maybe even despite his desires, he views every fine experience with the female sex as an enticement to disaster.

He has a saving grace: the Short Affair and Quick Escape Artist is not hard to recognize. He shows himself in many ways; in fact, he almost *always* tells you who he is. The trouble you can get into is not believing him. Then you can end up playing Mother Hubbard to his cupboard, crying when the goodies are no longer there.

How Can You Identify This Kind of Man?

Prepare to meet the Short Affair and Quick Escape Artist a lot. He holds a very popular spot among men. There are legions of him out there.

Because he's so common he displays a wider variety of surface traits, styles of dress and money habits than most other kinds of men. Still, all Escape Artists exhibit certain giveaway signs.

All Escape Artists have a way of coming on and pulling back at the same time. They have a nervous edge about them. The Escape Artist also likes to do just about everything slightly out of kilter or the opposite of everyone else. He starts work at an off time and goes in late. He eats odd foods or half meals. He's just a touch out of sync, enough to grind gears with normality and make sure no one – including you – can quite coordinate with him.

He holds back. Even in bed.

Often the Escape Artist had an early marriage, or at least a "big" love. But it was one with troubles in it from the start. It was one that was oddball, one that was fumbled from the word go, one from which, after he played defensive tackle for a goodly while, he escaped to the locker room. His escapades during or just after this early bond led him to find out exactly how many women he could meet and bed. His early union also now provides him with his best out: *he's tried permanent pairing and it didn't work.* He's afraid to try again.

When you meet him, however, he seems to burst into your life all eager for love. Instantly, though, if you listen carefully, he starts to tell you all the reasons it could never be. In fact, he assembles a veritable gauntlet of impediments.

To wit, the Escape Artist is always just about to go broke, so he says. He has always not yet gotten over somebody else. He has always discovered he wasn't cut out for marriage – "Some people aren't, you know, and I'm one of them."

Clearly he's afraid that by getting involved with a woman he will lose control. But it's not just with women he feels he will lose his hold on life. He fears it in general. He has trouble letting go. He's wary at dinners and parties. He thinks he doesn't fit in. He's possessed by worry of the future. The money's running out, he says. How will he survive? He can't get involved until things are secure. It keeps him from living in the present. He's always concerned about "What's next" and "Where everything will lead."

Outer Signs

Take the Escape Artist's dressing habits. He appears in many different modes, but he always wears a combination of chic or up-to-date along with old-fashioned or peculiar. Somehow his coolest clothes come out looking straight. His shirts are unbuttoned at the top, but not enough. He got a pair of pleated pants, but not until everyone else had moved back to jeans. He wears jogging jackets with dress pants, sneakers with virtually everything. He has cowlicks.

For some reason, Escape Artists are highly concerned with their feet. They will *only* wear doeskin Reeboks. Or they own an enormous collection of shoes, all acquired in the pursuit of comfort, but wear only two pair of them. The rest were mistakes. The arches wanted to move but, typical of the Escape Artists' simultaneous push forward-pull back, the toes said no.

Like his clothes, a Short Affair and Quick Escape Artist's manners and vocabulary allow him enough trendiness to interact smoothly, yet he is never quite completely with it. He understands, but does not use, the latest slang. He always manages to be sort of with it and sort of not.

Even his car is a strange combination of flash and reserve, economy and bravado. You might find him driving a gold...Volkswagen (not a Porsche), or the biggest...Nissan (not Cadillac).

When doing business, he uses normal hours. But in private, he returns to counterclockwise. He eats at odd hours or not at all. He gets down to work every day about the time everyone else wants to party. Although it's eleven p.m., he can't come out. He just started working. You call in the morning, and he's taking a nap. He knows all the food stands in his neighborhood that will give him Bar-B-Qued ribs (no salad or veggie) at 4 p.m. or 4 a.m. He may drink, but more likely he "almost" drinks. His favorite cocktail might be a Virgin Mary, or he might hang on the edge with just wine or beer. One glass is enough to make him loopy.

He lives just far enough out of the mainstream to be awkward. He likes oddball places and neighborhoods. He hides out where it's just a little hard to get to, and to where he can retreat. Home is usually an apartment – he might work as well as live there. If he owns a house, it's likely he leases it out and rents a less encumbered space for himself. His abode is the essence of bachelor style, very male and a bit Spartan. It generally combines tasteful bits with lots of blank space. He has some prints that are almost, but not *quite*, erotic, a big couch (well used), a small collection of favorite records that he plays over and over again. His refrigerator is empty, except, perhaps, for a six-pack of Lite Beer. When he does cook his specialty is broiled chicken.

Like the Man Who Would Be Mogul, the Escape Artist tends to be strongly involved in his career. Like Mr. Genius, his career probably involves some artistry or creativity, and almost certainly autonomy. His labor, especially when he's his own boss, offers a flexible blockade: he can always manage to have unfinished business, strive for the next goal, or achieve the proper income before he can consider a union. Only then can he risk involvement, he tells himself and you.

The Escape Artist controls his life extremely well. For each barricade you conquer, another takes its place. He's always keeping track of when to bail out. But under the surface command, he doesn't have all that much control. While he instructs his mind to take care of things and hopes his body will follow suit, often it does not. He's frequently a little too skinny or too fat. He catches colds, a handy way to get out of things. He overreacts to drugs, drink, and even coffee, or he thinks he overreacts. He doesn't exercise with any regularity (or his feet or back won't let him). His diet is inconsistent.

He shows you in no time, and proves, that he is better off alone, that you are better off without him. It doesn't matter how magnetic your affair was at first.

Sex Signals

Still, there is one tremendous advantage (which can give you quite a problem) with the Escape Artist. He is a very sensual man.

A glutton for tactile pleasure, he loves to be stroked, petted, rubbed, and sucked. He really, really likes sex. Of course, he cleverly turns this into another excuse. He says he loves sex too much to confine himself to one woman.

The Escape Artist is a man in whom you find thrilling and delightful discoveries. He loves to hug and cuddle. He likes having done to him exactly what you like having done to you. You can explore his hidden places and turn all his daring moves back on him and it works. He loves to go down and be gone down on. He is usually a very good and versatile lover. After all, he's learned from lots of partners.

But it's often in bed that you get the first sign of his inability to give way. The Escape Artist tends to have trouble climaxing, especially at first. Willing or not, he holds back. Even when comfortable, he can take so long to come that the event becomes overly lengthy, something he sometimes rightly, and sometimes wrongly, considers to his advantage.

To make things easier, he adds the element of fantasy. Often the Escape Artist indulges in more sexual imagination than sex. The Short Affair and Quick Escape Artist spends more time dreaming up lurid escapades than almost any other man. Just the sight of a woman on the street can touch off scenes of amorous adventure, like a satyric Walter Mitty. But he doesn't necessarily play out these fantasies just in his head. He brings in a helping hand – his own. He loves to masturbate. When your most constant partner lives at the end of your arm, it helps to circumvent permanent pairing with a woman.

The Escape Artist throws himself into mutually satisfying sex with you during that first flurry. But no matter how exciting he may find his sensual experiences with you, at a certain point he begins to fear your blossoming affection. His assumption that you are a living, walking millstone takes control. He thinks maybe you have fallen too hard for him (a serious threat). Or he has fallen too hard for you (a more serious threat). It doesn't matter *what* you think. He retreats to his castle and pulls up the drawbridge.

He likes women. There is no denying that. He picks them with the care of someone selecting from an assortment of Godiva chocolates, but he goes through them as if they were M&M's. To ensure his freedom, the Escape Artist picks on slightly desperate and insecure women who want exactly those things that threaten him: a desire for intimacy and a hope for lasting togetherness. While he prefers women with unique jobs and interesting lives, he seems to have an uncanny ability to select isolated wallflowers with style, rather than the thoroughly autonomous. Such women are more vulnerable to his short-term interests. He avoids women who don't need what he doesn't have to give, protecting himself from ladies whose distancing matches his own by calling them "aloof" and "tough."

Between affairs he has fits of reclusiveness. He comes out again when a new flirtation appears. He whirls a while with yet another woman, then beats yet another hasty escape to his citadel. Since he sees all women as wanting to catch him, he flatters himself as the one who got away, but sadly he gets away with only his own skin and leaves the loot of a rewarding attachment behind. The spells of retreat grow longer as he grows older and more tired of his own pattern. The Escape Artist has never struck the fine balance between being with people and being alone. He does not live at ease with loneliness but battles with it. He keeps it at bay only with fits of work, movies, books, and fantasies.

Money Markers

Throughout his comings and goings, he deals with money as he deals with women: he spends it but worries about it. He doesn't want a fortune, but he wants a steady supply. The problem is, he's never sure he has enough money, and he can't do anything else until he's sure. Money provides him another obstacle. He spends money easily, even generously. He generally will take you out and prefers to pay. Perhaps it's part of his concept of give and take, since he knows your affair will last only for a short time. Or perhaps he's not shy about spending for his own pleasure.

Family Aspects

While he takes one giant step forward and forty-two steps backward with women, his pattern with his relatives is the opposite – forty-two steps backward and then one leap forward when they need him. He moves away from them in space, but stays in close enough contact to come running.

He usually feels that he had a bad or alienated childhood. He didn't learn how to relate to people because of his strange parents, his physical isolation, or some traumatic event. Although he sees his family as having scarred him, he doesn't harbor blame. But he does talk about his wounds a lot, as if to justify his behavior.

He thinks he would like children, but he doesn't always get around to having them, which he regrets conveniently late. Or he has children but doesn't live with them, which he *truly* regrets. If he has children, presumably by an early marriage, they are the only ones who can clamber over his great wall. All gateways are open to them and he is a loving father.

He has male friends among his business contacts and in his career world, but he rarely cultivates close buddies; his main friendships are with females. And he has a lot of them.

Obviously, the Short Affair and Quick Escape Artist has some distinct liabilities. Under his seeming independence, he has serious problems with self-esteem. He doesn't take criticism well. It ruffles his feathers and gnaws at his mind. Often he is wildly jealous of other men; he resents their achievements, successes, and especially their abilities with women. Going with an Escape Artist is short. Your turn lasts one to six weeks. When your affair ends (with your calling him instead of his calling you), it helps his self-esteem, but it doesn't help yours. And he simply can't believe that you had no nefarious intentions to acquire him.

But then the Escape Artist also has his assets. He has a lot to give despite himself. He is truly fond of women, a pleasure any woman can appreciate even for a short spell. He is interesting. He sports that kind of quixotic intelligence born of caution (or paranoia). He's fun for a while. And he can ultimately wind up a great telephone pal when you're low.

What Is in Store for You?

Let's say you're at the rodeo, and it's bull-riding time. The ride only lasts eight seconds. It starts smooth, then it bends, it bumps, it ends.

An affair with the Escape Artist is similar. You're still saying "howdy" when he's saying "adios." Escape Artists happen a lot to women who are out there "dating." There are armies of men who play a hard and fast game of "I don't want to get attached." Once you acknowledge the fact that a phalanx of walking walls may await you, you can decide what to do about it.

You can end up feeling like Pavlov's dog. For two weeks, every time you press a button, you get a bone. Then, suddenly, you get an electric shock, and you are deprived. You may also feel like a photocopy – another one just like the other ones. On the other hand, with some foreknowledge (since he forewarns), you *can* have a nice time, stay detached, and keep on trucking when he detours. Or you can refuse to ride. To choose among these alternatives you need to consider what comes at the end of the line.

Deep down, women frighten him. He can't get over envisioning every woman as wearing an apron and carrying a fifty-pound rolling pin.

He is also thoroughly unable to handle rejection, so he pulls a presto-change-o act that simply enables him to get out first. He makes you dumped; that way he doesn't get dumped on.

Obviously, when you're still trying to see him after he's finished and gone, you can get to wondering. Did your nose turn green? Does your bathroom have a trick mirror that doesn't reveal your flaws? You were so great a few days ago. Now you are treated like a homeless skunk.

To him, you *are* at fault. He doesn't find a multitude of failings in you, as the Woman Hater does, but just one: the fact that you want love, he says, means you *need* it. That's bad, he says; being needy is not good. He forgets that it's human and has no innate badness or goodness to it, and that in truth it's *he* who can't handle a heady brew, not necessarily you. Nonetheless, you can come out thinking that a desire for commitment is some sort of error, somehow unhealthy. You can wind up eating a plateful of rejection that he ordered.

The Escape Artist is different from the Hustler. At least he risks some involvement with you. The Hustler offers no emotional output at all. The tiny amount of time the Escape Artist comes out of his hiding hole is his saving grace. An affair with him does not usually end with sour feelings, only resignation. In a way, he represents a no-blame situation. You can't fault an armadillo for his scales and you're a fool to kick one and you know it.

Though the affair lasts only a few short weeks, quite likely he will give you friendship and favors forever, it's as if your relationship made you a disarmed sister. His phone is always open to you, and his schedule can almost always make room. After it's over, chances are he'll take you home and then leave. He is almost always a little afraid you want to start up again. And besides, now that you're a sister, sex is a bit abhorrent, like incest.

What Are the Telltale Signs of Trouble?

Listen for telltale phrases. Any sentence starting "I'm not ready" constitutes a blinking light. But listen carefully. He's liable to bury the "I'm not ready" warning in totally unrelated conversations, for example, about why Indian elephants have smaller ears. He doesn't want you to pay his early warning much heed. He is still chasing you when he tells you who he is, so he does it in such a way as not to scare you off. But he means it. Of course, you can scan for his style: the flash combined with reserve, the going bananas one day only to return to austerity the next, the way he edges about people, parties, and population centers, or the way the phone rings with calls from ladies whom he now calls "friends."

Some of the other signals are more subtle. For instance, he thinks that because he told you, no matter *how* obscurely, the affair wouldn't last, you are adequately forewarned. He assumes you know he's taken out walking papers from the outset. So when he starts to become unavailable, notice if he's surprised that you are surprised. These telltale tips should indicate the presence of an Escape Artist. Right off, this is a critical point for you. You can decide to go ahead or not, or what controls and attitudes of your own you want to muster up.

The next critical point arrives when the number of excuses *not* to see you equals the number of bricks in the Great Wall of China. His schedule gets more and more intricate. He has something else arranged. He has calls to make. Lots of old friends appear with sudden and pressing demands. At this point, no matter how hot the fire was, you are becoming an old flame. It begins to seem as if you see him only when he wants to see you, not when you want to see him. He pops over to make love and then leaves right away. When use becomes misuse, it's time to review who is going to pull the plug.

Then he splits. First go the tea bags, then the toothbrush. You call and his voice gets wary on the phone. You attend the same soiree and he acts as if you're a virus: he says hello but turns his head and covers his mouth. He tells you that your romance lasted longer than most of his, so you ought to feel lucky. This means more than a bend in the road. This means you are at the end of the line.

What Are Your Chances and What Should You Do?

Until the Escape Artist changes, if he changes, all his romantic attachments end. On the other hand, his friendships can last a long, long time. It's true that no one can get through all the protective layers of any other person, but the Escape Artist is such a true believer in "An ounce of prevention is worth a pound of cure" that you can never even get close to the treatment stage.

You could perhaps be his youthful early wife, but you will find that he is trying to grow into what he thinks he should be. In the meantime, what he is will sink your marriage.

Does he change? Some Escape Artists do, eventually. But they are very late bloomers, if they bloom at all. They're a decade behind everyone else. If they change, often they come out as Limited Partners. Short Affair and Quick Escape Artists have been alone too long, retarded by too many impediments, to find more total types of intimacy possible. They also only evolve alone. In all probability you can't ride out the change as a partner with one. You'll have to meet him after he gets there.

If you meet or know an Escape Artist, I advise against even trying, much less fighting for, a permanent relationship. In the first place, he'll probably run off. In the second place, if you manage to hang on awhile, what you get won't be very satisfactory.

But whether or not you should completely shun Escape Artists is another question. That depends on what you think about the other things he offers. With the Escape Artist you can either throw him – wheat and chaff – out, or you can gracefully toss the lover part and salvage the being his pal. (Though being on a long list of female friends might go against some women's grain). If you go for the latter alternative, letting the romance go gracefully and keeping him as a friend, I suggest some time between the romance and the friendship parts.

Depending on how hot your affair was, give him (and yourself) six months or more before you take him up on the new kind of bond. Keep in mind that you will probably have to call him. The calluses on your finger can get insulting unless you simply accept them, for his idea of friendship is being called, not calling.

Of course, as always, there is another way to skin the cat, especially if you don't want to get attached. You can take the Escape Artist for what he is and what he offers, know fool's gold when you see it and don't think you hit a mother lode. Enjoy the good stuff while it lasts, then when the affair washes out, pick up and pan somewhere else. Have a nice short union with him, then wave goodbye. Sometimes if you're biding your time and licking old wounds, a passing fancy is better than no fancy at all. An Escape Artist's flattery and sensuality can most assuredly boost you, especially if he's the one who likes to give the massages, instead of getting them. You also don't have to figure out right away if you want him for a long-term pal. You can make up your mind at a later date.

However, if you're the sort who can't come out of a short-term affair without feeling hurt and rejected, learn this about yourself and just don't get into it. Go for what is *good* for you. Don't repeat things that aren't. Wanting permanent intimacy is not a problem. It isn't a mistake and can't cause a breakup. It's a healthy desire that requires the right environment. It's *not* wanting long-term affairs that causes short ones.

If you're really in love with a Short Affair and Quick Escape Artist, willing and even able to hang in there, remember he is like the gingerbread man. He thinks you are the fox. This is not the most restful situation in which to put yourself. There will always be a nervous edge to your life, and you will have to bear in mind the fragility of the situation. He could get claustrophobic at any time. You won't know when. As he makes his break, a hysterical reaction won't help; a long, loose rope might. Don't tie him on a short tether. Stay calm, detached, and give him leeway. Meanwhile realize that having an affair with another man will throw him into a fit of male to male envy. He already thinks he's not as good as other guys. Therefore, think carefully.

Some Escape Artists attempting to become Limited Partners want to live together and not marry. I don't think I'd settle for it. "No marriage" means he is still holding out for all the old escape hatches. An old Escape Artist who wants to live alone – with you – isn't ready yet. He wants only to half-commit himself. He may want someone at home while maintaining a single profile without you. Good Limited Partners, however, acknowledge that they are attached, even if they have separate business lives. They don't carry on a single man's front in public.

Where Do You Fit In?

Escape Artists abound. You are highly likely to meet more than one in a lifetime, but if you meet too many, it might be time to sit down and examine yourself.

There is probably a reason why you link up with people who fly "Don't Tread on Me" flags. Most likely you are trying to stay alone but telling yourself you want to get attached. You don't want to stick out by not wanting what other people want, so you contrive a way of pretending you want involvement while ensuring it doesn't happen.

One way to handle this is to become a lonely and tragic figure with the dead horses of your previous affairs – a lot of them, lasting only weeks or months – always there to beat. It's a good obstacle against anything permanent.

Of course, such camouflaged intentions mean you have to get dumped *upon* rather than doing the dumping yourself. Otherwise how can you claim you wanted permanence? Also, lots of women have trouble rejecting any men, Short Affair and Quick Escapes Artists or not. Their parents told them long ago they had to do the catching, so it follows they should take on all comers.

Analyze your own behavior and see what it tells you. Then talk to the quieter voices in your head to find out whether you want to stay detached or whether you want a partner, at least for now. *No* decision has to be permanent. You may discover you simply don't want to tie yourself down to any one romance yet. You may uncover that you *do* want a long-term relationship but have fears that thwart you. You can either state openly that you don't want to get involved and give up the rejected role, or you can dismantle your fears. Sally did. She discovered she wanted a husband, but that her family's cloistered atmosphere had frightened her. She saw permanent alliances as choking to death in boredom. Realizing it didn't have to be that way, and with her own lively life it wouldn't, she freed herself.

Soon, when a man said, "I don't want to get involved," Sally said, "Well, I do, so see you later."

Remember, confusion of desires, being perhaps a little less independent than you act, being tired of being alone, getting over a broken romance, are all the things that make you a little shaky on your pegs and vulnerable. And that's exactly what the Short Affair and Quick Escape Artist recognizes, so be extra cautious with yourself.

You may just prefer short-term affairs. And that's perfectly all right. But if you accept that it's all right, then say so. Don't pretend you want forever when you refuse to act like it. If future, family, and farmstead seem too final, but you want some sometime men, indulge the Escape Artist. He has advantages. Make sure, though, that you are able to dabble in short romances without regret. Some people can live with here-today-and-gone-tomorrow better than others. And sometimes you can be high enough that no affair, long or short, brings you down, while other times you can be low enough that they all do.

During such lows, it might be best to go it alone for a while – make no attempt at unions. Escape Artists come into your life against your will more often when you are running away from sadness. You have to learn about loneliness sooner or later. Since you can't run away from your own feelings, wallow in them by yourself for a while. Learn to acknowledge when you are shaky and what kind of men that attracts. Certainly do so if you are recovering from an important union, because you do influence what kind of men are attracted to you. So be prepared.

Last but not least, check one final camouflage. Acting out the maid of constant sorrow is often a way the loner has learned to get attention. That way she can stay isolated and have people say, "Poor thing." Constant affairs with Escape Artists are like repetitive colds, a chronic illness. Rather, learn to seek out ways of drawing sympathy that don't involve the wear and tear of the six-week unions you told yourself – and everyone else – were finally the real things.

Some Short Affair and Quick Escape Artists, those who claim the reason they can't settle down is they have to make their next achievement, share a lot of traits with the Man Who Would Be Mogul. Others are similar to the Hustler, whose aim is only to bed lots of women and have affairs even shorter than six weeks. Like one night. If you're pondering over some Short Affair and Quick Escape Artist, you might want to read about these two other types of men as well.

I go on to another kind of man who, unfortunately, is also very common. He's far more disastrous than the Short Affair and Quick Escape Artist. He ensnares you in much longer affairs and even marriages, during which he undermines your confidence, self-value, and self-esteem. He's the Woman Hater.

Every women should read about him, because even if you're not romantically involved with him, you'll meet him somewhere. Sadly, many of us are, or have been, in love with him.

2

The Woman Hater

The Man Who Berates, Criticizes, and Emotionally Abuses You

Did you ever pluck the petals on a daisy, chanting, "He loves me; he loves me not," trying to divine your status with a seeming Sir Galahad?

Well, there *is* a courtship in which both petals tell true. You collect on both predictions, but the sequence is crucial. First he loves you, then he loves you not.

This dubious double fortune often falls to women who somehow stand apart. If you are – or were before you met him – intelligent and stylish, vivacious and admired, in other words "a catch," watch out. You are the most likely target for the Woman Hater.

The Woman Hater abuses women. But unlike the Woman Hitter, the Woman Hater does not strike or beat a woman up. Rather, he berates a woman with criticism and retracted love. He undermines the capabilities and scars the confidence of any woman involved with him.

Unfortunately, although he is one of the most devastating to women of all men, he is one of the hardest to recognize up front. He is a tidy time bomb. He treats a woman fabulously at the onset of the affair. It's only after the woman of his choice surrenders herself heart, head, and often hand, to a union with him that he abruptly reverses his behavior.

Perhaps its trite to say a man hates women. Certainly the Woman Hater would deny it. Often the woman with him would defend him.

But it doesn't come out in what he says or even in what he claims he feels about women. It comes out in how he eventually acts. As with most men, he chooses a woman who suits his character. Part of his concern is the conquest of something special. Part of his makeup is having excellent taste in the things he acquires. That means he wants the dollar jackpot or the highest mountain. He might pick a woman when she's young and snappy, just coming out and pretty special. He might choose one later on. But all in all he likes the Mercedes of ladies. He seeks the pretty, the sparkly, the noteworthy, or if older the independent, the adventurous, the self-assured.

Story

So often the Woman Hater happens to exactly the kind of woman you wouldn't expect it to.

Take, for example, the experience of one of the women I interviewed, Clarissa.

To say that Clarissa had zest wouldn't quite describe her. She was bright and alive. She couldn't stop herself from tackling everything she wanted – travels, love, education, work – while still being very social. It had taken Clarissa a while to get used to her own dynamism and the effect it had on people, but by her late twenties she no longer allowed the fact that she was attractive, emotional, and intelligent to be in contradiction. She rolled it all into a package that was pretty impressive. She was doing well with her career, her social life, and her store of self-knowledge. She cultivated rather than covered her flair. She was writing and teaching, wearing plumes and scarves. Her confidence and attractiveness were magnetic.

When Jon hotly pursued her, he already had what is called a "bad rep." He had treated previous women in a decidedly callous manner. Knowing this, Clarissa was resistant to him; otherwise, she would not have been an attractive quarry. She thought she had accumulated enough experience and wisdom to be interested only in a man who truly cared for her. She generally could say no to bad pennies.

But Jon was *so* caring that, even with her jaundiced eye, Clarissa began to believe the Good Ship Lollipop had arrived. He brought her perfect roses and bottles of rare wines. He cooked fabulous meals and showed her old films on his VCR. He was very affectionate. He took her prowling through antique stores and brought her to parties. He praised her, never said anything that diminished her. His respect for her seemed to be a given. Clarissa was careful to be her true self with him in order to be sure he saw her every side and still cared. She let her cranky as well as her carefree moods hang out.

She stayed a little detached and distant for a goodly while, but he was a match for it all.

When, after quite a bit of hesitation, she went to bed with him, all his elegance truly emerged. Jon had taken sex beyond sensuality and turned it into a rarefied and cultivated taste. Everything he did was both exact and exquisite. He sensitized every part of her body. She was so swept away by exquisite technique that she never quite noticed she didn't get held.

From early on Jon pushed for a permanent relationship with Clarissa, but she had been unwilling to agree. Finally, when the attentions lasted and the good things continued, Clarissa gave way. She decided he truly loved her and that she should commit herself to him. She said "yes" to him and she meant it. She gave her heart, moved in with him, and married him.

That was the turning point. It was all downhill from there. Jon changed radically. Soon Clarissa found herself living in an ever progressive nightmare of criticism and withdrawn affection. Everything about her that had been right before was now wrong. He criticized her looks, her work, her every deed. He never brought her a gift. When she cried he walked out the door. Usually he used all his money to buy himself belongings and left her to manage the household. When he did give her some money, he did it as if she were a leech. She received his consideration only grudgingly. When she did win some concession from him, he exacted a heavy price. For a night out where she wanted to go, he gave her the cold shoulder for a week. For help around the house, he belittled her in public. He excluded her from his business parties and dinners, and to Clarissa the sting of exclusion was far worse than carnal jealousy. Bit by bit she began to lose her self-assurance and to feel constantly beaten down.

She said to me, "The whole second half of our relationship was in twister perspective. It seemed that because he had put himself out to catch me, he was eternally angry with me and I had to make it up to him in spades. Every day, in every way, I had to win him. I had to cajole him for a conversation and sweet-talk him to get help from him. To get him interested in sex, I performed all the foreplay. He said I wasn't proper in public, so I tried to be better and regain the right to go out with him. I did everything at home, but it was never good enough to receive a piece of praise."

Clarissa was both confused and stymied. She wondered how her original impressions had been so misguided. She puzzled over what went wrong. She kept trying to please him, to discover what exactly he wanted, to carry on and wait for the *real* Jon to return, only he always found something new wrong. She knew she should leave Jon, but for some reason she wanted Jon to confirm again that she was special. She wanted him now as he had wanted her before. She planned to confront him, but the day before she intended to do so, Jon, accusing her of countless flaws and misdeeds, walked out on her. Clarissa was devastated. Slowly she picked up the pieces of herself. As soon as she did, Jon was back. Once firmly back, he started to criticize her again. Meanwhile he talked of his affairs with other terrific women. This went on two more times, until Clarissa realized the only way to break with him was a total break. She picked a small incident to force him out. Then, despite the fact that they by then had a child (he hadn't wanted any, but she "won" one), she never directly spoke to him, or allowed him in her home, again.

With the Woman Hater there is practically no indication of how the relationship will go until you are already over the dam. You commit yourself to a seemingly certain set of circumstances only to find them demolished. Such an unforeseen switch can reduce even tough-minded women to gibbering. You almost have to go through the Woman Hater once to learn to recognize him again. Nonetheless, different trees have different leaves. And, while the Woman Hater may hide his ultimate nature in a veil of foliage, he does have definite identification signs.

How Can You Identify This Kind of Man?

In the first place, the Woman Hater likes himself. In fact, he likes himself – or at least he acts like he likes himself – inordinately. Not infrequently he is, or he tries to come on as, a rather sophisticated, educated, and traveled man. He wants the best for himself; this leads him to a prestigious lifestyle. He may well know fine wines, buy himself the best liquor and special tobacco. It is not unlikely that he lives somewhat beyond his means. Getting himself anything he thinks he ought to have extends to realms other than the material. The Woman Hater tends to set high goals for himself in all respects. He chooses a difficult career, desires more than moderate wealth, and prefers glamorous social circles.

Usually he's gregarious. He's charming and gallant. He is as good at socializing as he is at other things. His story of who he is, what he does, and how it's going is mesmerizing; he has a great line. He's a verbal enchanter, spinning a golden web that's attractive to many, but sticks to very few.

Needless to say, when his pursuit of finer things includes you, he is absolutely magnetic. His constant search for prizes, and his assurance that he will win them, certainly flatter you. On top of that, he seems to adore the image of women. His bait is his love of the feminine flair you yourself love, his hook the fond hope that you will fulfill his quest.

You are the prize, that special woman.

Long before you decipher how much and how well he cares for himself, his charm might be your earliest signal. If you look carefully, he does not seek really to find out what needs, moods, and desires you might have under your feminine facade. And he is certainly more concerned with how you initially *evade* him than how you eventually give yourself to him.

Outer Signs

His clothes will probably be expensive. In a store, he walks right toward quality items and he is oblivious to anything on the cheaper racks. He demands pure, fine materials – wool, cotton, and silk. He likes scarves for his neck, and socks that come up to his knees. He has a conservative streak in his apparel. He tends to think the more traditional, reserved styles show more elegance. He usually wears a jacket, often a blazer. But he sometimes goes for the "casual elegance" or continental looks. He likes grey.

His hair is never too long and never too short. He doesn't seem to pay it much attention, but he must because it never varies more than an inch. He's very aware of his hands. His fingers are long, his skin smooth, his nails long and shiny. His second toe is longer than his big one, and he calls it the mark of an aristocrat.

He likes a fashionable car, one with a touch of class. He picks automobiles that are noteworthy, well known for their performance plus style. The motor is special, so is the trademark, and probably the price tag. If he drives an old car, it's the kind that had distinction in its day and is now almost a classic. Since a car is a highly visible belonging, he often has a better vehicle than he does a place to live.

He prefers to dwell in better-than-just-exclusive neighborhoods – he would like the most sublime location within them. He admires the highest hill, best view, or most unusual house. When he can't own such a palatial home, he may lease, rent part of, house sit, or become a permanent guest in one. Any apartment or house he chooses he picks for space and taste. He likes delicate fireplaces, alcoves, and arches. Yet, he places furniture formally, often stiffly. The air is still, and you feel you're in a museum.

Indeed, his environment is like a museum; full of stuff. He is a great consumer. You might find nine cameras, two cars, twenty-six silk shirts, and three unused rowing machines, plus gadgets for peeling lemons, opening champagne bottles, and clipping sideburn hairs. It befits a man with high self-esteem to match himself in both quantity and quality. He gets everything he thinks he ought to have, maybe two. On all these things the Woman Hater does not like spots or dents.

He wants things classy and kept that way. Interest in his collection of consumer items and admiration of his taste confirm his view of himself.

Public confirmation of his greatness is an important and touchy area for this man. Like any person, he wants to be living proof of his own self-image, but the image in his case is a fancy one. If he happens to be good at a particular sport, he will play to the balcony. But unless he can display some special ability, activities such as sports won't interest him. Large crowds are certainly not his style. Fear of heart attacks, excess weight, and ugly flab are his most likely motivations for physical activity. He pedals, runs, pushes, pulls, carries out exercise with the diligence that characterizes his other practices.

Sex Signals

The Woman Hater tends to pick what seems to him and others as the *best* of women. He is drawn to ambitious and creative ladies – education, talent, and beauty all rolled up in one bundle. Social position and money help, too.

His modus operandi in courtship is the bold announcement that you are special. He extends himself for you. He arranges special occasions and events. He does not say, "Hey, let's watch T.V. together." He takes you sailing in a *tiny* boat. He opens a *very* old bottle of wine. He brings out the linen napkins, unnerves you by wearing his desire for you on his sleeve. He wants to *have* you.

While some types of men regard the sexual conquest of a woman as the final goal, this is not so with the Woman Hater. He finds the surrender of your body useful, even encouraging, but not all that he desires. He wants more: he wants you to pledge yourself. If after some time, sex or no sex, you remain casual, he becomes upset. It is he who introduces the intensity into your affair.

Going to bed with him for the first time is never aggressive. Most likely it is the sensuous, seductive culmination to some fine evening together. It arrives like an elegant dessert – Cherries Jubilee and brandy. He is good in bed. After all, he has cultivated a lot of refined tastes. He appraises you with a connoisseur's delight, treats you like a princess, places accurate kisses just where you want them. He strokes, conducts a guided tour. It lasts a long time.

He is good, but he is not huggy. Sex with him is ornate choreography, an exquisite dance that is not really tender. The intensity of his lovemaking can carry the illusion of intimacy – in the beginning. Often it takes some time for the deficiency of his affection to become apparent. He would have to really *like* you as a woman to be tender in sex. And liking, unfortunately, is his weak point.

Since he pursues only to conquer, and in so doing discovers exactly what he sets out to discover – that his image of woman is not to be perfectly fulfilled – his attitudes change drastically when the victory is accomplished. Once his, you are in some ways more, in some ways less, than he bargained for. *Yes* is a key word to him. Once the word is uttered by you, the shoulder gets cold. Things differ dramatically. He shuts down your access to his life. He changes the lock on his office door and neglects to replace your key. He outlaws tickling. Suddenly you are too heavy to sit on his lap. He turns his nose up to a serendipitous escapade with you. He turns you down in bed. Slowly it becomes obvious that the cause is not fatigue, but the desire to slight you.

All this is quite characteristic of him; he is truly good at all these little things. Indeed, one of his give-away traits is his ability – all the things a Woman Hater does, he does well. He is expert at romance to start with and, later on, just as expert at rejection.

Money Markers

The Woman Hater's money belongs to *him*. He alone determines what he requires and how elegant his possessions should be. Your earnings, however, belong to *both* of you. They support your mutual household. So after he has indulged himself, whether you work or not, you're reduced to eking out your luxuries from the grocery budget.

Quite likely, during the course of your relationship, a great deal of money will be spent. To the Woman Hater, spending's what money is for, and the sooner spent the better. The Woman Hater can be very persuasive when it comes to buying things. Desperate and immediate necessities arise all over the place like little mushrooms. Credit cards and juggled debts become a way of life. He resents the sound of brakes on the cash flow and will surely release a torrent of charm or criticism to get your signature on a check.

Family Aspects

Few Woman Haters want children. They don't look fondly on becoming stepfathers either. Children represent too much of an encumbrance on his freedom and money. They require real care. They are messy. They break things. If you decide to have children, the contract will involve your tending them on a go-it-alone basis. The Woman Hater may claim to love his children, but he won't do much for them. He will act, perhaps, like a magnanimous father, but not be a wrestling-match-on-the-living-room-floor daddy, and the chances are few he will bend his plans to babysit.

The Woman Hater's relationship with his parents, brothers, and sisters will be marked by various estrangements. He generally feels he has moved beyond the social level of his relatives and views his ties to them as personally regressive. He meets his obligations to family only at the bottom line and only after he's taken care of himself, as well as what he considers the more important demands of his business and social life.

Rather than flirt too heavily with outside opinion, the Woman Hater finds that his estimation of himself is more easily maintained by himself or in a small circle. As a result, while he may charm many people, he tends to have few close friends. He also goes through friends. He manages his other social relations, minus those people he is courting as friends, clients, or social contacts, by remaining slightly unapproachable. He is the older, the employer, the expert, or merely the more formal. If someone's vision of friendship with him includes being direct about his inadequacies as well as adequacies, he or she has forgotten how narcissistic he is. He views directness not as potentially beneficial but as an attack. It's hard for anyone to be a frank and honest friend with the Woman Hater. He is not your humble sort of fellow, and he thinks other people are not quite competent or good enough to judge him. He also won't keep company with just any folk, that's why he leaves friends behind as he sees himself advancing.

The Woman Hater has numerous liabilities. He is selfish, overbearing, and critical, a river of no return. In his elegance there is arrogance. It may be impossible ever to be real with him. He costs a lot. Yet he is always a fascinating man. He has a big and exciting dream of how his life will be, what he will achieve, and how the honey will flow. He has flash, and he looks good – both on his own and with you. His very presence can be a sort of audacious compliment. If you dread sedateness, normality, security, investments, commitments, and boredom, he can certainly seem attractive and he looks good on your arm. But watch it!

What Is in Store for You?

What do you do if you are shown a Lincoln Continental and, only *after* you sign the contract, you discover that you have actually purchased a Volkswagen with no shock absorbers?

The first thing is to learn to spot Volkswagens lurking in the trunks of Continentals. Failing that, you can at least try to determine where you are going and what's in store for you. Then you can decide whether to bail out or get heavy-duty shock absorbers.

If you resolve that you are dallying with a Woman Hater, there are things to know. For one, the fact that the Woman Hater is a repeater does not bode well. The prospects for absolute permanence are poor. Maybe two years, maybe four, maybe much longer, but not forever. If not when you're most down, then when you're older, he will leave you. For another, like the foxtrot, a two-step pattern lies predictably in your future. At first, the affair amounts to a veritable treasure trove of support, flattery, and love. For anyone with the least bit of appetite in her soul, such treatment is both a temptation and a delight. But the criticism and withheld affection that appear in stage two are the most important factors. Like two bulldozers they gouge away the landscape of your early relations. The early features disappear so effectively you even wonder if they had been figments of your imagination. Sadly, his preliminary finesse is based on his sensitivity to you as an object, not as a person. Once you are acquired, he is not one to be in tune with you. No more do you receive words of love, affection, and praise. Quite the opposite. You hear more and more about your ever-growing list of inadequacies.

Once a woman has committed herself to a permanent relationship with the Woman Hater, his resentment for the tenderness he extended to "catch" her reveals itself. Withheld love gives him tremendous power over a woman who is trying to be his mate. In these gestures he exposes himself as someone who hates rather than loves, someone who is too angry at women in general to live and let live with one of their representative members. Some women stay because they are trapped by family or finances, but many women – secretly maybe most – stay with the Woman Hater in the vain hope that the former attentions they got from him soon, or at least eventually, will return. They search to improve upon whatever he thinks is lacking in order to reclaim the original conditions. It does seem as if he is saying, "I won you. Now you win me." Once committed, therefore, you may try to win him back. But there's a catch – he's unwinnable. Once having withdrawn the affection and flattery that marked the early maneuvers, he will not return them. Once having started to find fault, he will continue to discover more and more black spots in your character.

You can sing songs, do dances, write homilies in his praise, and try every program of self improvement. Still nothing will make him blow you kisses from across the room again. And criticizing him back only serves to confirm his accusations about you. You might go back and forth with this man several times. Leave him or get left, only to get back together. First off, once you're on your own, he likes to rewin you. Secondly, most women, if they can leave at all, find it very, very hard to become detached from him. They still want assurances of his love and a return of his flattery. Once you do end an alliance with him, you can rarely be his friend or have him for your friend, at least not for a long time. You will remain sensitive to his many mean deeds and his over-given criticism. He more than likely will not be able to resist verbally jabbing at you every time you do something he doesn't like. You might stay emotionally attached to him, but now through burning hate and rancor, not affection.

Besides the emotional hazards, some labor problems pop into your life with the Woman Hater as well. Don't forget all those purchases. Someone has to keep them clean. It is in his prospectus for you to play maid to the objects. Despite getting a gadget for every need, the Woman Hater's attitude is not that objects serve you, but that you, not he, serve them. No spots and no dents, remember? You will also have to do all the work and carry on all the burdens of ordinary daily life. Women in these partnerships tend to have to continue their careers, struggle under financial stress, and keep looking good while they become kitchen maids, housekeepers, bookkeepers, mechanics, childcare experts, insurance agents, and party givers. And, while with some types of men you have relatives coming out of your cupboards all the time, with the Woman Hater the job of keeping up ties to friends and family will be up to your conscience to decide and left to you to manage.

You will also have to take care of yourself. It will be hard to do the things you want to do as it is, but you could be in really difficult circumstances if you got sick or fired from your job. Considering his standards, he will have trouble putting up with you when you are not of the best quality. If you have children you will work yourself to a frazzle, for which he'll pick on you. To get away for work, rest, or social events you will have to hire substantial amounts of child care, or else stay at home. And God forbid you should get older.

What Are the Telltale Signs of Trouble?

Of course, there are signals that indicate that you might have taken on something that was not quite what it seemed. Consider it a sign of rocks on the road if his past partners cry about his abusive behavior, while you yourself are treated very well. Especially watch out if the women are much like yourself. You are hearing about the end stage of his previous affairs while experiencing the beginning of your own. Notice, too, if he enumerates the faults of former women. Chances are things will not go a different course with you. Note if even early on you get chastised for independent decisions that do not concur with his plans. This may be a signal that he is already secretly waiting for you to change yourself in response to how good he thinks he is being to you.

But the major warning is when his behavior abruptly changes. This happens almost certainly at points of commitment in your relationship – starting to live together, getting engaged, married, or pregnant. The first signs are small, but they pile up. Stupendous sex fizzles down to the mundane, then the nonexistent. He stops public displays of affection. Suddenly, at a party, he treats you like a spore from outer space. He says he is always telling you the right way to live and you stubbornly do it your own, *wrong* way just to annoy him. He starts to berate your overuse of oregano and underuse of Mop & Glo, your clothes, your behavior, or anything else. He won't help you because *you* made the mess. He uses you as the butt of jokes in company. He implies that, despite running five shops, four offices, three cars, and two households, you can't add one plus one. The start of stage two is the critical point for you to consider dropping him.

When the Woman Hater moves on to new goals in his own life, then it is *he* who may leave *you*. He knows you are hooked on retracted love, and he doesn't especially like the things he acquires to walk out on him. He's a keeper. Every time you are about to call it quits, a Woman Hater finds a way to reattach you. Most often he behaves more as he did at first for a spell. Offering bits of the old time, he fakes you out, until *he* is ready to go. That can happen early or late – when he decides you are no longer special and he deserves better.

What Are Your Chances and What Should You Do?

In short, despite what you do, most affairs with the Woman Hater sooner or later break up. Either he walks out or you decide to cut your losses. Some last, but they are not beneficial or healthy situations for any woman.

Unfortunately, within the Woman Hater there is little potential for change. Fortified by his high opinion of himself, he rarely sees any need to alter, and since he views himself so highly, your opinion of his virtues and failings will never match his own. He simply does not have the chinks in his armor that make alteration possible. He doesn't have a personal philosophy of change (i.e., he doesn't believe in self improvement or "getting better," he thinks he's fine the way he is). His friends aren't close enough to tell him about his faults, and you are liable to be the last candidate on his list of influential others. To change he'd have to get professional help, and the chances he'd "lower" himself to that are unlikely.

All in all, considering the balance sheet with him, I'd advise avoiding this type of man. I also advise fleeing from one already in your life.

Once you are pledged to the Woman Hater, it is a heads-he-wins-tails-you-lose situation. It's up to you to decide the possibilities you

MEN WHO ARE GOOD FOR YOU AND MEN WHO ARE BAD

see and the advantages you gain in a relationship with him, but some kinds of men are more undermining than others and the Woman Hater is one of the worst of them. It's a bit more than most women can or should handle to be above constant attack and to overcome loveless atmospheres. Why ask for so much difficulty when other situations offer more for less?

Calling it quits makes sense for another reason – liking yourself. If you *were* outstanding, you will find it hard to tolerate yourself for hanging on. You will save yourself energy and self-esteem if you get out early. Remember that the fault-finding and cold-shouldering grow like Hydra's heads. Self-confidence is vulnerable, even for a dynamo of a woman. So it's sensible to cut your losses and save what assurance remains.

There is, however, another possibility to consider other than outright shunning the Woman Hater. Perhaps the trick with him is never to say yes. In that light, you can contemplate collecting on stage one and saying "so long" before stage two. Take what he offers, then run. I personally believe that without giving yourself to a relationship you can't get much from it. But if you were not looking for anything serious to begin with, this suggestion has definite possibilities.

If you do want to stay with a Woman Hater for whatever reason, there are some skills for survival. Keep in mind that it was your class, style, and strength that attracted him in the first place. If he has any weak spot, that's it. Woman Haters rise up and pay attention to elegance. Keep your style and handle tough times with all the class you can muster. Also remember that he cannot be handed intimate knowledge of you with the assurance that he won't abuse it. Make and keep other friends outside the relationship. Better yet, don't stop being your own best friend. To avoid the criticism, cultivate your own opinions of yourself and stick to them. If you are vulnerable in any area of self-evaluation – your looks, your smarts, your abilities – techniques to help deal with criticism are available: learn them.

You can end up with lots of fears from a Woman Hater: are you or will you ever again be special, attractive, adventurous, financially solvent? One strong foil against such fears exists. Remember, *he is not the one to quash your doubts.* As I said before, many women are held by an invisible string of hope that the Woman Hater will once more flatter and reassure them. But he is *not* the one to go to. Asking a criticizer for a faultless checkup is backwards strategy. When you need confirmation that you are still you, find someone *else* who thinks you're great.

If your relationship goes all the way to breakup, just knowing that's par for the course for the Woman Hater will help fortify you against self-doubt. He did think he was madly attracted to you in the beginning and even that he loved you. It's a great memory.

Where Do You Fit In?

Admittedly, Woman Haters are attractive men. They are out of the ordinary, ambitious, energetic. They have an air of excitement. But if you find yourself consistently attracted to this type – going through both stages, and ending up worse for wear – some insight into yourself might be gleaned from it all.

Also consider that many very independent woman still have dependent urges hidden within them to which Woman Haters appeal. Perhaps you maintain the old fantasy of being carried away or taken care of. Some loving companion will make it all easier for you, even though you have chosen a complicated life.

Woman Haters, in the courtship stage, fall right in line with those fond, secret hopes. They seem as if they *want* your sassiness and still will romance you. Perhaps also you might feel that without *needing* a man there will be no way to connect with one, and so you actually fear being independent. In truth, clearing up those last remnants of dependence frees you from endlessly riding the roller coaster of your partner's good or bad opinion or the illusion that some Woman Hater will really take care of you.

Do you feel you have to be flawless to be worthy, extraordinary to be loved? Did you seek a classy man possibly to obtain prestigious outside opinion, just as he did with you, or perhaps because you needed a challenge or match? Take stock of what you want out of life and love right now. If it's any or all of the above, do it with a Woman Hater. If not, *don't*.

In terms of the lack of attention the Woman Hater eventually pays you, and also his desires for wealth, class, and luxury, he can be much like the Man Who Would Be Mogul. He can also share many characteristics with the Idle Lord and Mr. Genius. Worse, he can slip over into the Woman Hitter, if his abuse gets physical as well as mental.

The type that is most like the Woman Hater is the man I go to next. Where the Woman Hater's dislike of women is subtle and his hate not voiced as public doctrine, the Male Supremacist is the tried and true, old fashioned man who thinks men are superior. He acts on it, too. Read on.

The Male Supremacist

*Men Who Think Men Are
Superior and Women Inferior*

Once upon a time all creatures made babies by splitting in two and cloning themselves. Then, one fateful day, somebody, two of them, to be exact, invented sex. Ever since, there's been a whole lot of merrymaking, but a lot of trouble, too.

Now, although it looks by and large as if the female was the basic form biologically, and the male was the afterthought, some members of the masculine variety got it into their heads that they were better than the original sex, namely the ladies. There is virtually no evidence, other than what they've written themselves, to support such an assumption. Still, myriad descendants of these upstart specimens meander around in the guise of the Male Supremacist.

It's the Male Supremacist's *mind* that's the problem. He believes men are creation's highest creatures. Men are, and were meant to be, superior to women and women must remain inferior to men. Of course, a lot of men think their sex is preferable. They feel the are endowed with facilities sadly lacking in the opposite gender. Due to these specialties, they wouldn't want to switch, not even in reincarnation. Many women feel similarly, that the female got the better end of the deal. Theirs is the sex par excellence, with benefits unparalleled, and they wouldn't trade for the whole wide world. So both sides end up figuring, O.K., our sex is best. Certainly men and women are different. But in most ways, still, we're roughly equivalent.

Not the Male Supremacist.

The Male Supremacist subscribes totally to male supremacy. He feels that men not only have precious paraphernalia, they have inherited superior qualities and special privileges as well. They possess a singular hold on intelligence, ability, and rank. They have an exclusive right to mastery, mainly over the opposite sex. And they are free to do what they want, while women simply aren't.

For example, men must have sex. They need it. They are by nature highly sexual animals. Consequently, the Male Supremacist chases almost *anything* feminine to see what he can get. He believes that women come in two classes, the "loose" and the "pure." Yet his classes overlap. He always tests a woman, even a seemingly pure one, to see where she fits in and find out just how "loosely" he can make her behave. When he pairs up permanently, he wants his woman to arrive almost holy, never look sideways at another man, yet bust all her buttons in the sack with him. Meanwhile it's a woman's – his woman's – job to raise the family and serve him.

Story

In my travels I've met many Male Supremacists and have known numerous women who lived with them and had stories to tell. Of all the tales, Teresa's is the proverbial. Her man Dean wasn't just a partial Male Supremacist. He had every trait in the catalogue.

Teresa grew up in a small city and part of a culture where longstanding, commonly-agreed-on ideas influenced everyone's life. Her hometown and social milieu taught that while boys "sow wild oats," girls "gather reputations." Men were the proper and "natural" family heads and decision makers. Women, at best, were second lieutenants. They had leverage, but they lacked the mental capacity and physical stability to lead.

Teresa's family and friends repeated other traditional edicts as well. They said that once married, a couple should live and love as a pair and never divorce. A couple should also be true to one another forever. As a result, Teresa unquestioningly looked forward to a traditional marriage. And she stayed "good" to win it. She was perfectly agreeable that her and her man's domains would differ, hers to be the home, his, labor, and that he would generally take precedence as the most important member. But she thought all else between them would be equal. Both would instantly become, and permanently remain, loyal to each other. Together they would operate as two sides of a coin. So, innocent and starry-eyed, Teresa eloped with her high-school sweetheart Dean when he returned from the service.

But Dean's view of marital bliss diverged from Teresa's. According to him, couples didn't intertwine, they followed the lord and

master's dictates. Whether single or married, males had prerogatives. The only thing that changed with the wedding cake was how
Teresa could behave. She belonged to him now and did what a
woman should – kept the domicile, followed his commandments,
served and serviced him and only him. She could no longer do anything of which he didn't approve. She didn't wander around
without him; when he wasn't there, she stayed home. In the meantime, he could do what he liked.

On their wedding night, Dean drank so much he passed out
before she undressed. Then, in the wee hours of the morning, he
grabbed her – and that was that. The next night, he didn't come home
till three. Despite her anger, he insisted that they make love then anyway and that she do things to him she never imagined were possible.

As time went on, she told herself that they had a wild sex life. But
she couldn't deny that, if there wasn't force, there was always an element of coercion in their sex. Dean insisted that Teresa would like
whatever he did, or at any rate she would *learn* to like it. She
frequently pretended more delight than she really felt. She had little
say over when or how they had sex, except for occasional "headaches" she claimed, or during her period (which he always held
against her). And since she never knew when or what he would next
expect from her sexually, she was always a little anxious.

At first, in bed and otherwise, she did what pleased Dean. To do
so seemed the rule for women and she had no other footsteps to follow. But she began to realize that while she willingly gave up her independence, a lot of her personal freedom slipped away with it.
Dean dictated what she was to wear and how she was to keep her
hair. He tore up all her jeans. He wanted her tone of voice sweet, her
manner compliant, and her hospitality to him and his friends ever
ready. If they weren't he would throw a monumental fit, even break
things. She wasn't allowed to work, but he gave her only a minimal
allowance on which to run the house, buy food, and cover all her
"extras." So she had little or no money for herself.

As they slipped past the honeymoon era, Dean began to stay
away more and more. Hunting and fishing trips grew more frequent.
So did nights with the boys. Sometimes he didn't show for dinner
and occasionally was out all night. He'd have powder on his collar,
and his socks would be inside out. People started cooing and consoling her and wouldn't tell her why.

Then, when Teresa got pregnant, Dean hardly came home at all.
On the night of the big event, he couldn't even be found. A neighbor took her to the hospital, and her sister held her hand. When Dean
finally arrived, he seemed to like his day-old daughter. Still, he told
Teresa, "The next one better be a boy." And though he bragged about

his child, he wouldn't pick her up. Teresa had three more daughters before she bore him a son. She kept trying for Dean, who wouldn't give up, although he never helped with the home and children. He came and went as he pleased.

Finally, at long last, his affairs, his temper, his domineering, and his absences got too humiliating. She locked him out. He followed her like a possessed hound dog – watching for another male – until she let him back. But after three weeks of good behavior, a new joint bank account, and a two-day vacation, the old pattern reappeared.

Now Teresa has told herself and Dean she'll give him one last chance. She has said that before. She doesn't expect him suddenly to transform, but she does expect him to alter certain conditions she will no longer tolerate. She claims she doesn't mind most of the restrictions but does mind the belittlement. He still chases every woman he can. And she has cooking, church, and children, but no cash.

She's not sure she could be anything but a traditional wife. She still thinks the man of the house should hold a dominant place. Dean does provide for her and the family and is fatherly in his own limited way. But she doesn't mean to be ill treated or deprived of respect again.

During one separation, she really began to enjoy her single state. She got to drive and go out to lunch. She even camped with the kids on her own. She began to realize that giving up the idea of a one and only man might not be so bad. She isn't kidding about the last chance. Nor is she holding her breath.

The Male Supremacist comes in all degrees, from minor to major. Surprisingly he is quite easy to discern, though his case might seem moderate at first and, once you are with him, turn out to be extreme. The trouble is, what the Male Supremacist *is* seems to concur with some women's own conscious or unconscious expectations of what should be. So you find it hard to object to him. Still, presuming that being of a different sex involves somewhat different conduct is not the same as living with someone who insists on flagrant, unfair disparities. The Male Supremacist doesn't just expound his assumptions as matter for discussion. He's a literal man. He practices what he preaches. After a union with him, his opinions end up your personal conditions, and they are not necessarily congenial conditions. Since you may or may not find that you can chew what you bit off with him, you should stop to analyze his assumptions before you get involved.

How Can You Identify This Kind of Man?

The Male Supremacist thinks everything – from can openers to honor to women – exists in limited quantities. His worth and esteem, therefore, depend upon getting as much of everything as he can (certainly more than his rivals), protecting what he has from others, and presuming that everything anyone else has means so much less for him (hence, taking theirs away when they're not looking).

With that view, homes become castles. Women become pearls. His own – wives, daughters, and sisters – should stay around his neck; the rest are for diving after. Prestige becomes outdoing and out-owning other males. He becomes a conquering warlord. He adds to his territory and guards his valuables like a shogun. He likes guns. And he's a very jealous man.

Outer Signs

Being, looking, and acting like a man are of utmost importance to him. There's nothing froufrou about him; he's bold and he's heavy. He shops in men's stores, at men's departments, or from Sears. Anything tagged as "unisex" he avoids. He only dares to go to second-floor ladies wear to purchase a gift to lure a woman. Even then he asks the salesclerk to pick one for him.

He wears his pants a little low on his hips and anchors them with a big, thick belt. He likes large patterns and prefers blue, black, and red. His suit material is twill or plaid. His jackets aren't loose or fitted; they're long, straight to the hip, and often Western. He wears his leather coat the most – it's black or dark brown with one row of round buttons down the front.

He prefers flashy cars – the newer and larger the better. Often he owns *two* station wagons, or maybe Broncos or jeeps. He also hankers for pickups, trailers, and campers; they fit his idea of pleasure, and all of them give him his kind of ride – hard, bumpy, and rough.

Before he pairs up, the Male Supremacist cares little about how he lives. Concern about decor just isn't his style. Often he lives where mothers and sisters can do the upkeep that he won't. When he does have a bachelor abode, he leases a furnished place or else gets the trappings from a furniture rental company. He picks big square rooms, an enormous rectangular coffee table, carpets, and conveniences. He wants his hideaways not so much near work as near the after hours action. He dwells downtown, near the campus, or music and tavern section of town. He rarely cleans his place. He always eats out. He sends all his clothes, towels, and sheets, of which he owns one set in stripes, to the laundry. And if he forgets to pick them up, which he often does, he sleeps on the bare mattress and wipes his face with yesterday's shirt.

Once coupled, he likes to live in quite the opposite manner. If he can afford it, he wants an isolated house away from the bustling metropolis. Whatever he picks, city or suburb, preferably suburb, he treats like a castle and says is "good enough." Especially if you don't think so. Given a choice, he prefers modern houses. Since he wants a good amount of turf, he idolizes corner lots – the fewer neighbors surrounding the better. Of course you'll be the one who's there while he goes daily to his man's world. You'll find it's very easy to get to schools, churches, and shopping, but hard to reach downtown. With him, even if you live in a downtown flat, somehow it's hard to get out of your neighborhood.

He loves appliances. He defines them as making your life better. The purchase of new gadgets comes high up on his list. Your kitchen will probably have three ovens – upper, lower, and microwave – not to mention toaster (although a car comes first and if you only have one, he takes it). He puts in washers, driers, and compactors, builds a huge counter. He doesn't know much about small things, but he's aware of all the big ones, especially if they're expensive and obvious.

He wants the living room to shine like an old-fashioned parlor. It's rarely to be entered and never messed up, so it holds your best furniture. Here you entertain guests – when he's present. The family has its own, run-down room, or stays in the kitchen.

He eats a lot. He drinks a lot, too. He loves red meat, especially steaks. He has a barbecue on the patio. He alone is in charge of the fire. He insists that you put on enormous meals and keep the freezer stocked with food. He tends to get portly as he gets older. He doesn't like it, but he's very bad at dieting. No matter what you do, he eats on the sly. How could *you* know what's good for him better than he does?

He's usually a sociable fellow, though some Male Supremacists are quiet and severe. Certainly he's lively around men, whose company he prefers. Often when he's out just with you, he talks more to the restaurant owner, head waiter, or bartender. He exaggerates. He likes to be on the go. He gets agitated if he's not at some active spot every other night or so.

He has information about all those things that men should know about. If he doesn't play sports, he watches them and knows all the current statistics. If he doesn't do business, he knows about it. If he doesn't fish and hunt, he used to. If he doesn't take a car apart, he "hasn't got the time," or else he's waiting for his son to grow old enough to teach.

He may or may not treat himself well in terms of luxury, but he always treats himself well in terms of allowables. That is, he does anything he wants when he wants to and blows up at any attempted limitation. In fact, the only emotion he readily tends to show is rage. He so armor-plates his psyche with muscle or fat that when a feeling does come through, it's usually explosive.

Authority means he gets to make a lot of rules and restrictions that all apply to you. He gets mad, rowdy, and sometimes even dangerous or violent when you neglect to do things he told you to do, particularly if he's been drinking. He has a big vocabulary of curse words and profane phrases that he uses mostly around his buddies. But when he gets angry, anything and everything pours out in front of anyone's ears.

Sex Signals

He chases after any member of the female gender, except *perhaps* the *present* mates of his *best* pals. He's a howler, a chaser, and a prowler: nurses, secretaries, and waitresses aren't safe around him. He doesn't approve of women higher-ups, such as lady lawyers, doctors, bosses, or officials, but he'll still give them a bit of a sexual come-on. Distinctions such as married, single, innocent, or wise don't faze him, but he usually doesn't go after very young women unless they know what they're doing and can satisfy him.

He'll only settle with a woman who proves she'll quite probably remain his private property. That doesn't mean you have to be a virgin till you go down the aisle. But he has to court you, meet refusal, and give commitments before you succumb to his charm. And there should have been no more than one other before him, a man he despises in retrospect. Your resistance assures him you won't give away what is rightfully his, although he's never absolutely sure of you. It helps his security if you're relatively young, i.e., haven't had too many years to play around. A first wife will be in her late teens or early twenties, a second not much more than thirty, and only that if she's come out of one long marriage.

His version of courtship is to take you with him where he goes. He also calls a lot on the phone and shows up at the door unexpectedly. He's persistent and relentless until you're won. Once that's done, he installs you at home and proceeds to take you with him less and less.

There's never a moment that his attention isn't sexual. Part of his definition of masculinity is his closeness to a hard-on. His presence is heavy, musky, odorous. His eyes roam your topography. So do his hands, at any opportunity. He makes the first move without hesitation – also the second, third, etc. You're constantly in the position of "fending off" or "letting happen," in the kitchen, with the kids around, anytime.

He's not a relaxing companion. He treats you like a gopher, himself like a tiger. Bedding down with him is not usually a sensitive or languorous experience. He's too much like a starving man released at a banquet, even when he has feasted on another feminine morsel only a few hours before. He sees himself as the doer and you as the receiver in any sexual action. He tells you what to do and what position to move to next. Since he interprets independent gestures on your part as aimed for his pleasure and not your own, he tends to interrupt you just when you are enjoying sex. He thinks good sex means length of time and speed of rhythm. He varies some, but in actuality he's rather limited. If the proper body parts don't reach standard contact somewhere along the line, he gets unnerved. Occasionally he has a problem with impotence. When he does, he involves you in a mutual campaign to help him overcome it. Pretending it doesn't matter just won't do. And if all else fails, he'll wait until you're asleep, get an erection, and wake you to prove himself.

Money Markers

Sometimes he's a steady earner; sometimes he's a drifter who changes jobs and locations, with you following along. But however he works, he considers all wages his to give out. He dispenses dollars like paper towels: They should be used only when needed, and they should go a long way. You and the house run on what he doles out when the mood hits him, though he'll sometimes buy you a big expensive gift. He pays the bills himself. Often he travels around by car on Saturday and settles accounts in cash.

Now and then he does secret things with money. He always considers his expenses none of your business and lies about many things: he may invest without telling you, purchase things without consultation, or, despite stringent finances, gamble. He spends freely on drinks, bets, sports, guns, and pals as the fancy strikes him.

He doesn't like you to work or have money of your own. If absolute necessity drives you to seek an added salary, he may see that you lose more jobs than you hold. Certainly he demands that your occupational position be below his own, perhaps menial or temporary, and that your job take place where few men abound. Your boss equals one other man too many. He'll drive you to work and return on the dot of quitting time – or five minutes early. He expects your earnings turned over to his control.

Family Aspects

The usual Male Supremacist wants about four children, but only with his wife. With "other" women, he uses condoms. Some Male Supremacists have vasectomies after they've sired their kids, to keep themselves out of trouble. All your children reflect on his virility, but having boys is better. It takes a whole flock of daughters to give him the same bravado as one boy. He isn't quite sure what to do with girls except spoil them, buy stuffed animals, and watch over them like a hawk. With boys he's rough, strict, and he pushes sports over school subjects. He likes all his kids to call him "sir."

He *respects* his parents. However, it's *your* job to serve them in his stead. He expects you to take second place and an underling role around his mother and father and sometimes even his brothers and sisters. He supports them against you. He never settles a certain animosity with *his* brothers and *your* sisters. Unless he can win their undying admiration, he stays very distant from *your* kin. He even posits himself against them and divides your loyalties.

If he's close to anyone, it's his male friends. He and his pals seem unable to admit how much they care for one another in any way other than to seek each other's company. To call it love isn't "manly," but love it is. Often his chums come clear from his preschool days. Others are from later times. But all in all, they're just like him.

He makes a statement that separates the men he trusts from those he regards dimly: "I'd trust him with my wife," he says. If a man's not his friend, he's an enemy. As friendly as he appears to *all* men, he lets his hair down only if he's sure he's safe. He tends to socialize with a very limited circle.

He rarely forms true friendships with women. Occasionally a Male Supremacist has a woman pal he sees on and off, sort of mistress-fashion, over many years. She alone becomes a friend and adviser and gets treated like one of the boys, but she's never brought home. Generally the Male Supremacist would have even *you* shun women friends. He'll accept ones from your childhood but view new ones as a threat. He prefers you to keep company with the consorts of his buddies. So, often, you tend to spend all your time with the same six or eight people – for years and years and *years*.

He does have some sort of allure. His male confidence is highly persuasive. He emanates something that's somehow...comforting. He can give you the feeling that he'll take care of you, that all compliance will be worth the price. He makes you think only *he* can turn you on, that he's hot and without him you're not. He gives you the assurance he can handle anything from a hurricane to a broken toaster. He himself may not be safe, but at least he protects you from those who are worse.

But his liabilities double, then triple, then quadruple over time. The fact that he's a jealous tyrant and invades your freedom seems natural to him, never a drawback. He grows even more resistant to new ideas or changes. New notions make him pull back farther and get even worse.

The predators from whom he protects you are usually invented. It's the Male Supremacist who makes you a victim; he just calls it guardianship.

Before going on I have to tell you about the Male Supremacist twist. No, it's not a cocktail. It's a modern-day, old-fashioned, double-standard man whose ascendancy is threatened. In response he decides that if women want equality they're going to get it with a vengeance. He knows all the latest liberated social customs and uses them as weapons against the women involved with him. He not only demands that you pay half the restaurant tab (that's fair, though taking turns has more grace), he insists you pay the cover charge at the club *he* chooses and knows is beyond your range. Then, when you refuse, he leaves you at the entrance and goes in himself. He wants his ex-wife (especially one who's left him) to pay him alimony. He asks for child payments on the months he has the children or counts how many meals he provides and deducts the price. He fights for custody every time you get a boyfriend. He serves you with restraining orders every time you turn around.

Though he seems in almost all ways different from the regular Male Supremacist, the essential element remains. He believes women are malicious and untrustworthy as much, or more, than the old version did. Under the guise of splitting things down the middle, he forsakes all kindness and reciprocity. While he may look up-to-date, underneath he's the same old thing. Now, back to the regular Male Supremacist.

What Is in Store for You?

One thing is sure as shooting. Sooner or later, he'll say he's going to make you feel like a natural woman. That's a signal to stop and reconnoiter. "Natural" might be fine for a forest primeval, but how does it do on twentieth-century cement? There's another trouble.

What exactly *is* "natural"? Anybody who tries to tell you what nature is and isn't actually is preaching personal opinion. Nature boy isn't telling you how it *is*, because nobody knows for sure – he's telling you how *he* wants it. He can fool you. You can even fool yourself. You might agree with him and never find cause to change your mind, or you might find what seemed sweet and natural ends up artificial and smacks of domination.

You may start with a Male Supremacist thinking that your coupling is as simple as Tarzan and Jane. (Strange that their only child was Boy, not Girl, isn't it?) But the Male Supremacist believes that differing things are meant to stay that way, like oil and water, or apples and oranges. Mating doesn't mean blending to him. Two separate elements – your genitals – attach for certain purposes, but the dividing line remains. And that dividing line is unbreachable. To the Male Supremacist, a double standard not only refers to who gets to hustle and who doesn't, it also stipulates who gets to use what space, what time, what things, what clothes, what words, and what etiquette. It even states who gets to stand behind the altar and talk to God and who has to sit on a bench and listen to the sermon. So with the Male Supremacist, you lead very separate lives that overlap *very* infrequently.

To him, women need limits and restrictions, while men get all the permission. You live with the implication that you are by nature recalcitrant and hard to discipline. Only incorrigibly mischievous creatures deserve so many no-no's. Instead of being an innately good person who might occasionally do wrong, you are, to him, basically bad stuff who must try to do good. You're walking, talking trouble. You're ever so slightly tainted.

You don't exactly have stages ahead of you; you have a permanent condition that comes with the category *woman* and starts as soon as you're his. When you can't make a mistake without it meaning you're not good, shame and fear enter the picture. You become your own constant rebuttal. Whatever you want to do, you watch and check. You stop yourself. You police yourself, and you lie a lot.

With him, as a woman you have to move in tight circumferences: you go from home to the store and trek back again, plus church, school, and a job if necessary, but you have no unknown whereabouts. You reappear at home by six and never wander after dark. You can bake, boil, or fry your food, but you can never trap it in the wild. You can drink wine or add soda to your whiskey, but you must restrict yourself to two. You can say "heck," "darn," and "shoot" but have to censor anything stronger.

Even in the house your reign extends only so far. He's the dictator; you follow orders. What power you get comes with age, his debility or death, grown sons and married daughters. Meanwhile you get the kitchen, the wagonful of kids, and the work that goes with it. He doesn't cross over to do your work.

He holds forth over the living room and sits at the head of the dining table. You can wear your halter in the back yard only, but he can wear trunks in the front. He owns all the major machines; you own all the linens. All the items the double standard attributes to females become your personal burden. You come to accept that you're mindless, less capable, and confused, that you can cause a lot of trouble.

Every time you approach his realm, you threaten your own self-worth. You're doing what a bad woman does, or acting like a whore. Therefore you have no choice but to stay away and grow ever distant from him. That's the only way you're sure you're doing the "right" thing. A relationship with a Male Supremacist eventually bars almost every avenue to intimacy.

Many women who at first want closeness with a Male Supremacist eventually give up trying. As he continuously puts you down, it makes your skin grow thicker, and living in a separate world tends to make you deaf, dumb, and blind towards your disjoined bedfellow. A woman with the Male Supremacist tends to become more and more disinterested in her mate's existence. The link that holds the partnership together becomes progressively more elusive and less real, until even the sex disappears. She usually ends up devoting herself to home and family and simply submerging herself. Her children become her life and her future gets lived through them.

What Are the Telltale Signs of Trouble?

You don't need a radio to receive the Male Supremacist's frequency. He comes on loud and clear, from far and near. Tune in and take note of vocabulary. A Male Supremacist has a hundred terms for females; none refers to them as humans. He never says "woman" and hardly ever "lady." To describe persons of feminine gender, he chooses words for small animals, vegetables, inanimate objects, and morsels of food: "chick," "bird," "fox," "doll," "tomato," and "piece," to name a few. He also uses a number of pejorative terms: he calls certain women "cunts," "twats," "slits," and "whores." The females among his friends and family he calls "girls." "Woman" is just too grown up, and grown up is too close to equal. Or if he says "woman", he says it like an insult, like he's saying "cunt." He expresses his interest in mammary equipment with terms like "knockers," "bazooms," and so on.

Male Supremacists think sex will cure rebellion, depression, sadness, anger, and bursitis of the hip. It's a black day when a man says, "All you need is a good fuck" to cure a mood he objects to. If he identifies himself as a member of the men's 4-F club (whose motto is "Find 'em, feed 'em, fuck 'em, and forget 'em") consider the fact that he may well plow you over and plant his seed elsewhere as well. If he mauls you, then says its not nice to stop him after *you've* gone so far, send him away. And if you hear that other old standard, "Keep 'em barefoot and pregnant," it may be prophecy, not joke. Put your shoes on and get walking.

He has notions that your body's not quite wholesome. He blames things on your period, which he calls "the rag" or "the curse." If you do anything different from normal, he asks you if you've got "it." Either he won't sleep with you those days or else he says it's "better" then – for him. He thinks you have to clean yourself up before and after sex, but he doesn't because he's as pure as Ivory Snow.

He opines that women can't drive, add, plan, build, make, or do anything; that they're natural companions of Clorox and smell best in Cascade. He doesn't necessarily say it right out. Rather he blasphemes lady drivers, lawyers, doctors, executives, and everyone he calls "women's libbers." He sees no need to squire you once he's got you. You're supposed to stay home. This is the critical point. It's time to remember we're living in the twentieth century, and change your living conditions.

What Are Your Chances and What Should You Do?

You can keep a union with the Male Supremacist now until forever if you so desire, but the conditions give cause for pause. What you can't do is change him. Remember the ice cube in hell? Or the sun rising in the west? Altering this man is just about as possible.

The Male Supremacist holds his convictions as self-evident and himself as their proof. He is, after all, a superior specimen. He doesn't even listen to contradiction seriously. He just bellows, teases, or ignores you back into place. Or he shows you his biceps, asks if you can match it, and then says, "See, *there's* the evidence."

If he changes at all, he's inclined to get worse. The Woman Hitter lies but a step away from the Male Supremacist. Yours may not include violence in his bag of tricks, but when any man believes he has the right to keep a woman in line, it means violence is always a little too close for comfort.

Personally, I advise you evade any Male Supremacist who comes within your range. I also suggest saying "so long" to one you've got around, sad as it may be to do so. He is *not* (now hear this!) the Intimate One – The Loving Traditional Man. There's nothing wrong with different realms or with the man as chief if that's your expectation and desire. But there is a built in problem with a man who disrespects all womankind. And ill winds come your way when a man takes liberties that debase his mate. Men should be pleased to be male. But Supremacists belong in another time and place. Maybe they never belonged at all.

You're the one with all the reasons to alter a Male Supremacist re-lationship. (There's no reason for him to change things). Forever is a long, long time with him. Dissolving a Male Supremacist connec-tion, once cemented, can be quite hard. He often sees your breakup as a reflection on his reputation. Besides, he has both his cake and his cookies by remaining hooked up with you. Chances are, you have a lot at stake as well: home, children, financial security, and your own upbringing. You may even come from an ethnic back-ground where one man is all you're supposed to get.

In such a situation you may want to try for some adjustments. De-clare your tolerance limit and outline what's due for your self-re-spect before making a break. You may achieve some discretion about his affairs, and even improved treatment from him when you draw the line.

I suggest *against* baiting the Male Supremacist as a means of teach-ing him a lesson. To taunt the Male Supremacist with exactly what he can't stand is like playing with fire. Don't slide over to another male, tease him with hints of adultery, or dishonor him for the world to know. And make sure your brother and father are on your side before you use them as a back-up force. They may subscribe to male dominance, too.

If you determine to end your relationship once and for all, muster your courage and do it cleanly, clearly, and legally. If you truly want out (and not just an explosive reaction) use documents, distance, and doors. And *you* do the doing. Applying tactics in an attempt to make *him* leave you is simply too dangerous.

You can stay and try to make the best of it. But before you go "total woman," make sure it's right for you. Don't be intimidated into echoing his standards if they aren't *your* standards. Trust isn't built on restrictions; it's based on faith and it goes two ways.

Where Do You Fit In?

Almost inevitably a woman who falls for a Male Supremacist once does so again, if perchance she goes another round. Such a penchant cries for revelations.

The Male Supremacist doesn't exist in isolation; he's always two for tea. When you consent to his domination, it means you concur with his dogma as well. But if your unwitting compliance to his ideas of dominance leads to misery, you'd better examine your dormant assumptions before you do the Male Supremacist again.

Do you hear yourself say such things about the feminine condi-tion as "It's our lot?" Do you hide your Tampax and pretend you don't have sex (while he goes around boasting about it)? Do you think a woman has to accept any advance from any man? That's either the old "a woman has to take what she can get 'cause they're the pickers and we're the picked" theory, or else you respond to all men as bosses. Do you feel that if a woman does not stay a virgin (or at least highly discreet) till she makes a permanent alliance, her union will always bear an invisible scar, but that a man's past never carries a taint? In fact, men "improve with experience" and you wouldn't want them otherwise? Or what about the idea that men can always find other woman, but a woman, once used, cannot? Once you mate, therefore hold on for all you've got or else head for the junkyard?

To find that you may unknowingly agree to ideas of female inferiority – and there are more than those listed above – is not such a terrible condemnation of yourself as it seems. After all, the Male Supremacist learned the double standard; so might have you. I say *learned*, not possessed innately. Women do belong to the same culture as men. They absorb the same lessons and pass them on. Did your mother say sex with all men was bad, then tell you your marriage would be made in heaven? It's just as hard for us to undo such unfounded assumptions as it is for men. Except for one factor: we're on the bum end of what turns out to be belief instead of fact. And since we are the ones who suffer for such assumptions, it pays us to find out what is real and what is not.

The double standard implies that your femininity causes men to behave as they do. Just by being female you tempt every male. His arousal is all your fault. But the chromosome that bears gender doesn't contain character flaws and no man's behavior derives solely from your sexual presence. His actions belong to him; likewise, when you do the seducing, you really can't claim your flesh was weak. *You* are responsible for what you do; and for the grief and pleasure you derive from it.

Many women, especially the traditional kind who lean toward the Male Supremacist, want to live out a vision in which they love one he-man who loves them back for life. But you must weigh that fantasy against the cost of its reality. When you haven't got love, and life is not so good, what's the point in living out a dream?

When your relationship with one man doesn't work out (and with many of us it doesn't anymore) the fault isn't necessarily your intrinsic character or your behavior. It didn't work out because it didn't, and that's that! Saying "adios" may not be what you wanted. But you've still got what you've got – yourself and the chance to love again!

The Woman Hitter isn't the only man who lies but a step away from the Male Supremacist. The Disaster Broker and Mr. Genius are also sometimes Male Supremacists underneath. So sometimes are the Woman Hater, the Man Who Would Be Mogul and the Idle Lord.

But the Woman Hitter. Ah, the Woman Hitter. He's the most dangerous of all the men who bear some Male Supremacist notions within them. He's the subject of my next chapter. You may, happily, not have run into the Woman Hitter, but far too many women have. Amazingly, crazily, his number is growing, not declining, so he's one of the most important men for you to read about, learn to recognize, and avoid.

4

The Woman Hitter

The Man Who Physically Abuses Women, Hits Them, Slaps Them, Pinches Them, Beats Them

The Woman Hitter is a physical abuser. He hits and he hurts. He comes from all walks of life – upper, middle, lower classes, different races, all religions. But he has one common denominator: he takes out his frustrations violently, and only on weaker people. That means women and children.

He's public enemy number one. And yet he never looks the part. Who would ever guess he's a wife beater? He seems just a little *more* than a regular guy – a little more ambitious and driven. He appears quietly contained, thoughtfully assured, decidedly masculine. He reeks of admired traits. But sniff a little longer, and you'll find out his confidence is not comfortable – it's assertive, and despite his drive, he's stymied. Under that extra-crisp exterior lies a half-baked chicken.

He usually hits where it doesn't show. And when nobody is looking, he twists arms, pulls hair, locks you in the closet, socks you about the body. He does it at home, at night, or when the company is in the other room. Closed doors and clothed bodies provide his shield.

The secret is known by one other, of course – the victim. He contrives to keep you as a co-conspirator. No bean-spilling allowed; he coddles you with elaborate apologies, frightens you with threats of further abuse. And he plays on the theory that if he is "more of a man," it makes you "more of a woman."

He believes that you too think it's manly of him to let you have it when you're out of line, that he's a tamer domesticating the lion in you. He thinks that's why you stand for it. He depends on your silence. Even if the battering shows, you cooperate – you tell people you fell down the stairs or slipped in the tub. And you don't wear bathing suits in public. He needs a woman whom he can threaten, to whom lack of a caretaker, lack of money, or lack of a he-man spells disaster. A Woman Hitter's favorite date is Snow White. Without the Prince, she just can't make it on her own. He prefers women whose upbringing included a heavy dose of female despondency. As a result, she buys the bit that she should take *anything* to make a relationship work. She heeds such garbage as "That's a woman's lot" or "You may never get another chance."

The Woman Hitter makes a special deal. Unlike the Father Knows Best, who wants a child to control, or the Loving Traditional Man who wants a stay-at-home-but-equal pal, he offers care and feeding in exchange for a whipping woman. It's a bad deal.

Story

When Jeanine from my high school married Bennet, we all thought she had made a hit. Hit was the right word, all right. Only years later did we learn she took a quick trip from blushing bride to battered wife. Jeanine had completed only two years of junior college. She was biding her time, waiting for Bennet to graduate. Then she dropped out of school and into a "perfect" marriage. When he took a job as the new go-getter in a real-estate development firm, they walked down the aisle.

People called Jeanine a living doll. It was an accurate assessment. She never picked a major in school. She never held a job more serious than McDonald's french fry packer. She could hardly spell "insurance policy." And it never failed to surprise her that checks could bounce. That Bennet held the purse strings, signed all the documents, and bought all the big purchases didn't seem fishy to her. He was taking *care* of her. Life was a queen-size polyester comforter. Not that she didn't work. But they never considered what she did as valuable labor. She kept the house clean and cared for the little cadets; *that* wasn't called work.

While Jeanine produced two children, Bennet came up with no promotions. Despite the early promise, his flash fizzled. And while he managed a very capable exterior, which had made him the envy of his high school, Bennet was fragile underneath. He couldn't keep a lid on his frustrations and envy. In private he flew into rages and flipped into uncalled-for jealous fits.

He thrived on man talk, he thought the love-'em-and-leave-'em philosophy was the way to go; he resented he hadn't tried it out. His father had been concerned that Bennet should be raised like a boy and become a *real man*. He had hit Bennet when he was a child, and often struck Bennet's mother. Even though Bennet feared his father, his parent's "masculine" strength impressed him. He translated violence into power. So once he was in his own driver's seat, he began to attack Jeanine.

Each time he took his rage out on Jeanine, he made up to her. Ever so romantically and sweetly, he apologized and seduced her back. Soon they really got good at their fights. Together they would accelerate some little fuss until she got hurt and they could kiss it all away. But then the beatings got more brutal.

One day Jeanine realized she was making up with him out of fright instead of the subsequent fun. But now her protests were stifled in a vacuum. He expected to kiss and make it better. Why should a broken rib be different from a slap? She was his property, and property took whatever you did to it. Once he even threw her out of the car and threatened to run her down. Jeanine was terrified. But by now Jeanine had a one-sided scoreboard: employment record – 0, children – 2. She had no money and nowhere to go.

One night, Bennet knocked her unconscious. Concerned that he had gone too far, he called an ambulance. Unwittingly he dropped the drawbridge that gave entrance to his kingdom. Outside authorities marched onto the scene. One by one, counselors, social workers, police, and legal advisers visited Jeanine's hospital room. She resisted their efforts. But only until she got back home. It seems in her absence Bennet had turned on and hit the children.

When he went to work the next day, she mustered her courage and made for the telephone. She quickly packed up and moved out. Luckily for her, an age of social enlightenment was beginning to dawn. She found many agencies ready to help her. It took a while, but now she is on her own.

It can happen to any woman – more educated women, career women, working women, married women, unmarried living together women, just going together women, women who have had only one relationship or women who have had any number.

I cannot avoid giving opinionated advice on the Woman Hitter. Without qualification, I say LEAVE HIM THE FIRST TIME HE HITS YOU AND DON'T GO BACK. If all women everywhere walked out *immediately* when struck by their men, wife beaters wouldn't have the chance to practice their perversion.

Having given my advice, I will continue for those who don't follow it.

How Can You Identify This Kind of Man?

Where the Woman Hater thinks he likes women but probably does not, the Woman Hitter does not even think of women as something to like. He never learned he was supposed to. A woman is something to show other men, to want for sex and servility.

The Woman Hitter is almost as hard to identify in the beginning stages as the Woman Hater. During the mating dance, his ultimate abuse remains obscure. It's not so much when he thinks you are his as when *you* think you are his that he changes. By becoming jealous, forceful, or possessive, he announces you belong to him. If you don't protest but comply, you play Pandora. Later on, bad spirits will pop out of his box.

He shows some early warnings: jealousy, perhaps a forceful, he-man heat to your romance. But also note these: his competitiveness with other men, his pursuit of women as part of his public image, his tight hold on emotions, his blaming others, his need to appear the dominant member of your twosome in the eyes of the world. He might strike before the wedding. If so, he works quickly to seduce you into a romantic parody of passion. Any "Tarzan is sorry he hit Jane and to prove it he will give her fifteen orgasms and a bouquet of flowers" line should ring like a five-alarm fire signal in your ears.

The Woman Hitter covers up serious problems of self-esteem with a veneer of storybook masculinity. His doubt mostly is in such areas as success and failure, strength and weakness, respect and disrespect. In each he measures himself against men, not women; he fears how he stands as a man among men. A submissive wife, maybe some side affairs, confirm his manhood. He blocks out much of the vocabulary of emotions and is left with largely negative feelings. You rarely find a Woman Hitter radiating joy or overcome with awe. He considers those emotions "feminine." When his emotions do erupt, he blurts out anger, often rage, that astounds even him. His fury covers envy. He agonizes over a secret measurement chart of other men whom he cannot control. What other men get and he doesn't – sales, promotions, prestige, money – he considers things his wife has lost or mishandled. She flirted, spent too much money, nagged, gave hospitality to some bum. Soon her body comes to symbolize his rotten world. When he wants to kick the world, he kicks its representative – his old lady.

The Woman Hitter needs order and regimentation. He wants his women to walk in all the squares, on time, in place. He keeps a code of criminal offenses in secret so he can constantly revise it. It's more fun and provides an excuse to hit if you slip up without knowing what you did wrong. Forewarned is forearmed, and he doesn't want you that way, unless he can depend on you to start the fireworks for him by conveniently forgetting or infringing on the rules.

Outer Signs

He dresses with precision. Whatever his occupation, bus driver to lawyer, he usually wants his uniform in order. He may drop towels everywhere, but his drawers must contain neat stacks of shirts like so many toy soldiers in a row, his jockey shorts clean as flags of surrender, his pants creased as straight as laser beams.

To say he is not a very flexible person is an understatement. He doesn't like unexpected company. Chance meetings make him agitated. He resists parties. He cuts off conversations with strangers. Especially *your* conversations with *male* strangers.

His life runs on schedule, according to routine – breakfast traditional, dinner hour set, children sitting down, relaxation planned, exercise rigorous. He likes sports and plays with other men. Ball games, squash, and boxing pit him against foes in a male atmosphere. Football and basketball give him topics of talk. He converses only with men. Sometimes he works out with strange devices in a gym. He thinks by looking hard he'll mean business to his cohorts.

His hourly demands become your life's clock: you make sure to get the shirts from the cleaners before he comes home. You leave shopping with a friend in plenty of time to get dinner on. You show up when you are supposed to and where you were told. You fill up your days with chores he wants you to do even if you don't want to do them. You hide your children's misdeeds from his attention. You pick what you say *very* carefully.

His environment is a blank. He doesn't live singly very often or for very long. He's a marrier. A firmly attached female is part of his image, so he almost always has one. He weds young. He has to prove that, like his old man, he can have a family. He reattaches to another woman quickly if a union ends, to prove his masculinity wasn't faulty.

He drives a manly car, never a flighty one. No Subaru for the Woman Hitter. He'll drive anything from an enormous Chevy Van to a Chrysler, as long as it's heavy.

A good deal of money goes into his upkeep. *He's* the public person, you're the private one. *He* needs the office, tools, automobiles, and suits – you can do with less. That is, until party time. When you come to the office or go out to dinner, your presentation becomes important. He'll demand you get your show together. He wants money spent on the public part of the house, the part that can be seen. You decorate and dust the living room and dining room, but you hold the laundry machines in the basement together with hairpins and bubblegum. They don't matter.

Sometimes he wants his mate like a mannequin who does not work at all. But even if his woman labors hard, he promotes the image that she is an expensive item he deigns to keep. If you throw that picture into doubt with your work, money, or independent purchases, you cause major blowups.

Sex Signals

To help his owner-provider portrait of himself, he seeks women who are ill-prepared for survival on their own, who believe they can't survive on their own or that they're weak. He likes conformist women. Not those who march to their own music, but those who sass just a little before they back off. Frequently he selects women already burdened with young children and having trouble supporting them. He can spot a woman who has not fortified herself from a mile off. When a woman has no degrees, skills, investments, experience in life, or willingness to go solo despite whatever skills she has, he knows it full well. If she hints at wanting to be possessed, he's ready to make the purchase.

He presents a very strong image to such women. He knows they are attracted to shows of masculine might. He makes decisions. He always drives the car. He announces he doesn't like a dress or hairdo to see if you do things his way.

And sex. Sex with him is lusty, not lovey. Maybe it's a little aggressive, as if he's spearing so much meat. He's not one for long and tender foreplay; he insists on a hard, driving rhythm. He always makes you take his approach. He likes the missionary position, the role of leader. No questions asked. A little rape is not unlikely, especially if you resist him or if he wants to reconcile after a battle. There's no question that as his property you are at his disposal. He doesn't like turn-downs. He comes back for more, three, four, or five times in a row. Lovemaking is through when he's through and you're thoroughly wiped out.

Money Markers

Money is a primary key to the relationship. If you take the monetary support, you take the licks: it's the Woman Hitter's idea of getting what he buys. He may only bring home a monthly paycheck. He may have you on a diet of diamonds. He may have you living on hope. You still end up as a two-bit target.

You see, all the money is *his* money. If you have personal income or funds, he commandeers them, and he keeps the checkbook. More than likely he won't let you work. If you do help support the family, he makes sure you never earn as much as he does. He insists you quit jobs, or he makes you lose them.

He wants everything you're wearing and using to be bought by him. He forbids gifts from the family. You may think you're a wife. To him you're a bought woman. He alone makes major purchases. He holds the titles to car and home. And he's tight. He may let money out, but he keeps tabs on every expense. He resents medical bills. You do not need to waste money, according to him, seeing doctors. He expects food budgets to be small, but he'll smash the dishes if dinner doesn't suit him.

Money is power to a Woman Hitter. Psychological dependence may rope you into the relationship, but the economic knots he ties keep you from getting out.

Family Aspects

Naturally he demands the role of head of the family. No guff allowed. He's an authoritarian father as well as husband. He usually wants children, though some cold and lonely ones do not. Generally children help support his masculine self-image and keep a wife in her place. He wants to make a perfect world for his kids, but he usually ends up hitting them too. Wife abuse and child abuse go hand in hand. Children make the most defenseless targets of all.

He relates to his mother, brothers, and sisters only as a dictator and authority. Relations often spot his wife-beating first and call him on it, but he has probably bullied them for years, so they no longer affect him. His father is another matter. A passion, probably negative, exists between father and son. The Woman Hitter forever tries to make his father treat him as the new head man.

In-laws represent a threat and interference. A Woman Hitter will attempt to completely sever your ties with your own family as early as possible.

He attempts equality with male friends. He *has* no female friends. It's a man's world, and he spends a lot of time there. Among men he builds a false camaraderie: men's talk, men's jokes, men's pursuits – all to the detriment of women. His alliances lack intimacy and are extremely status-conscious. He plays know-it-all and who's-doing-better in money, business, and sports. He flirts with cocktail waitresses. He cultivates the idea that other men are like him.

As far as the Woman Hitter's liabilities go, he doesn't have one – he *is* one. He's a walking, talking fatality, a wrong-way ramp on the freeway of life. It's not that he doesn't *like* women. He utterly disrespects them. You don't turn someone you love into a punching bag. Let's face it. There's no saving grace to a man who threatens your health and your life.

What Is in Store for You?

Consider the Woman Hitter like a pack of cigarettes. No matter how slick the package, how long, short, mild, strong, filtered or flavored the contents, he is hazardous to your health. There are many ways to play with fire, but only one rule – *Don't!* You could get killed.

Admittedly the Woman Hitter may be the man of some women's fantasies. But there's a big difference between reality and imagery. In your daydreams if a man passionately overpowers you, *you* control it. *You* arrange all the circumstances. You plan who the man is, how far he goes, and exactly what things he does to you. But when the Woman Hitter is a fact in your life, not a fantasy, you're not in control. *He* is. He doesn't know your boundaries.

He probably doesn't even know his own. Once he starts, he'll go as far as his frenzy carries him. It's best to keep brutes in the fantasy world. There they can make your heart beat and your lips moisten, but they can't break your nose.

With the Woman Hitter there are no stages, just rages. Once he hits, you can predict how the relationship will go – from bad to worse. The beatings can stay low level for years. Then maybe they suddenly accelerate. Or they can gain at a slow and steady rate from twisted thumbs to broken bones. If you think the first time was just an oddball circumstance, for heaven's sake you sure know when it happens *again*. He has no reason to quit if you don't stop him. Unfortunately the ways to stop him are ultimately only one: RUN.

As long as you don't hit the road or call the authorities, you're in for a condition of chronic battery, and a life of secrecy. His brutality gets more regular, the intervals between less lengthy. His abuse also spills over to the children, perhaps your sister, even an aged mother.

He may remain forever cool, always hit so it won't show. But it's possible that *some* blow, *some* day, will be too hard. Neighbors hear. Some friend sees the black and blue on you. A doctor comes into the scene. In that event, your life can go from secrecy to total publicity. Outsiders and officious strangers will come into your days. Each is from some agency that you thought would never touch you. Police, the district attorney, social workers, probation officers, juvenile protection officials, get to know your name. Or your death makes the headlines.

What Are the Telltale Signs of Trouble?

There are a number of telltale signs to the Woman Hitter. If a man interprets any offer of assistance as an accusation that he's weak, it bodes no good. In fact, if the subject of weak and strong concerns a man a bit too much, I'd be wary. Being weak is a sensitive issue with a Woman Hitter.

Meanwhile notice that while some men just *say*, "All a woman needs is a good screw," other men act on it. If the man you're with follows through on the "good screw" idea when he thinks you're out of line, the "good punch" theory might be coming, too.

Notice also if a man says women need to be put in their place, then gets angry when you step out of it. If so, it's a red alert. Who knows what he might do to put you back where he thinks you should be?

If a man *threatens* to hurt you or hit you before he really does hurt or hit you, it should bring you to a test. *Call* the threat. Tell him to go ahead and hit you. It's worth it to find out. Only three ends can result and from them you can decide what he is and what you should do. First off, he'll stop threatening you, never, never repeat it, and never, ever hit you. That's fine. Secondly, he'll continue to threaten you, but still never hit you. In that case you should leave him anyway. He's keeping you in line with fear. It may not hurt your body, but it hurts your mind. Or thirdly, he'll go ahead and hit or harm you. Then you know. Go immediately.

In any of the above cases find out if the man you know has a childhood history of abuse. Consider it a danger sign if he still admires the parent who abused him.

There are no mild alarms with a Woman Hitter, only major ones. Any of them means you should make a break.

What Are Your Chances and What Should You Do?

The likelihood of changing a Woman Hitter is almost nil. Certainly it's nil when you're his target. He needs professional help and he needs it badly. That requires time, money, and desire. Unfortunately he's unlikely to invest any of these. He's even less likely to confess that he does harm you. He can't take criticism. He's afraid of being thought weak, or emotionally disturbed. He's terrified of the depth to which his anger might really go. And anyway, he thinks other men are the same.

The trouble is, the Woman Hitter feels little or nothing unless he boils over. Because of that he doesn't recognize when a blowup is coming, or why, so he rarely admits he has a problem. He's also always *sure* it will never happen again. Your leaving him, the police, the threat of jail, assault charges and court may bring him to seek change. But even with therapy he's a risky gamble. He doesn't change easily and if you were in his "before" picture, you probably won't be in the "after." Besides, if he is caught, he often just plays along pretending he wants to change until he's left alone again. Then he goes right back to the way he was.

I advise flight at any cost. And as soon as possible. Even if you have been with a Woman Hitter for forty years, have suffered *many* beatings, have children, have no money: GO! Go *naked* if you have to! Call for help, go to the neighbor, lock yourself in a room, use the arm of the law, before the next blow falls.

Next, *don't go back*. That's the hard one. The Woman Hitter needs you and he'll try to get you back. Your leaving ruins his idea and public image of how perfect he is. And after all, you're his possession and his hitting object. You've been in cahoots with him, a game for two; how dare you walk out and leave him with no playmate? But, believe me, he's not going to change any faster than a leopard changes its spots.

Many women who've been with Woman Hitters are terrified of leaving for good, and for many reasons. There's the money, the shame of it all, the feeling that you've allowed yourself to be a victim. Or you believe you can never stand on your own, feel confident, or trust yourself again. And there's the fear that he'll find you. But remember, there's help out there. You don't have to manage it alone. There are battered-wife centers, hot lines, social workers, medical officials, and safe houses. If not those, then try the police, district attorney, private counseling, family counseling, clinics, friends, and family. Find the people who can help you. Spouse abuse and battered women are national issues receiving congressional attention. Many states have programs for aid to get you back on your feet. Secret shelters exist. Jobs can be found. Friends and family are more aware. Use every contact and phone number you can get. When you decide to get out, it's not the time to be shy.

If you do stay with the Woman Hitter, whether out of fear or hope for a brighter day, or if you go back to one, at least attempt to change the conditions. Get counseling for yourself, even on the sly. Shore yourself up and sort out your situation. Many psychologists now not only offer ways to self-enlightenment, they also offer fight training and instruction in healthier ways to quarrel. If your Woman Hitter has *any* ray of hope, perhaps you can convince him to go with you.

See if somehow you provoke the beatings. Not by doing the things he accuses you of – he'll use any excuse – but in subtle, psychological ways. For example, perhaps you think you should be punished, then unconsciously set him off. Avoid the explosive phrases, little flirtations, or forgetfulness you know will trigger him. Also, begin to learn how *not* to be a victim. Learn quiet, firm stands for self-control. Slowly get tougher. Learn self-determination, an occupation, even a martial art! Leave him short a punching partner and don't slip back again.

Very likely these methods will still lead to the termination of your relationship. But perhaps you will be stronger when you finally walk out. If nothing else, they may help you avoid truly serious injury. On the other hand, they may work in the opposite fashion. He may resist your changing with further and accelerated violence. Then, all I can say is – save yourself and the children. And above all else, don't just threaten to leave him. *Do it.*

Where Do You Fit In?

Who ever heard the sound of a hand slapping nothing? No one. The Woman Hitter is a two party game. You hold an indispensable role.

If you find yourself catching what a Woman Hitter is pitching, it's time to start thinking that possibly, for whatever reason, you may be a willing victim. The key word is *willing*. It may not be consciously willing, but it's willing just the same.

If you are, then masochism has a hold on you, and it's time to explore it. Many women have a touch of masochism, the "sweet suffering syndrome." It's built into us culturally. We can have it mildly, like apologizing when someone bumps into us, being long suffering wives and mothers, or taking job abuse. Or we can have major cases, like being ready victims of physical and sexual violence. Stop and think about some of your notions and patterns. Do you believe the weaker/stronger theory of sex? Do you think you should "take" things and be quiet about it? Are you always at fault? Do you think subjection is natural, maybe beautiful, or even kind of sexy? Do you have the deep secret notion that you deserve to be hit, that maybe you're bad? After all, you do bad things, think bad thoughts, and get out of line, don't you?

Perhaps you also accept that you are a man's property, that it's wonderful to be owned by, or belong to, a man. That's an easy belief for us to accept. Since women have been "purchased" in our society for so long, it's easy to forget that you're not a possession, but a person. Still, in the old days, even dowries or bride prices didn't include a pound of flesh. And the fact that a man supported his family never meant he was paying for a scapegoat as well. Remember, you're not property. You're a person, your own person.

True, realizing that you own yourself means giving up illusions that the man who possesses you will also protect you. (Is getting hit protection?) He'll care for you, feed you, and most importantly, *decide* things for you. But it doesn't make you more of a woman to have any of these things done for you. It only makes you more of a victim. Your womanhood, like your self-hood, is something you own alone. And when you don't care for your belongings, including yourself and your womanhood, somebody else is liable to knock them around. Asking another person to handle your life for you, be your owner, keeper, trainer, and decider, costs. Being responsible for yourself, whether you're mated or alone, also costs. But you pay a hell of a lot more when you play punching bag. No matter what you get for it, from Jello to jewels, you certainly overpay. It may be simpler and cost less to go from Snow White to Scarlett O'Hara and start taking care of yourself. Dreams are hard to give up, but the illusion that the Woman Hitter is a prince bursts into extreme reality every time he hits you.

It's possible to get over the idea of being property and over masochism. Nothing is worth self-denigration and flagellation. Try assertiveness training, courses in confidence and self-assurance. Get job training. Find classes on insurance, mechanics, and child raising. Make friends with efficient, operative women and watch how they handle life, and imitate. It takes a lot to leave an abuser and to go out on your own. Sometimes a known evil looks better than what's unknown. But here's one reminder that should help shake you up and out: whatever you let happen to you will be passed on. If your man hits you, later that's what your children will do, and they will lose what means the most to them – the most important people in their lives, those who love them. And that's a hideous legacy.

As I've said, the Woman Hitter is closely related to the Woman Hater and the Male Supremacist.

I go on now to a man who is far less dangerous than the Woman Hitter. However, if he doesn't physically hurt you, he *can* leave you exhausted, frantic, and broken down. He's much harder to recognize than the Woman Hitter. It fact, you often don't want to recognize him. He seems to be – finally – the right man, the great love, come along. He's compellingly, electrically exciting. He intensely adores you, is intimately involved with you. In fact, so involved with you he seems to swallow you up. And sometimes he does.

5

The Compellingly Intense (But Crazy) Man

He Draws You to Him. He Is Magnetic, Intimate, Wonderful. Only He Sucks Your Energy, Your Spirit and Almost Your Life Away

He's a reverie. He's a nightmare. All for guess who? You. You know you've been had from the first look into his eyes. Or rather, his first depth charge into your eyes.

When you return from your first meeting with the Compellingly Intense (But Crazy) man, you feel feverish, exhausted. You feel as if you've been through the heavy soil cycle in a Maytag.

And it's great. He's so there. He notices the changes in your eyes and moods. He keeps track of your strong points and your weak spots, your appetites and dislikes. He wants to soak them up. Watch them. Appreciate them. He has a marvelous vocabulary of affectionate gestures. He calls you by a pet name, concentrates on what you say, joins in when you tease. He's silly with you, wise to you. He seems as if he has perfect insight into you. He turns you inside out.

But here's the rub. He's just as intense in other parts of his life, too. He walks the line between genius and craziness. He's fused into his own mind. So everything he does, he does to an extreme. Everything he does, he does without relief and to the hilt. He plunges as deeply into thoughts, music, oceans, crime, or drugs as he does into you.

Either he wants to be with you incessantly or else he leads a crazy double life. When he's with you he's so obsessive, you become obsessed as well. As a result, when he's with you, he is *so* with you. But when he's gone, he's *so* gone. And you know he has some other intensity going. He has another woman. He's leading a life of crime. He's in the underground, or something equally grave. You care. It pains you. But you don't cut him off.

He tends to choose intense women, too. They're cerebral, vivacious, explosive, or deep. Or he gathers turbulently dependent women who are despondent, perhaps attempt suicide, get pregnant, or have other crises. In fact, it's not unlikely he has one woman of each sort. The Compellingly Intense man almost always has a second woman. He always seems to need yet another soul to explore (on either a long term or temporary basis). Or he has to have another full time bond, as involving as yours, in which to struggle.

Often his women are the opposites: one blond, one dark; one frantically energetic, one hardly moving; one vital and verbal, one ponderous and petulant. Extremes fit him. He's black and white, on or off. The Compellingly Intense (But Crazy) man wears no shades of gray.

Story

Everything my friend Caroline does she does to perfection, though she claims to be riddled with indecision. A visible passion marks her life. Perhaps that's why she has a penchant for Compellingly Intense (But Crazy) men. They meet her standard of how *grand* a love affair should be.

From the start, she always has a glimmer that such a furious fusion will be a disaster. Then she forgets and plunges into the emotional whirlpool the Compellingly Intense (But Crazy) man creates. She fell head over heels for one man in particular, Kevin, and their involvement lasted for years.

Kevin zapped Caroline from the first minute they met. He wasn't especially handsome, tall, suave, or anything else that would normally call attention. He was simply *electric*. His first look seemed to go right through her, as if delighted to find her and be fixated by her. And Caroline's nerve endings leaped to attention. He focused in on her, engulfed her, and shut out everyone else. His presence gave off an almost pungent, mesmerizing sensuality that seemed to extend around and enfold her. He suggested they go out alone for coffee or wine, and she went.

When she got home, Caroline was already obsessed. She felt half way to orgasm. She couldn't get her mind off him. She floated up and down like a helicopter. Kevin called the next day. Seeing her again, he touched her hair, cupped her face in his hands. Next time she melted madly, frantically into his arms and bed. Soon Kevin and Caroline knew each other so thoroughly the world seemed to contain only the two of them. They had names, phrases, and gestures only they used, games only they played. They read each other's minds. They were braille to each other's fingertips. Life became steps in a private dance. They'd break into one another's houses and leave notes. Gifts that appeared bizarre to anyone else had secret innuendos for them. Their love became narcotic for Caroline. No one but Kevin seemed to exist. After a time she could hardly function without him.

Yet he was *gone* a lot. They never really lived together. He always had some place of his own to go to. He said he wasn't prepared for total involvement. He had to have his independence; he'd call when he wanted, be there when he wanted. She'd have to wait, and wait she did. She practically slept with the telephone and framed herself in the front window hoping he'd arrive. Yet when he came, he was so intently intimate that she never complained.

His own place was a one-room hovel where he burrowed. His clothes lay heaped in piles. His bed was always unmade and without sheets. Books and music, tapes and paper, funny substances, lay scattered around. The curtains remained always drawn, the room dark.

One day Caroline received a call from a strange woman. She, too, was involved with Kevin, she claimed. And Caroline should know they were very, very intimate. When Caroline queried Kevin, he confessed. The other affair, though, didn't hold the same significance to him as

Caroline did, he said. The other woman needed him. That's why he couldn't leave her. He feared what she would do to herself if he should go. Caroline listened, but deep down she knew the real reason was he liked the drama and keenness of the triangle. Other women popped up without warning as well. Kevin would lie as he went off with them. They were "old friends," colleagues. But somehow the fact that they were more than this always became known. Unwittingly, women came to the door looking for him. One turned up pregnant. Another had venereal disease.

Finally, one day a different kind of call for Kevin came. The vice squad was looking for Kevin. For that matter, so were some gunmen. Kevin claimed he was only trying to make money. But since he loved

acute situations, his deals had been dangerous and his partners un-
scrupulous.

Enough was enough. Caroline knew her whole being was being
sucked away into Kevin's intensity. She'd gotten the jitters, in-
somnia, was smoking and drinking. She knew she had to grasp control of her own existence, or forever stay linked to his delirious, yet
depleting, absorption. She thought about Kevin night and day. She
was living her life through him, not through herself. He exhausted
her without promising any returns. She decided to cut him off and
began to pick up her pieces. She plunged herself in work and went
away on a long meditative journey.

Kevin lingered in her mind a long tome. She missed the rapt tête-
à-têtes. She longed for the sex, and the incredible engrossment. But
she had a very stable streak in her. She liked the freshness of a simple
life and she didn't want to be crazy, even vibrantly crazy. Slowly her
passion for Kevin died.

Indeed, the Compellingly Intense (But Crazy) man makes a better recollection than a daily diet. Some women figure him out fast,
that he takes too much from them. They lock their doors. But to
others, he seems that "once-in-a-lifetime experience" of total absorption in another person, of wonderful complete intimacy. These
women only recognize him after the Maytag spits them out, spun
flat.

How Can You Identify This Kind of Man?

The Compellingly Intense (But Crazy) man is a sort of sexual pole
vaulter. He leaps before you look. He's inside your skin and headed
for your inner sanctum before you know it.

When you piece together all the parts of his behavior, you realize
he's not unlike a spontaneous combustion engine. He spends energy,
consuming every ounce he gets. His skin looks as if he'd drained his
vitality away. His hair has no spunk left to do anything but lie there.
He's reminiscent of a creature from a faraway place with a dying sun
who comes seeking thriving environments and needs to absorb new
humanoids.

He doesn't prepare for the future or dwell in the past. He's *now*.
Whatever he does he *does* with an active verb. He penetrates. He expends. He dances. He wears things out: people, places, clothes, machines, concepts, and you.

He treads close to the Disaster Broker. But unlike the Disaster
Broker, he doesn't invite crisis. Rather, crisis beckons *him*. He's prone
to his own destruction. If the police don't arrest him, his thoughts
do. If death doesn't claim him, dissipation does. If he doesn't end up
at a mental hospital, he lives in fear that he will.

Outer Signs

An air of exhaustion hangs about the Compellingly Intense man. He has bad breathing habits. He exhales more than he inhales. He probably smokes. His head, sometimes his whole body, leans forward with an air of preoccupation. He forgets to eat and frazzles himself down to the bone. He walks a tightrope. He looks as if his energy leaks right out of his pores. He strains his eyes, which grow dark circles. He rubs his eyesockets with his fingers and fists. He needs glasses and uses eyedrops. He looks a little shiny and transparent, even when just out of the shower.

He's not a careful dresser. His style is either camouflage, to blend in anywhere, or he wears entirely black. (Though he may wear an earring and go slightly punk.) He prefers you in camouflage or black as well. He likes the brilliance of soul, not silk. Why draw attention to your private tea party with lots of bright colors?

He's a user. He can render a coat elbowless in no time, reduce jeans to ravels in a fortnight, scuff his black boots or brown oxfords instantly. His heels wear as thin as crepe. His soles flap. His shirttails fall haphazardly about.

You don't love him for his sense of dress (unless you're into dark as well), or for his looks. If he's good-looking, he doesn't notice. If you do notice, he denies it. His style lies in the elegance of his nearness. His attraction is his intense involvement with you. You're like an art object to him, the only art object he desires.

He has a place of his own, although he's rarely in it. He's idiosyncratic, a loner. He's not the roommate sort. He only wants togetherness of a furious kind. His sheets don't match, if he has any. His books are scattered, and he throws all their jackets away. His place isn't meant for comfort. The bed doesn't fit in the alcove. He has little or no furniture. The part of town he burrows in doesn't much matter to him, but he likes depressed and scruffy areas best.

His car hardly matters either. He purchases almost any kind, as long as it's secondhand. Then he uses it till it falls apart. It's always battered. Terry towels cover great holes in the upholstery. The tires could be used for the "One Of These Things Is Not Like the Others" game on *Sesame Street*. One door is a different color, too.

Obviously the Compellingly Intense (But Crazy) man doesn't treat himself very well. That is, if you judge by exteriors. He treats his inner self a bit better. He follows his passions with a vengeance. Like a child whose parents have bought a candy store, he can't learn to feed on treats slowly. He'll risk malnutrition rather than lead a meat-and-potatoes life.

Sex Signals

As for women, he likes the unique, the feral, the exotic, the individual, but definitely sexual types – types with something heady about them. An extreme flavor is necessary to satisfy his palate. Once he likes a woman's spice, he wants to devour it. What intrigues him are women who mirror him, women who are, somehow, overly *keen*. Looks, elegance, and flair seem to have little to do with it. But once he spots you, he hovers around. No longer do you breathe oxygen, you inhale his presence. No longer do you exist isolated within the shell of your skin. There is somebody in there with you.

Sex is one part of you he *must* know. When he does know it, he is the ultimate in intimacy. Lovemaking with him takes a long time. It moves from rug to bathtub to bed. It's a feast of places, of twists and turns, of straight in and to the depths. He looks into your eyes. He wants to hold your head, wants your ears and mouth, wants to share *thoughts*. Sex becomes a song you continuously sing to each other. When the two of you are together, you always smell as if sex has just occurred. Everything about you is moist and warm. He leaves phallic, funny gifts you learn to open alone. The woman he loves would leave Eden willingly.

He may not mean to victimize his women, but he does. He certainly dominates the relationship. He devours you like you're the fatted calf and he's the lion, though he probably doesn't realize he's doing it.

Money Markers

Money is the Compellingly Intense (But Crazy) man's foible. He doesn't seem to know how to get it, how to hold onto it, or exactly how he spends it. If anything, it's fuel for his madness. It drives him to do mad things. He almost always manages to lose it, or somehow to use it all. In reality, he doesn't much care about money, but he knows he's supposed to have it and he doesn't know how to deal with that.

You almost always have more money than he does. But he hesitates to spend yours. He wants to spend you, not your cash. You split things and do what he can afford, which isn't much. And yet he resents being broke. He refuses to solve monetary problems by normal means, but hatches schemes. He'll try to free-lance a wild idea, take a crazy job, sell things he shouldn't, get "gigs." Or else, eschewing coin completely, he'll try to make a fetish of a nonmaterial life.

Family Aspects

The Compellingly Intense (But Crazy) man is often angry with his family, or perhaps he pities them, but he can't break with them. He tends to be the oldest child and has never figured out his mother's love and what to do about her. He's secretive. His parents don't know how he lives. He feels he's departed from them too much to tell them. He thinks he's different from his brothers and sisters as well, though he adores them (especially his sister.) He can't understand how he achieved such a different character than theirs. They're so nice, he's so disreputable. Perhaps he's an alien invader, a genetic mishap, or a secret adoption no one will admit. He puts himself through visits with his family, though every time he finds them unbearable.

He doesn't really want children. They terrify him. But often during his passionate involvements one is conceived in accident. A budding embryo catches him between the devil and his deep blue guilt. The odds on your terminating a pregnancy are fifty-fifty. (He's possibly been through a number of abortions.) But if by some incredible chance he does become a father, he's an intense and close one.

As for friends, a Compellingly Intense (But Crazy) man selects pals as odd as himself. They are mostly men, some women, as long as they burn as brightly as he does. His companions run from priests to criminals, geniuses to gamblers, but they're solid friends. They need one another. They may be separate from his love affairs, people he's never been romantically involved with, or maybe they are. Some bi-sexuality is not completely unlikely for him.

The Compellingly Intense (But Crazy) man is an angel and a monster. A delight and a disaster. Those not involved with him consider him a crazy, a loser, or at best, peculiar. But those involved with him dote on him; they can't do anything else but be his playmate. He takes them into time-warps. There's no avoiding him when he's around, no reading of detective stories, no television.

What Is in Store for You?

Have you ever heard of Space Mountain? It's the ride of a lifetime at Disneyland – a roller coaster that runs in the dark. The Compellingly Intense (But Crazy) man is similar to Space Mountain. The ride entails thrilling climbs, devastating dips, bloodcurdling curves. You never know where you are. Everything passes in a breathtaking rush. Then, hiding somewhere in the middle, is a big loop back. Oh, after that there are still more swoops, rattles, bangs, and crashes. The speed is still speedy, but the highs are lower and the pace down. Then, suddenly, it's over. The end always seems abrupt, even though you've known for a while it was coming. And when you finally get off, somehow it seems you wind up pretty close to where you started.

Part of the thrill is the edge of potential calamity. Might a car career off the tracks? An occasional person get bashed or broken? Might you fly right off into thin air?

Getting off is really hard. You want to keep going. Staying on is unhealthy.

The Compellingly Intense (But Crazy) man is the same. However, there's one major difference between Space Mountain and him. Disneyland advises those with weak hearts not to chance Space Mountain. But the world does not forewarn you about the Compellingly Intense man so clearly. The real trick with him isn't spotting him from the start. It's getting away on two firm feet. You hardly know you're on his ride until you're already over the first hill.

That uphill climb, and the curves and descent that follow, are the first stages of a relationship with the Compellingly Intense man. Every new feeling you have is sheer delight. But then there's that U-turn. Despite the passion, the relationship with the Compellingly Intense man gets older. Stage two comes along. You mark time's passage by his departures and arrivals. You settle near the all-important phone. You drag it into the bathroom and leave the shower door open to make sure you hear it. You take it off the hook when you're out so he'll think you're chatting and try again. You install a very loud doorbell and look out the window a lot. He dominates your existence whether you share a home or not.

He gets bemused and sad when you're not home. He acts as if *you're* the one cutting *him* out. He pretends he's your second choice, that you have someone else, or more important things to do than be with him. You soon feel that you're stabbing your true love in the back. Rather than risk that, you tie yourself back onto his marionette strings. You're a lifeless doll until he moves the sticks. And you know that you are always less important than the fevered pitch he seeks and that the involvements he has apart from you threaten your survival as a pair.

In the second stage, he becomes critical of you. If you don't live up to his expectations, he gets petty. If you make a mistake in perceiving his motives, he snaps. God forbid you should ask him directly what he's doing. You're supposed to understand all, so you pretend you do.

Despite the intensity of your relationship, a great deal between you goes unspoken. It turns out that your special language, your gestures, and looks are very inefficient. Neither of you really knows how the other is feeling, much less what the other is thinking. You don't really talk. You don't really say anything. You only collide and meld.

In time the utter joy ebbs away to agony. His other passions chain you. His disappearances devastate you and make you jealous. The ride you're on now becomes one of negative emotion, more dips than pinnacles. The problem is how to stop a tailspin into unhappiness. The true hazard of the Compellingly Intense (But Crazy) man is an overstretched relationship. When the two of you become totally dependent upon one another, you pass the point of a healthy breakup. All too quickly, "suicide" and "nervous breakdown" become part of the vocabulary. Your family or a doctor steps in to terminate your affair, because you can't. With the Compellingly Intense man, the fuel does burn out. So do you. Six months – or twenty years – later, you become a burn out case.

What Are the Telltale Signs of Trouble?

You can't see without looking. With the Compellingly Intense (But Crazy) man, the trouble is you don't want to see. Funny flaws exist from the beginning of your union, but not many people want to notice them. Indeed, the warning signals of a Compellingly Intense man are exactly the ones everyone always tells you about and you wish weren't true, but they are.

Intimacy that's too good to be real ought to make you stop and take heed, especially when it happens fast. No matter how much you want to believe it can happen, real intimacy takes time. Sharing yourself, as opposed to losing yourself, is a delicate procedure that evolves step by step.

To have a good relationship, you also have to stay down to earth. When little games you two invent separate you from others, it's hard to notice, but it's an inkling that things are amiss. A playmate is pleasant, but if it's carried too far into a realm of very exclusive words and meanings, you're out of this world and into one of your own.

If you find yourself hungering for only one kind of company, consider yourself addicted and ask, "What happens when he's not here?" You've become overloaded on him. No matter what, that's an unhealthy sign. You aren't *fused* so much as you've become each other's circuit breaker. No him, no lights. You've let love become a drug instead of life's best additive.

If you're not yourself without him, you fit the definition of clinically depressed. Rather than become a couch case, consider calling a moving van before you get worse. Sooner or later, your own sense of survival will make or break the habit. The deeper the addiction, the harder the withdrawal.

What Are Your Chances and What Should You Do?

It's sad to be sage, but cheap thrills do cost more in the long run. The Compellingly Intense relationship seems to come ready-made, but it has it's price. You're just billed later, in monthly payments that can go on and on.

If the Compellingly Intense man you know is in his heyday now, chances of your reaping a harvest many years hence are minimal. Some Compellingly Intense (But Crazy) men do indeed change. They weather their own storms, mellow their intensity, and become some other type – often, the Loving Many-Faceted Man. But they do it alone. Only their own upheavals cause them to change. And the loss of a partner is one of the upheavals.

In other words, the best Compellingly Intense (But Crazy) man is an ex-Compellingly Intense (But Crazy) – a man, usually over forty, who was once a zealot, but who has deintensified himself and become a positive person. By then, in order to steady himself, he has usually whittled balancing beams for himself. Yes, he might still fall off the tightrope occasionally. You might have to add ballast. But he has usually learned the right proportions. He's still intimate, but not so consuming. On the other hand, an older, *unreformed* Compellingly Intense (But Crazy) man still means troubled waters. He's almost like an Amoral Passion Monger. Beware and steer clear.

Certainly you need some sense of when you've feasted long enough on a Compellingly Intense relationship. He's like a devil's food cake. One piece is sweet. But if you eat and eat and eat, the odds are you will suffer. He makes it all too easy to play tit for tat – the "I can be as crazy as you" approach. Maybe you don't want to use it, but some women succeed in holding him – by guile – playing "poor me," having breakdowns, constant colds, agoraphobia, and other self-defeating manias. Who needs that? Not you. His vividness makes other experiences pale. And who needs that, either? There's a lot to be said for pastel affairs.

Since I seem to be saying "He's great" *and* "He's terrible," what do you do? If you're a heavy romantic who falls in love with the dream of love, don't do this man. Remember the warning: not for women with weak hearts. But, if wild rides don't fluster you in the least, go ahead and enjoy it. Just memorize your name and address before you leave.

If staying on with a Compellingly Intense (But Crazy) man should somehow become important to you, here is something to work for: *Hang loose.* It's hard, but healthy. *Stay detached* from his comings and goings. When your existence starts to get dictated by his appearance, rub yourself down with Cling Free. Don't cut yourself off from good times with other people. He's not the only person who can give mouth-to-mouth resuscitation when you're drowning. Don't play victim. And watch your emotional scale. If unhappiness outweighs joy on a constant basis, reconsider your relationship. It might be time to lighten the load.

Where Do You Fit In?

More than any other kind of man, the Compellingly Intense (But Crazy) man tends to pick women similar to himself. So, if you lean toward the Compellingly Intense type, or you've keeled over all too often for him, what does it mean?

Perhaps you expect the impossible dream, stupendous engrossment in the name of love, perfect intimacy, an Eden of enchantment for just two. But *expect* can be a million painful miles from *get* when the realm is anything but real. Not every aspect of love is stupendous. Romance can't stay a paradise of total intensity for two. Somebody still has to go to work, shop for groceries, take out the garbage. And everyone still has to carry on his or her own existence.

To ease your personal wear and tear, sit down and decide which outfit you want to wear in life. They come coordinated, no mix and match allowed. In the passionate set you get very bright colors, but you also get short term and continued searches. For the stable set, the colors are prosaic and trimmed with routine, but you get long term and someone on hand. Either choice is O.K., but be advised that the one set clashes with the other. You don't get search and stability, vivid and long-term.

Admit it or not, if you constantly keep company with turbulence it most likely means that you *too* like crisis. Count the upheaval level in your life. Maybe the day-to-day existence frightens you. If it does, if routine seems like living death to you, consider that it may be *dying*, not men, you have to come to grips with. Consider also that you may be depressed. Under all *your* intensity lurks a hidden, chronic, stalking low. A Compellingly Intense man can provide a good escape from depression for a while. But if you're down when he's not there, the problem isn't him. It's you. You can't look for your connection to someone else to serve as your upper, your energy, your hold on liveliness. If you do, consider yourself a lover-holic – and seek help. Relationships don't thrive on addiction.

Conversely, you might need to pick dependent men. When you think about it, the Compellingly Intense (But Crazy) man may call the shots, but he desperately needs somebody – or some several bodies – to be addicted to. He needs to recharge, and he can't do it alone. Sure, it feels good to know you're needed, and it's thrilling when he comes back. But you can get so caught up in the gratification he offers when he's there you forget to order up somebody who loves you for *your* sake, not his.

No one ever forgets what it's like to be with compellingly intense and absorbingly intimate men, but remember – even ambrosia must be sipped, not gulped.

As I mentioned, the Compellingly Intense (But Crazy) man can overlap with the Disaster Broker. He can also come as the Courtier, a young, passionate man who likes to, needs to, must absorb the glories of older women.

Still, there is another man I also mentioned before who most resembles the Compellingly Intense man, and hovers all too close to him. He's the Amoral Passion Monger and he's dangerous. He's so dangerous in fact, I go on to describe him now. It's important that *every woman* learns to differentiate between the two and beware.

6

The Amoral Passion Monger

A Dangerous Man Who Will Do Anything in the Name of His Love: Chase You, Haunt You, Imprison You, Hurt You, Even Kill You

Remember the man who threw acid in the face of a woman he claimed to love? Or the one who sealed up a summer girlfriend in his basement and kept her there? How about the suitor who burned down a club full of people because the woman he desired went there with another man?

The amoral passion monger is dangerous. He believes he can do anything in the name of love. He does what he feels is necessary to keep you for himself because *he* loves *you*.

It doesn't matter how you feel.

To say he overvalues his own passion is too mild. He thinks that by securing his love object he can secure his own reality. He goes beyond buying or begging. He leaves the realm of rules and reason.

You usually aren't a singular victim. Amoral Passion Mongers pursue one woman after another, even several at once. Many marry and still continue, wedding one woman after another without divorcing the others.

Recognize the very early warning signals and avoid this man at *all* costs. Notice a threateningly heavy pursuit after only one or two meetings. Pay heed to demands from a man that you give up your freedom, remain true to him, wed him or come live with him long before you would normally conceive of committing yourself. Watch out for inordinate jealousy from a man. A man who follows you. A man who calls incessantly. A man who shows up at your home or work.

Beware of a man who sends uncalled-for gifts, especially if they reveal knowledge of your personal habits he could only gain by watching your every move. Doubly beware when a man threatens you with harm if you don't become his. Believe him and guard yourself.

Some men do wacko, wonderful things when they're in love. They send a thousand roses or singing telegrams, or paint your name on a bridge. But what they do never threatens you physically. Their loony, extraordinary gestures are *for* you, not *to* you.

Use your feelers. They should tell you something is wrong. The passion is too extreme. The timing is off. The movements, the words, the gestures, and the demands are not ordinary. Whatever you do, if it happens to you, don't flirt with fire. Use any legal and any other means to end it totally. Call the police. Don't contact or communicate with the man. After a certain point you might have to leave town on the midnight Greyhound carrying only a pair of pants and a new name. If necessary, do so. You can't be blamed for his fixation, but you can for not heeding your knowledge that such excessive ardor is dangerous and crazy. So before he hurts you . . . get help. Have him removed. Just plain *go* if you have to. But do something.

The Amoral Passion Monger is closely related, and often at first seems like, a Compellingly Intense (But Crazy) man, only he goes much further. However, sometimes a Compellingly Intense man can turn into an Amoral Passion Monger. Disaster Brokers can also come dangerously near to being Amoral Passion Mongers. After all, Disaster Brokers love risk and danger, and will do anything for glory. Why not for love?

You often meet the Amoral Passion Monger in the same ways you would a Hustler. He hangs out in the same places, bars, beaches – wherever he can meet women. He comes on in a similar manner, wanting to know your name, your phone number, your address. The next chapter is about the Hustler. Every woman has met some, usually many of them. Even so, it's surprising how few women can tell that they're *not* good for them, and fall into their hustle.

7

The Hustler

The Man Who Is Only After Sex

Love? There's no such thing. There's only lust. Anyhow, love doesn't matter for tonight. Talk? Waste of time. There are faster ways to "get to know each other," don't you think? Why not just pull down the blind and take off your clothes. We'll have a good time.

For some types of men, sexual surrender is only *part* of what they want from a woman. Oh, they want the sex, but they also want more. For the Hustler, sex is the beginning and the end of it all. The Hustler wants no attachments, no deep conversation, no dinner and dancing (though he may buy you a drink). He wants a roll in the hay and the more the merrier. He may go from bedroom to bedroom. He may bring one partner after another to his own boudoir. He may like having women one by one. He may think groups are groovy. He's the cad, skirt chaser, lecher, libertine, seducer, and bounder of old in today's form. A combined voyeur and conquest collector. And he's good at talking to strangers, especially female strangers.

Just as some automobiles are exercises in sensory deprivation (they have cushions to keep out the bumps, tinted glass to keep out the glare, air conditioners to keep out the heat and odor), the Hustler is an exercise in emotional deprivation. He offers sexual encounters only. Please, no extra feelings. No tears, no fears, no clinging, no love, no tomorrow, no jealousy. He gets all his highs and lows from new sexual rides in previously untried bodies. He doesn't want to deal with wants and needs or real contact. Just your first name and phone number.

He comes in two present forms. Occasionally he appears as the playboy or swinger. More often, he comes on as the fern bar, beach, party single. (Though neither type much cares if you happen to be single. They just care if you're available and ready.) Since any woman is liable to meet a legion of Hustlers through her life's course, albeit in different circumstances, I'll describe them both.

Story

My neighbor Rhonda recently reported what she called a "double hustler day" to me. First, she and another woman had dropped into a bar they didn't know, but that "looked nice," late in the afternoon to celebrate finishing a project. They were sitting at the almost empty bar, having their white wine, engrossed in conversation with each other, when a man came up and sat at Rhonda's side. "Hello," he said, "I haven't seen you around here before." He was dressed in clean, tight Levis, a dark, open shirt and sports jacket. His hair dipped ever so seductively over one corner of his forehead. "I couldn't help but notice how beautiful you are," he went on. Now, Rhonda clearly knew she was being approached, but the flattery was so quick, so open, and so refreshing. Besides, you never know, not at first. He could be an all right guy, one you'd really like to meet.

"Thank you," said Rhonda, "but I'm busy talking to my friend."

"You can talk to her anytime, I'll bet," he replied, "but I've just met you."

"Well, we haven't really met," said Rhonda. To which he answered, "We could solve that in no time. Why don't you come over to my place? I'm a great guy. You'll see."

"I'm with my friend right now," said Rhonda, now knowing he was jumping a little too fast to be a man she'd want to meet. "We could meet later, after you've split," he suggested. At that point Rhonda's friend said, "Look, I've got to be going anyway."

"See," said the man. "You're free. You could come up and we could get to know each other. Did anyone tell you you have the most beautiful smile."

"Don't go," Rhonda yelled to her friend. "I'm going with you." But the man followed her out. "At least give me your phone number. I'll call you sometime. What are you doing tonight?"

"My phone is dead," Rhonda replied. "The cat peed on it."

"I could follow you to your place," the man suggested. When Rhonda declined he replied, "You really don't know what you're missing. We could have a great time. I'm really good, you know." He touched a piece of her hair, edged towards her just a bit, smiled intriguingly. "I can make you feel really good, like you've never felt before." He was obviously pretty successful. When Rhonda insisted on leaving anyway, he offered his number and asked her to call him.

Rhonda noticed, as she got to her car and he meandered back to the bar, he headed up to two new women who had just sat down.

Rhonda was relieved. She'd fallen further down the same track before with guys like that, ended up the next morning being thanked, hurried out the door, told they'd call and never hearing from them again. Or having the guy athletically jump her bones one more time at dawn, take a cup of her coffee, then casually dress and leave forever. This time she spotted it. Rhonda seemed to suit Hustlers. Pretty in a sorority-girl way, still she looks wise, not innocent.

But her relief was short lived. Back home the phone rang instantly with a man who'd been pursuing her for months. "Hi, it's R.J.," the voice said. "I'm in the neighborhood. I thought I could drop over."

"R.J.," Rhonda answered, "you know I don't get involved with married men."

"That's O.K.," R.J. replied. "I just have a bottle of champagne here and I thought you might enjoy it."

"R.J.," Rhonda repeated. "You know I don't go out with married men."

"We could just sit around and talk. Or we could drive over to my boat."

"Sure, R.J."

"Come on, Rhonda. Don't be one of the up-tight women. I could even get a little party going," R.J. suggested. "Me, Jerry, some of the girls at the marina."

"No, R.J. Good-bye, R.J."

"Well," closed R.J., "no harm trying."

Rhonda didn't happen to fancy a frolic with either man that day, but she appreciated that, now that she'd learned to recognize them, Hustlers didn't leave her guessing. Though they didn't directly state it, they always made it pretty clear what was offering. And you could come and get it. Rhonda didn't feel like getting it. It always made her feel "gotten."

By being fairly transparent, the Hustler expects to deal only on a superficial level. Then, he assumes, if you're at all willing, your intentions are the same as his. No underlying motives are allowed with the Hustler. He offers exactly what he offers. You know what you're getting. And no one has responsibility for anyone but himself or herself. He tells himself he operates on a basis of free will. But his kind of free will means he won't deal with anything more serious than passing intercourse, and he won't take the buck for anything that happens. Not every women knows exactly how skimpy the package he offers is. She expects more to come of her union with the Hustler.

But when all is said and done, a relationship with him is . . . well, not a relationship. It's sport.

How Can You Identify This Kind of Man?

Hustlers like entertainment. Life for them is a parade of passing people and trappings. Safety lies in numbers, escape in variety. There's too much happening to limit themselves, too much happening to do much thinking or caring. "Good times" is their philosophy. It's also their geography. They think there are lots of easy women in Europe, even more in Asia. But there's plenty here, too. And they go where, hopefully, they can find them.

All in all, Hustlers are pretty literal fellows. They don't go for depth in meaning, feeling, or relationships. If life is a wave, then they are body surfers. True, some hustlers are complex and angry loners who knowingly use women. Others make a fetish of being "light." They try to avoid any and all ties or thoughts. All of them loathe the idea of psychotherapy, or facing themselves, though they may participate in encounters and "enlightenments," especially on weekends. None is sensitive, at least sensitive to women. They want all the internal stuff to be put in a deep freeze, and only to nibble on trifles.

As a result, the Hustler reduces reality to one of two mottos: 1) Everything in life is so wonderful you ought to have a good time; or, 2) Everything in life is so awful you might as *well* have a good time. It's a singular optimistic or pessimistic stance, with no explanations. He probably subscribes to other modern but prosaic policies: freedom, owning yourself, open unions, space. When he wants to persuade you into bed, he can rally all of these as pressure over what you aren't, and over what you should be. He can flip them over and call you up-tight, old-fashioned, or hung-up as well.

Outer Signs

The Hustler in either form, single or playboy, takes care of himself. He's the only person he *has* to take care of. He leads a sort of stripped-down existence – unencumbered emotions go with unencumbered apartments, sleep, cars, and scanty dress. He doesn't wear undershirts. You won't find him buying underpants, either, except perhaps tiny nylon bikinis. He can't always be bothered to get a pair of socks when he puts on his shoes. He goes for half-dressed – or undressed, because no matter what, he wants to look sexy. He owns a lot of jeans and tight T-shirts, sleeveless T-shirts, or tight "Alligator" shirts. Some own a lot of short gym shorts. He wouldn't be caught *dead* in old fashioned baggy boxer shorts.

He's a very casual, but good, dresser. Semi-silky shirts worn with two open buttons. Tight jeans or well-cut, form-fitting slacks. Butter-soft leather loafers, boots, or boat shoes. Miami Vice jackets. If he has to don a suit, it's Frenchified, and probably has a vest with a paisley back. He runs or works out in sweats that somehow manage to be both low and tight across the bottom.

When he's a little older, his garb becomes a bit looser, your basic *comfortable* sexy appearance. He probably sports a beard by then, maybe wears tunic tops with plunging necklines. Under the neckline glows an inordinately deep suntan, flashing like a neon sign saying *Nudist Colony Ahead* (though he'll call it a "discovery center.")

Perhaps the Hustler adds a touch of rococo. A gold chain, an I.D. bracelet, an onyx ring, a turquoise belt buckle. Some of the playboy types have taken to hair dye and maybe just a touch of makeup.

Youth means a lot to the Hustler, even when he's young. He can't envision all the sex without it. He has unspoken but obvious worries about age. He will try to stay and act very young. Yet he probably looks older than he is. His life doesn't wear easy on mind or body, despite his seeming attempts at youth or ease. His skin, eyes and neck reveal it. He plays too hard and thinks too soft, and it shows.

The Hustler's style extends to his automobile: it's meant to please him, and it's definitely not family oriented. It looks game. Often he drives a sports car, especially the more suave and seductive types – Porsche, Corvette, Alfa, Datsun 300 ZX, or Mazda RX7. Its sleekness and image mean as much to him as function. If he thinks big, he thinks Mercedes, Pontiac, or Mercury.

Often the Hustler owns, or would like to own, a boat. He sees yachts and cabin cruisers as going with carnal picnics and orgiastic clambakes. He likes to take one person, or maybe small groups, to out-of-the-way places. He doles out drinks and bologna, and tells you what a good time you will have, are having, or have had.

He has an apartment of his own (after maybe college roommate days). Often it's in the sporty, singles part of town, and located in a complex of buildings. His pad is a little bit modern and a little bit expensive, with not too much furniture or attention paid to the decoration. You know, some framed posters. The complex probably has a pool, steam room, and Jacuzzi. (Or his own tub has jets.) If he owns a place, it's more likely a condominium than a house. It lies near the beach, hills, or woods. The backyard deck is very private. The closet has been turned into a cedar sauna. The deck supports a hot tub. Wherever he lives, he *always* has a couch – a big one. The tables are blond wood, the television large. There are mirrors, sometimes everywhere and curiously placed – like on the ceiling. A king-size bed with no bedspread fills one room. He owns a supply of huge towels and a couple of spare terry cloth bathrobes.

There are a few paperback novels about. He reads John D. McDonald, Dick Francis, Stephen King and sci-fi. Heavier books than that appear, but he doesn't finish them. Some Hustlers subscribe to *Playboy* ("for the articles," he'll say) and *Hustler* (for the obvious).

He uses services to make his existence more convenient – he sends clothes, sheets, and towels to the laundry. (Although younger Hustlers might go to the laundromat or laundry room to meet girls). He knows the way to local pizza and Mexican restaurants blindfolded. He has a favorite nearby liquor, quick food, and drug store. Playboy types know liquor stores that deliver.

Surprisingly, though, he doesn't eat out much except for breakfast. He centers his activities around home. All kinds of things can happen over there, especially over "dinner" if you can call it dinner. You see, his refrigerator is bare except for juice and a bottle of mustard. When he needs food he makes quick runs for it. He thinks in terms of chips, dips, and cheeses when having company over – less fuss that way. Or, he brings in the pizza and the tacos. If he does cook, it's a steak on his hibachi and salad from the deli section. Basically, he really only provides one regular food – and it's not soul food. He *does*, however, stock a lot of ice cubes.

His bathroom cabinet is his real pantry. It contains abundant and diverse supplies: Tampax, Vaseline, body oil, baby oil, Close Up, and Scope. But no condoms, although he is getting worried about sexual diseases. Also, he still considers birth control *your* responsibility.

The older, playboy type of Hustlers also equip one other department – the liquor reserves – for every preference. In general, they purchase the cheaper brands – gallon jugs of Ye Olde Wolfbreath vodka, quarts of Uncle Unknown bourbon. The younger single Hustlers have beer, maybe wine. And all of them have tried marijuana. Whether or not they liked it, they often offer lots of not-so-good grass. Say, Tijuana Tan.

Unfortunately, most Hustlers tend to have a job that requires regular hours and a certain amount of attention. (Though some have made a pile of money or have a family inheritance.) Usually, the Hustler is not the boss. But he manages to have a good enough position to dress fairly well and have free time. He might be a sales representative or a computer expert. He might be in the business office of Ma Bell or the gas company.

Most Hustlers, while they may not treat their souls terribly well, treat their bodies all right. They care about physical fitness. They jog, exercise, lift weights, or play racquetball. They can be swept away by new ideas on diet and vitamins. Some eliminate sugar and red meat from their diets for a while, and try alfalfa sprouts, lecithin, or bran. Cardiovascular systems intrigue and frighten the Hustler. But cancer is the real forbidden world.

Sex Signals

The Hustler generally aims either for youthful slender or youthful sporty women. The key word is youthful – even into their late thirties. He'll try almost any woman, but he prefers pretty ones. He'd rather avoid bookish, intricate, fragile types. Instead he heads for those women who have been taught to appeal to men, who wear attractive clothes and make up, and who look like they try to be sexually appealing. He also prefers women who, by where he finds them, seem to be making themselves available, who aren't too intense or bust out with too much analysis. (Caustic remarks don't put them off that much. Hustlers think that these are a front.) The singles type Hustler also likes "free" women, while the playboy type likes "good sports."

Neither type of Hustler is shy about meeting women. They easily talk to any woman who comes into a fern bar, sports shop, gym, beach, or party. They get you to establish who you are and what you do right away, usually by asking semi-impertinent questions. They flatter you. They doubletalk their way around telling you about themselves, dismissing their work or other matters with a single word, or saying it isn't worth discussing. Rather they engage you. They hook a response. Hoping to spear something beyond a response, they soon challenge you to prove yourself. A lot of women seem to rise to it. They may query you on your habits to see if you're "old fashioned," or "up-tight." They imply how great they are, and that if you don't go off with them it's you who'll be missing out.. They mention "good times," freedom, feeling good. They offer to "fix" you. Not too much preliminary comes with their offering. Dinner and theaters, dances and dates, are not on their agenda. Once you've met, the next step is directly to his place or yours – preferably his. It's more set up and has the things he likes.

Sex with the Hustler goes beyond proficient – it's virtually *acrobatic*. He's read the *Kama Sutra* upside down and backwards, and that's some of the ways you find yourself with him, too.

He insists on getting himself as well attended to in bed as he attends to you. Maybe he insists on getting himself attended to better. He shows you where to apply yourself to him the way it feels best. He expects right off the bat all the added extras that sometimes go with sex. Hesitation signifies hang-up and not fully entering a "casual" good time.

In performance he gets excellent marks. He has lots of acts down pat. If you prefer prowess to profundity, he's right down your alley. But cuddling and cooing are not in his bag of tricks.

Money Markers

The Hustler tends to earn pretty good money. He also tends to spend quite a lot of it – on himself. He makes investments, but is unable to accumulate much. He lives just a little over his means, or just a hairsbreadth under. He pays a pretty sizable nut each month for his easy way of living. He often likes to do expensive things, take skiing trips, fly to Mexico. He owns or rents expensive things.

He doesn't use a woman's money much. After all, he entertains you without coughing up much of his own. He doesn't take you out. He doesn't buy you things. Women are a pretty common and available commodity to him. They're easy to get. He's attached to no one. So why pay?

Family Aspects

He seems to have no family. You rarely hear him speak of them. Phone calls from them never interrupt you. No pictures of them seem to exist. Wherever they are, they're distant. Their world and his rotate in different orbits.

He has a number of male friends and a larger number of acquaintances (some from the places where they all hang out). He plays tennis or eats lunch with his close chums. Both his friends and acquaintances are used to leading the Hustler to other people (especially women), and to parties and picnics. They make up each other's entertainment circuit. Some Hustlers start up friendships with men only to meet the man's women friends. When he gets the women's numbers, he disappears.

All in all, the Hustler is pretty much a textbook case of self-centeredness. He cultivates distance, and often mindlessness, in most aspects of his life. If and when you reach for him, he's like Casper the Friendly Ghost. Gone invisible. He is not only hard to get through to, he pretends there is nothing there when you do. Or he pretends it's unfriendly of you to ask for anything from him. True, he has his assets. He offers light entertainment and serves up physical gratification without strings attached. Maybe you don't want any strings either for a night, a month, or forever. Then he suits you. However, perhaps the best plus he offers women is one of which he is unaware. With him you can learn just how much you want to carouse or how lightly you can take sex. For that reason, it can be worth trying one or more Hustlers in your life. But if you don't feel any need to carouse and sex isn't light to you, don't.

What Is in Store for You?

You can't exactly say you have a *relationship* with the Hustler. You can meet and greet, talk and make love, but can't see each other, go together, or head for the altar. The Hustler will put your name in his black book and, if he's the playboy type, call you for parties. If not, he'll forget you. But there's no emotional bond with him. He's not even a telephone buddy like the Short Affair and Quick Escape Artist. You only get to call the Hustler for a feather bed bender.

Mind you, you can also only stay on his list – if he's the kind who calls again – if you participate in what he wants. He scratches edgehangers and no-sayers. And, if you ask for more than he's giving, he'll disappear fast. Sex is the only ante to his game. If you don't pay up, he doesn't play.

Sometimes you have to learn the odds and study the form like in horse racing to learn the difference between men who are bad for you and men who are good. In the Hustler's case, he's a fast start at the gate, but he's only good for a very, very short run. If you're looking for a quick sprint, fine. But if you're looking for distance, choose another kind of man.

When a man asks you over, not out, at your first encounter, or if he begins to talk about sexual prowess before you exchange names, the underlying invitation is pretty obvious. Once you go with him, the action will be pretty fast. Hustlers will carry you as far as they can get you to go, until you stop them with a very firm *Whoa*! Also note, as far as a Hustler is concerned, a no from you is still a yes until you back it up. He's hard to rein in. If you go any place with him, his place or your place, he'll put the jump on you. He'll assume just by accompanying him you meant to go the whole course.

Most women use certain ploys to protect themselves until they get to know a man. Consciously or unconsciously, you choose to meet someone new somewhere away from your bedroom, a little in the public eye, and with open avenues of escape. A Hustler will try to circumvent these protections – they mean time and trouble. His intention is singular, so why fuss around?

He expects sex and makes it seem like you agree to it. So *you* become the one who is remiss when you withhold what he claims was understood. If he gets his way and has sex with you, and you seem upset afterwards, he will use guilt tactics and tell you it was your choice. You wouldn't have done it if you didn't want to, right? If you're not upset, he'll say a pleasant good-bye. He also has another approach he rarely wavers from: if you've taken one or two steps with him, talked, necked, or petted, you *must* go all the way. (I've had men follow me out of places ranting that I have to give them my number or go off with them simply because I've talked to them.) The rule has a variant: it's not fair to lead a man on; if you intend to back out, you must do so at the beginning. And so on.

Don't buy it. It's bunk! Whatever there is between you, it's short. If you say no, he'll move on pretty quickly. If you say yes, that's it, the whole schmeer. The event is over. You might be offered occasional repeats and escapades – adult field days – but his track runs in a circle. It's not a highway.

After it's over he doesn't want you to call unless you want to come over. He may not even give you his name and number. Hanging on the telephone is not his idea of fun. Physical contact is. You don't go on gradually to learn more and more about each other. No introductions to family follow. Once around the course, the Hustler usually moves on to another track.

Since you can't go anywhere with him, what's important is how you end up with yourself. Win, place, show – or lose. You may meet other people through him, but only to encounter the same sort of horse.

What Are the Telltale Signs of Trouble?

The Hustler flashes his calling card pretty quickly. So if you have any suspicion that you'll come out with losses, don't place your pennies on his pony. His outer signs pop off like so many firecrackers – all in a row and in speedy succession. You reach a critical point of decision often within the first few minutes. His Mae West act ("Come up and see me sometime") is a definite storm warning. So is a barrage of questions that get more and more personal.

If you do go up, or have him over, a set of irregular ripples crisscross your pond. He stands just a trifle too close. You feel as if you have to keep from backing up. He brushes by you when it wasn't really necessary. He nuzzles your neck, as if you were already intimate, when you are not.

He's waiting to see your reaction to all these things. No reaction means he moves one step farther. If you do react, he'll try again to see if you really mean it. If you've gone to his place, he might grab you behind the bar, slither up to you on the couch, or head you to the bedroom. Crossing the threshold means going all the way – he'll try.

Balking on your part produces a bombardment. He'll question your "with-it-ness." If you say you have another man, he'll accuse you of being property. If you say you prefer to love the person you have sex with, he'll say you aren't liberated. Refusing is utterly *neurotic* of you. It's certainly self-denial. Who but a disturbed person would turn down such pleasure?

If his maneuvers unnerve you, it's time to take a stand – a negative one. If you absolutely say no, the Hustler tells you that you're "nice." It's his way of saying he's decided to jog off.

Any point can be critical with the Hustler. You may find yourself, out of curiosity or whatever, having gone along with him pretty far. The idea that you can't back out, that you're "mean," is ludicrous. You can say no any time! And you never have to put up with grabbing. If the usual gesture language – taking his hands off, moving away, staying behind the kitchen counter – doesn't work, then muster up every way you have of saying stop. In fact, *yell*: STOP IT!

Politeness is his greatest advantage and your greatest disadvantage. So toss it. Your mother isn't looking.

What Are Your Chances and What Should You Do?

Let's be serious. There's not much chance of turning *People* magazine into *Time*. And there's not much chance of turning a Hustler into a scout leader. He has no concern or respect. Sharks have little regard for the spirits of the tiny fish they scoop up, devour, and excrete. The same goes for the Hustler.

Considering the all-around rewards, my advice about the Hustler is to say "Sorry, but no." You can find more intimacy in other versions of short relationships that are still primarily meant for sex. Certainly you can find more things to do and a wider variety of communication elsewhere. At the bottom line, what the Hustler offers soon gets boring. Personally, I think a spin with the Hustler means you aren't taking care of yourself too well. I read even a cool, calculated go-around with him as a sign of depression. In so many non-words, the Hustler says you think you can do without any caring. In most cases, I just don't buy that.

For pure physical contact, with no friendship or commitment attached, at least he's safe emotionally, although going with him can raise serious health concerns. (Remember, you're making love to whomever he's made love to.) You can try him and if you don't like him, you can leave. Also, at certain points in your life, you might want to test your survival equipment. If you can take the Hustler for what he is and come out fine, you'll know you are guaranteed to survive arctic conditions.

But please – only do him if you're in the same frame of mind as he, if you too want sex and no attachment, if you want performance. Then also see if he just wants to get pleasure or is willing to bestow some as well. Some Hustlers only want to get massaged, not to rub in return. They hate feeling they have to do anything. After all, they aren't good sharers to start with.

If you do decide to romp with Hustlers, your chances for a good experience are best if you have good eating habits. Stop when you're full. If you do too many Hustlers for too long, an uncomfortable feeling can result that takes a long time to go away. You can't find an Alka-Seltzer for too much Hustler at your local drugstore.

If he uses shame to persuade you, he's not the one who ends up guilty; *you* are. He'll take advantage of your shady areas – what you think you should do, how you don't want to make him angry, how hard it is for you to say no directly. He doesn't suffer your confusion when he's happily getting it on.

As for group sex – it can be fine; it can incorporate love and care for all involved. Or it can be forced by social pressure and have a circus atmosphere. You certainly ought to be the one who decides on your own participation. You might derive more satisfaction from a strong no than from a muddled yes.

Where Do You Fit In?

If too many men who just want sex come through your door, it's possible you might need company so badly you will take anyone and anything.

Perhaps it's time for you to realize that you can find *yourself* entertaining and sexual enough not to require provisions from the outer world. Your life doesn't have to be a parade of people, jokes, and good times to fill it up. Think about sitting down with just you. Make *yourself* your favorite date and go to your own living room. Admittedly, it isn't always an easy task. It can be hard to break through loneliness. But, once found, the world inside your own head can be spectacular, multicolored, and infinite.

That means taking personal charge of your sex life, too. You can fulfill your own desires, say, during those long in-between-men spells, without frantic forays in search of someone, anyone, to satisfy you. To do something you don't particularly want to do just to answer a sexual drive means you allow a need to become a blind compulsion, if not a fetish. It means you're admitting only one solution where there are actually many. Abundant techniques for loving yourself sensually and sexually exist. Masturbation can be healthy and delightful. You can explore it as a stop-gap measure if not as a full-time pleasure. That way you can hold out for the partnership, not just the anatomy, you crave.

Check out just how far you will go to prove you are (pick one) liberal, liberated, not hung up, guiltless – or whatever other definition unnerves you and is important to you. Demonstrating or not demonstrating does not make you good or bad, right or wrong. Zero in on your *own* comfort zone – what's right for you according to when it starts to feel wrong – and set your limits accordingly. Otherwise other people's definitions will push you around and their terms will intimidate you. At least let the things that threaten you be *real*. The fear that you won't be with-it isn't real. Tell anyone who manipulates you with accusations to go and shove it.

Romping with Hustlers could also indicate a backhanded way to get attention. Do you have a history of repressed rebellion? Is doing something shocking important to you? The high of a "they'd never guess" secret? Did you smoke in the bathroom at sixteen, knowing that, despite opening the windows, some scent remained when your folks came home? Or did you wait till you left home and you've been on a surreptitious free-for-all ever since?

Sex tends to be one of the very first forms of rebellion for women, the first break away from parents and childhood. But it doesn't have to remain a continual way of announcing your identity. Once you've run down that street, you can try others. Graduate from adolescent ways. When you learn to tune into *all* your needs and not just your nocturnal ones, you'll leave the Hustler's one-track, boring mind forever.

The Short Affair and Quick Escape Artist is similar to the Hustler. In fact, he can *be* a bit of a Hustler when starting up a new affair. But at least the Escape Artist offers a longer spin and considerable care for a while.

The man I come to next is also a kind of Hustler, but a very special kind. He chases only a certain kind of woman. And more than wanting just sex from them, he wants control. I call him the Baby Chaser. He only goes after very young, or passive, or foreign women, women who seem newly, purely, artlessly sexual and at the same easily manageable. At least they're manageable for a while. His system doesn't work in the long run. Not every woman needs to learn to spot the Baby Chaser or what it's like to have one, since some us are not his métier. Still, some of us are, others have had him once, and all of us have seen Baby Chasers chasing only babies and rued them.

8

The Baby Chaser

The Man Who Goes for Very Young, Passive, or Foreign Women

The Baby Chaser goes for either very young women (twenty-two is about his limit) or else passive women from cultures other than his. He believes such women are lusty or exotic.

Of course what he doesn't admit is that with such women he can keep the upper hand.

You see, a female equal means too much trouble to the Baby Chaser. No, when it comes to a partner, he wants something easier. He desires someone who will yield to him completely and blend right in with the way he wants to live. He doesn't want someone with much will or strong direction of her own. It also helps a lot that, young or exotic, the woman he seeks seems a sexual prize.

There are, actually, two types of Baby Chasers. The one has always been drawn to babies or foreign, often Asian, women. Frequently his modus operandi is that of individualist. He's a writer, a musician, an oil rigger, an archeologist, a racer, a surveyor. The other is a late comer. He was a Man Who Would Be Mogul, Mr. Genius or the like, who as he passes forty-five suddenly discovers that he's made it. He's become rich and powerful and his old relationship doesn't seem quite so sparkly anymore. It's no longer the right gem to decorate his new status. He leaves his old union. He now wants something – a much younger woman, usually a very pretty woman – that will show how grand and powerful he is.

This is not to say that fruitful unions cannot occur between older men and younger women or between couples from diverse societies. Age has no rules and background doesn't either. But the Baby Chaser doesn't start with a plan for a balanced or mutually fruitful union. He *seeks* a relationship where age and cultural criteria decidedly *do* matter. He assumes that with a hardly grown or less knowledgeable woman, he can get sex, care, company, and his own way for practically no strife. He also acquires a certain cachet with his love object. He acquires a sexual status symbol as good as, or better than, a Cadillac.

The first type of Baby Chaser, the one who has chased young women from the beginning, is a great man for infatuation and he knows it. He's usually a kind of lone ranger, distinct, musty smelling, so male. He's got all the aspects of fantasy romance turned real. He's masculine, independent, a formidable guide. He drinks, he strums guitar, he calls you "babe." He plays on being a first sexual turn on for a woman. Sex is part of what he sells and what he wants to be sure of. The second kind of Baby Chaser, who becomes one in later life, has other attractions. He has money, position, luxuries to lavish on a woman. And if he wasn't a particularly sexy man to start with, he becomes so by the time he starts to acquire younger women.

Both are older, wiser, and have resources you haven't. Both by and large want a settled union, but both are repeaters if a union breaks up. Once again, they go for a woman just as young as the last one, the age gap getting greater and greater every time.

Meanwhile you're supposed to take his lifestyle spit with spittoon. You also learn that jealousy is a no-no – since one young thing is rarely all the Baby Chaser ultimately desires. (He usually chases others on the side.) What he never stops to realize is that when the baby grows up, she grows up to buck him.

Story

I've known many Baby Chasers. Lots of men at least flirt with the idea, if not the reality, of becoming one. I'll tell you about two, one of each type.

Jake picked up and packaged Pam when she was just eighteen. With her Japanese features, small stature, and coloring, she looked even younger. A classics professor, 32, Jake was quite a compelling man. He ran digs in Anatolia, wrote poetry in ancient Greek, played the guitar, always dressed Western. He met Pam when he advertised for an upcoming dig. He'd broken up with the woman he'd been with before, also a student who'd lived with him a few years, then abruptly left him. Pam, however, seemed so demure and docile, he thought she might well make a permanent placid mate, but ... well, on with the story.

Jake has such presence, such maturity, and depth, that Pam felt overwhelmed by him. He was, after all, a professor, she a mere freshman. Freshmen weren't usually allowed on digs, but he selected her out and made an exception. As soon as he met her he also paid her other special attentions that made her feel honored and privileged. He asked her to join him for beer and Mexican food, showing how earthy he was, not at all effete like you'd expect a classics professor. He took her country and western dancing where he knew the whole band. He smelled slightly musky. He had a sensual aura and a wry sense of humor. He teased her, like a "man" would tease a child. He surrounded her protectively and at the same time flirted with her and impressed her with his knowledge. She felt a little off balance. He had so much to say, so much to teach her. She felt she'd never be his equal, never be as good as he was; the best she could do was emulate him.

The second time they went out he lightly implied that she was naive. He could lead her into worldly ways and even unlock her womanhood. He showed up unexpectedly and very late at her door. He brought marijuana. He'd written a new poem. And so Pam went to bed with him.

Pam wasn't a virgin, but suddenly with Jake she experienced a blast from sex and sensuality her former high school lovers had never equalled. Jake was like an express ticket to a brand new garden of delights. He thrilled her with all kinds of new erotica. Next day he took her to his house. She stayed for several days. Finally, she simply went and got her clothes and moved in with him.

Jake got a lovely, docile, house and bed mate he meant to keep. Pam, for her part, thought she'd got her own individual guide to knowledge, information, and experience. She wouldn't have to go through all the steps most women do. She had an older, wiser leader. To be the mate of such a manly man, not at all a boy, was irresistible.

Pam happily blended herself into Jake's life. But being happily settled with Jake didn't mean Jake meant to settle down. Just because they were in bed a lot – their erotic activity became daily fare – didn't mean he wasn't in other beds, too. There were other students, girls on the road when he gave lectures, girls at digs. Meanwhile, back at home, he disclaimed the need for civilization. Cities were abominable, society a crock, other professors and university life something to be shunned. If Pam was to stick to Jake, she had to stick to the sticks. She had to live his ways, heed his philosophy, go by his schedule, his plans, his classes, his trips. She had no life of her own. Meanwhile he went on his digs and did his teaching without her.

But a life of one's own has a way of growing on people and anyone who thwarts it seems to become, like a parent, the enemy. Pam began to cry "foul" and make some moves of her own. She returned to school. She had to commute and it was hard. So, in her next independent step, she took her own money – she'd never contributed to their living, Jake had paid for everything at the start and she'd resisted any of his offers to change that – and without Jake's permission, bought a little car. She made a friend or two, and then she joined a woman's discussion group. Slowly but surely, Pam turned Jake's home front into a war zone. She refused to cook and threw his dirty clothes out a window. When he brought a new young student over, Pam threw her out of the house. She contradicted him, yelled at him, did everything just the contrary to how he wanted it. Then when he didn't come home till late one night – she'd heard from friends he was wining and dining another young thing who'd applied for a dig – she locked him out.

Gavin was quite different from Jake. He didn't start a Baby Chaser, he became one when he walked out on a marriage of twenty-three years when he was forty-seven. His business had finally caught on and made him a wealthy man. He had a Mercedes, he could do anything he wanted, but somehow he couldn't see himself with a forty-five year old, familiar and rather tired looking companion. He'd always liked to dress well and spend on himself. He'd put his wife through some lean years, while he still had the best car, money for restaurant lunches, and a flock of racy friends. Now he wanted his whole share of the good life. He began dating women in their early twenties. He met them at bars and through friends, some of whom dated very young teenagers. Gavin wanted a steady companion though, a permanent mate who would show him off well. Finally, Gavin found a woman he particularly liked and found attractive, Penny.

Penny wasn't quite sure what to do with her life. Just turned twenty, she saw that some people lived really well and she wanted to try it. Gavin seemed great. He had things she couldn't afford for herself. He was sexy and older. Certainly he took her to places that were sexy, and he lavished her with gifts.

Soon he suggested they live together, and together they found a big penthouse condo. The place was wonderful, but Penny quickly began to feel like a trapped bird. She had nothing to do all day. Gavin only included her in his night life. She shopped and drove around. Not knowing what else to do, she began to nag for marriage and Gavin married her. But somehow she was never treated like a "wife." Gavin's friends, while greeting her nicely, ignored her and treated her like a bit of fluff. The friends' wives' conversations fell flat around her and she could see she didn't fit in with them. Gavin treated her as if she weren't smart or capable. He hardly talked to her.

But Penny was smart. She soon demanded to know more about his business and Gavin became upset. Finding herself excluded, she read up on business, took some classes, and began to follow the stock market. She said she wanted to do something, he said go ahead. But when she asked for money to start her own business, Gavin pooh-poohed her. So she got angry. Gavin also never wanted to do what she wanted to do. He danced before they got married, not now. He went to rock concerts then, too, not now. The trips stopped and so had the flow of money. He complained now if she spent too much, and she found that now she was expected to perform lots of sex for him while he paid very little back.

Penny began not to be home when he arrived. She made her own plans, then she invited a young man she met over just at the time she knew Gavin would arrive. She began to nag. She dropped demands on him like bombs the minute he got home. When he was off with friends and their young women – and she knew Gavin was occasionally sleeping around – she started having affairs, too. Like Jake to Pam, Gavin became the enemy to Penny. She turned against him. Almost consciously she decided to make his life miserable, not seeing that she was making her own life miserable as well. Finally, she decided there was another way to win. She moved out, filed divorce on Gavin, and asked for a bundle.

Penny received quite a lot of money, but not as much as she'd hoped. Gavin fought her hard and he'd tied up a lot of the money in his first wife's name. For some funny reason, though Penny left Gavin, she also ended up the one who was bitter. She found herself shallow, a dirty fighter, and untrusting of anyone.

Both Jake and Gavin had made a mistake. They forgot to foresee that older and younger, or wiser and more naive, all too easy turns into oppressor versus oppressed. With Penny and Pam, age and cultural difference took on the color of revolution. The Baby Chasers looked great at the start, but quickly became tyrants. The more Pam and Penny felt devoid of power, the more they discovered age-old female ways of fighting. Like time bombs on the shelf, they ticked off until they grew up and blew up. Both Pam and Penny ended up sexually radicalized and angry. Each had seen the enemy – and it was man. They found it very hard to like or be nice to any men for a long, long time.

Sometimes the Baby Chaser is a little crazy, sometimes evil, sometimes soulful, sometimes power packed. But he's always awesome, always sensual. Trouble is, the Baby Chaser isn't after women who have his number. He bedazzles the ones who don't. Learning to spot him doesn't always change the fact that you fall for him, but it does help you take the experience with a grain of salt.

How Can You Identify This Kind of Man?

Both kinds of Baby Chaser play a trump game with one face card. The man who has always been a Baby Chaser plays the mystery of the unknown male, the Jack of Spades or Knave of Hearts. The late comer plays the King of Diamonds. Each of them suspects the card they hold as their main attraction isn't the highest, so they don't pull it on queens and aces. Rather they drop in on little deuces and treys.

They bluff. Eventually the bluff turns back on them. They claim their preference for young or passive women is sexual desire, but it's really the desire for dominance. As a result, they usually end up taking a loss.

The Baby Chaser seems like he has a lot of dimension, but if you look closely he's pretty thin, a paper poster. He can't get close to women of equal age, rank, and moxie. He has a lot of fears. He can't face age. He either tries to sidestep cities and the rat race or buries himself in both. He hates being out of money or having secrets people know about him. A long association with the same person scares him. Let's face it, *women* terrify him.

Outer Signs

Almost always the younger type of Baby Chaser cultivates a recluse image. The cowboy mode suits some; you can do a lot with hats, belts, and boots. Others go for the offbeat editor image, the eccentric writer, the nonconformist director, the international photojournalist, the skittish star, rock or otherwise. Somehow, the Baby Chaser makes himself unique and makes himself a character. He tends to be skinny and restless. He has a distinct and definite maleness. Often he has a southern or western drawl he never quite loses. He's macho in style and looks, but not in talk. He doesn't need a line about male superiority. Quite the opposite, it falls in place naturally for him.

Older Baby Chasers are sleek and expensive looking. Even if his coat is bulky and brown, it's cashmere. He's quieter. He *talks* to you and flirts, but doesn't have that much to *say* to you. He seems a man's man. His nails are buffed.

Both kinds of Baby Chaser find professions where they can work more or less alone, or else ones where it's lonely at the top. But the work has to have, or lead him to, one added aspect. It has to attract groupies. The Baby Chaser loves groupies. He loves to be in situations where he has something women don't, and they come to him.

Young or old, he almost always looks older than he is. Even his dress reads "well aged." It may be his poncho, his old worn jeans, his very conservative suit, his wild or sleek grey hair. He cultivates his "well aged" look, his air of maturity.

His act has an oldness as well. He's a repeater. As each relationship ends, he tries again. The disparity in his coupling grows larger over time. He gains in age against your youth, in power against your weakness. In trying again, he often goes for an even less resisting girl- child in the hope that this time it will work.

He smokes or has smoked, or seems like he *should* smoke. He drinks bourbon, beer or tequila. No sports really interest him, except for individual sports. He may do martial arts, run, or admire a good rodeo, but no teamwork for him. He has secrets. He doesn't like to be talked about, mostly because he carries on differently in each aspect of his life and he wants no mixing. His behavior with women contrasts with his business behavior; his social self contrasts with his loner self. It's not unknown for him to hide or lie.

The long term Baby Chaser prefers his transportation almost bizarre, definitely not your usual sort. When everyone else has a European car, he has a Jeep with Charlie Pride singing on the tape deck. Or he has an enormous station wagon, ranch style. When the others go American, he'll get a battered old sloop-backed Saab, or an ancient, unrestored Packard. If a late comer, he probably drives something sleek. He may have gotten caught on the idea of a younger, fancy, two seater, sports car as his preferred women became younger. A Corvette, Porsche, or Mercedes sports car. Or he drives a Jaguar or Lincoln or BMW sedan. Whatever he drives it's a Lonermobile.

The long term sort of Baby Chaser often likes folksy, ethnic stuff, items with roots. Blankets and quilts, menorah and mezuzahs. It fits his image as older, wiser. He finds comfort in the texture and flavor of a poor or distinct people, even if they aren't his people. He studies Indians. The late comer, though, likes expensive, expansive, modern convenience. He likes people to get things for him and people to take care of them.

The Baby Chaser's home is usually somewhere removed. He lives across the bridge, high up in a penthouse, or at the outer edge or out of town altogether. Some Baby Chasers bounce between an urban and rural existence like a ping-pong ball. Almost every occupation compels him into the city, but much of this thinking focuses on loneness. Or he lives in, then out, then in again. On his boat, then off, then on again. At his cabin, then back, then there again.

The Baby Chaser, you see, doesn't really want to be a modern man. That's why he treats himself to a fantasy female and to a situation that doesn't threaten his illusion. If he can't really live in another age, at least he can hedge around contemporary times, steel buildings, enfranchised women, and equal wives. His nymph-chasing is

more old-fashioned than you think – rather like a warlord's preroga-
tive.

But the strain is hard on him. He doesn't always handle it well.
He may have bouts when he overuses drink or drugs. He follows up
with stringent periods off all chemical influence. Or he may be
rigidly pure and healthy. He may be unpredictably taciturn, tactless,
or prone to temper. And he may offend people enough to gain some
real adversaries.

Sex Signals

Women of the same age and stage of life usually don't especially
admire either the long term or the late comer Baby Chaser (though
some become restrained "friends"). But then females his own age
must always contend with the smart of rejection from him. Single as
he may be at times, or attractive and worthy as these women may
be, he doesn't choose to tarry with them. Rather, he heads for the
feather bed of the young, the docile, and the less knowledgeable. It's
not just that he wants his women passive or dependent. He's into
putty. He wants his women able to be shaped.

Like the spider in the parlor, he usually has a web – an *advantage*
that draws women to him. You find the Baby Chaser, for example,
when you have material (he's an agent, editor, or buyer), you're a
student (he's a teacher), you're an admirer (he's a politician or per-
former), a model (he's a designer), or actress (he's a producer or
director). He invites you to meet his colleagues, to attend a party, to
join the group. Then he suggests a drink or some such. He offers no
frills or goodies, just a one-thing-leads-to-another approach. To his
home and his bed. Eventually you simply become the women he
brings along to his gatherings.

He tackles you pretty quickly once alone. After all, he lusted for
you from the minute you walked in the door. His penchant for young
women, black women, white women, Asian women, sweet women,
comes across with a lot of eroticism. He's hot to trot. You're soon on
his couch, floor, or office chair – even the car seat. And then to his
bed.

There he likes to take you and render you senseless. At least at
first. He enjoys knowing a lot more than you. He's certainly not
standoffish about showing his wide and varied knowledge of positions and the *Kama Sutra*. He plays tour guide, you're the tourist, and
he shows you the back roads. But notice that he wants to *make* you
have thrills instead of *letting* you have them.

But it's only at first he gives more then he gets. He uses sex for
position in more ways than one. He hopes for a later recoup on his
efforts. He leads you to learn and like what *he* wants to do. He then
expects you to do them to him in due time.

When he wants you for keeps, he can be very good to you. In his own way that is, and when he's around. He does love having his baby at home. He probably loves you. Certainly he likes having you there adhering to his ways and whims. But he wants to fashion permanence without contention. He thinks your early silence means you'll never fight with him, so assuming all is well with living how he wants, he becomes a ready victim for manipulation. He even ends up giving to some degree as you rebel and start to make demands. He doesn't want to go out and find a new baby, start from scratch and train someone else.

But usually he's also an extra chaser on the side. A few Baby Chasers are sexually true, but only a few. The majority are prone to poaching. Infidelity is almost a game for them. And most Baby Chaser's women eventually do some poaching back on him. To bring information home about how you have affairs is one way to backstab. When a Baby Chaser's baby starts having affairs, the Baby Chaser is utterly dismayed. He's even more dumbfounded when the baby threatens to leave him or totally break up. He pretends he'll change. But an ounce of persuasion is worth a pound of alteration to a Baby Chaser. He may say he's going to change, but he doesn't.

Money Markers

The Baby Chaser – long term or late comer – almost inevitably ends up footing the bills for everything. They don't always like it, but they do it anyway. They pay for your mutual keep, but also for the extras and their other adventures, too. After all, you don't have the earning power or income that he has. Even when you do, the one thing a baby can do is withhold her money. To pay at first is part of his come on, but over time he's not too sure how he feels about the arrangement. As part of his image he can't make too much fuss about supporting his young woman, but he's not really an easy giver. He's a silently grudging one. Beyond household expenses, he can get a bit tight with money. There's a limit to the flow. And he gets grumpy if the flow goes too fast.

He prefers to spend money, not on frivolity, but on his stability. He likes to be an unusual man, but not a down and out one. Running out of money strikes close to his panic button, so he never cuts himself totally free from the business or employment that binds him. He doesn't take too many monetary chances. He keeps his pennies if he can. They go towards his home, his bank account, and to pay for any children from past unions.

Family Aspects

When the subject of having babies comes up, the Baby Chaser says no. ("Maybe later" is one of his favorite ways of saying it.) But that doesn't mean he won't get anyone pregnant. In fact, he often does. That's how he acquires progeny, or the marriages he might have gotten in. He's ambivalent about children. He thinks they will slow him down, take his time, change his ways, or catch on to his number. At the same time he wants descendants. So, somehow he often manages to slip up and have some. Once such an accident is fact, he can face it.

Since he follows his masculine image, he usually becomes the strong sort of masculine father – very male, reliant, protective. He's especially protective when his own daughter gets to the age he finds attractive, usually about five years younger than his present companion. (Although an occasional Baby Chaser has been known to come on to his own daughter.)

As for parents, brothers, and sisters, most Baby Chasers maintain good ties. They don't break with the family, no matter how much aggravation there is. Live apart, yes. Break, no. The family is a unit, a little corporation. He likes the way it carries on in time, so he stays in touch.

Friends are also very important to the Baby Chaser, especially men friends and especially *similar* men friends. Sometimes he gets real raunchy with them. He may have them over or you meet up to go out with them a lot. He uses one vocabulary with men, another with women. When he sees a woman who is just a friend, he doesn't bring his baby mate along. When he's with men only and a woman joins, a very quiet competition starts.

The Baby Chaser does have great assets along with his liabilities. He imparts quick lessons in life, and he fulfills all those dreams of white knights and supermen, at lease for a little while. He's an indulgence in fantasy, money, power. A male protector, caretaker. He can be a great first fling. But he doesn't have the flexibility towards your development that real love demands, and that's his failing.

What Is in Store for You?

Once you know the Baby Chaser's script, you can guess the end. In the final scene, after the Baby Chaser thinks it's all settled and going his way, his little sidekick says to him, "What do you mean 'we,' white man?" And, it might be you.

The Baby Chaser's scheme always backfires one way or another. When he picks women with another ethnic background, he lets himself in for her society's ways. Each ethnic group has tactics only natives know, use, and expect. He doesn't understand them. When he chooses a young girl, he can hardly end up as anything but an obstruction to her growth.

If he didn't meet change with resistance, perhaps the Baby Chaser's pairing would last. But since he *does* resist changes to his woman, soon evolution becomes revolution. Whenever you stretch your wings, he seems to be standing around with poultry shears. Breaking with him is almost like separation from your parents. You probably went from one to the other, or overlapped, so freedom from him symbolizes breach with them all.

What starts as the chamber of love winds up as a hotbed of devious aggression. Once you've seen his soft underbelly, you can oh-so-secretly attack from the passive position. Fussing begins. Nagging trickles in. You forget errands. You somehow arrive late, then later. You start rubbing salt in wounds and picking bones.

Maybe, just maybe, you follow him one night. Or you find a few phone numbers and call them. You appear where he is expected, but you are not. Some night on a dark street (not yours), you sabotage his steel-belted radials.

You start to do the same kinds of things he does. You lay down new rules. It's your house, too, by George. The boys and beer are out. You start leaving evidence of your sexual encounters. Inch by inch the big breakup comes; usually it's volatile by now. A friend, some emerging anger, or some book tells you that his shaping of your life or his independent carryings on are just plain unacceptable. Roles switch. He becomes the innocent one. "I don't know why she turned so vile on me," he wails. That makes you even more angry. You think he knows how much he molded you. He hadn't seen it and is amazed. But he doesn't learn enough not to do it again.

Unfortunately, the aftermath of the Baby Chaser entails a lot of black bile and anger. An overlord overturned rarely receives your sweet forgiveness. And when you don't come back, he gets very angry, feels taken, or is very hurt. Each of you feels an anger that often lasts for years.

What Are the Telltale Signs of Trouble?

The Baby Chaser's warning signs depend a lot on his and your physiques and circumstances.

I'm sorry to say that if you're young, sheltered, or nymphlike (small-bodied, small-breasted, with a woman-child air), or from certain cultural backgrounds, you'll have to be extra wary of the Baby Chaser. That's just the way it is. It's smart to recognize those to whom you'd be especially tasty. You don't have to get angry – just don't make it your *problem* and don't get exploited.

The next step is to learn the Baby Chaser's trail signs. Since you might lack an experienced eye, scout for these markers: when his age, skin color, facial features, mop of curls, or *something* is definitely different, it means be wary. Certainly if he says anything about opposites attracting, don't just nod in agreement. Consider taking another path.

A masculine, loner image or sleek older man should flash a hunter's red vest. Note his approach. You go to him with some mission in mind, but somehow business turns to pleasure; he's one up on you.

Next he takes you as a tag-along. If you not only follow, but feel furry, remember there's an unequal status between him who holds the leash and her who follows it.

Reputation is one of your biggest warnings. He had to start somewhere. And it probably wasn't you. Follow the clues. Ask about past relationships, or note the left, older wife.

Once involved with the Baby Chaser, sooner or later you start to think about splitting his pen. Perhaps you've been doing things his way because you didn't have a way of your own. One day you realize that you had no say in the rules. Maybe what's going down begins to come up – his other women or the nights he spends away. If things no longer seem equitable or tolerable, you've reached your first critical turn; you're about to find out if he's going to like you full-fledged. If you're seething with resentment, it's time to either introduce plain speaking as your household language or break camp. If you're about to exact revenge, it's better just to backpack away.

What Are Your Chances and What Should You Do?

If the Baby Chaser is stalking you, should you (a) run from him, (b) flirt with him only to flee from him, or (c) fight for him? Considering how much you'll change and how little he will, I'd say go for (a) or (b).

In the first place, if you really *are* very young (under 18), run far away from the Baby Chaser. You can experience serious injury in very fragile areas. I personally think men who chase teen, or younger, tail ought to go to jail. And I've heard every justification about "modern teenagers and their sophistication." I find both the excuses and the excusers repugnant.

But for you more of age, you on your own, consider how you want your Venus to climb off her half shell, with Adonis or Lazarus? There exist any number of ways to grow into maturity, independence, and self assertion. The Baby Chaser simply is not the greatest of them. He prolongs the child in you in some ways and causes you to skip your youth in others. He postpones your individualization and renders you younger than you should be at a later date. He deprives you of experiencing emerging adulthood as you would with a mate your own age. You take on a bogus age to match his.

He *is* one way to grow up, and he often looks like a good one. Certainly he imparts enormous experience. He's sensual, assured; he propels you or he has such goodies and resources. But remember, there's a catch to solutions (b) and (c). Due to inexperience, immaturity, and lack of awareness, most women who take up with him are unconscious of what they are doing. Even what looks like a one-night frolic can affect you adversely. You might go through a blind passage in which you can't see yourself. Only once you are older and looking back do the events that transpired become clear.

If, however, you fall in love with him and you get involved anyway, try to do him for the right reasons. Be sure that you have a sense of yourself and little desire to wind up a victim. Don't dally one day longer than the first day you feel dominated. When you discover he wanted only a passive or childlike quality, try to have your feet firmly on the ground. Look at it rationally – you can't stay a nymphet forever. And you shouldn't, either. Maintaining your baby face into advancing age or remaining submissive to your detriment can lead you into massive insecurity and a huge life crisis. Recognize that change will come and get ready for it.

One final thing: if you've been with a long-term mate (probably you hitched up young) who turns into a Baby Chaser and is going out with young girls behind your back, consider a quick, blunt walkout. Worries about inexperience, a sheltered existence, children, and so on can detain you for years, but the situation rarely improves. Acting sophisticated about it leads nowhere. Let the satyr go stag and get yourself into the thicket with someone else.

Where Do You Fit In?

It's hard, but it's possible – you *can* be a baby more than one time over. When you do the Baby Chaser once or more, you want to wonder why.

Could it be you nurture a touch of toddlerhood that's tough to eradicate? You want someone to do it for you. You hover between walking on your own and wanting to get picked up. You want someone to make your decisions, break your trail, raise you, praise you. Someone to take your chances and make your mistakes – then get the blame for the blunders.

But in real life no one can make the breaks for you or suffer your consequences. Even the Baby Chaser dishes out a brand of growth and a type of growing pain you'll have to go through. Maybe he can protect you from *you*. But who is going to protect you from *him*?

Men are not heroes, or gods, or gauchos. Perhaps you expect a man to be superhuman, to notice your every anger, hurt, or dislike; you think he should see without being shown, hear without being told. But *no one else* can look through your eyes, and no one can read your mind, particularly if you docilely pretend nothing is going on.

Men are just regular people. Sometimes they're sensitive, sometimes not. Sometimes they're super and sometimes they're weak. Sometimes they do right and sometimes they do wrong. So you might as well go for one who admits it right from the start.

Still, if you did one Baby Chaser in naiveté and found he didn't suit, don't blame yourself or him, but consider one thing. Living alone into and through your twenties has definite advantages. Everyone needs time, space, and an empty place in order to find herself. You only learn to know yourself by living with *you*. The sooner you start, the faster you get there. It's hard, but there's nothing in the world like it. There's no other way to get over the "alone is lonely" syndrome. To discover that alone is *not* lonely is a good lesson to get under your belt early.

The Baby Chaser often doubles up with another form of man. Frequently the long term kind of Baby Chaser is also a Disaster Broker, racy and raunchy and having to have young things. He can be a Male Supremacist looking for a virgin, or almost virgin, to be his mate. The late comer kind of Baby Chaser has often been a Man Who Would Be Mogul, so you can find many of his traits in that chapter. Both of them often act like the Father Knows Best.

Baby Chasing can also be an aspect of the man I talk about next. More than just being dominant, and more than being a supremacist, he thinks he is personally superior to other people. He is special, more talented, more artistic, wiser, better than anyone else, including you. He's quite common, or at least a lot of men have aspects of him, so if you haven't met him yet, you probably will.

9

Mr. Genius

*Who Thinks He's Better, More Talented,
Smarter, or More Artistic Than
Anyone Else, Including You*

Don't be fooled by appearances. Just because a man looks like an ordinary person doesn't mean he is one. He might be a Mr. Genius.

Mr. Genius may invent grand inventions, make nuclear accelerators, splash canvases with zigzag lines and/or cover everything with coats of plastic. He may make underground films, proclaim a revolution, supposedly save souls, or expound on enlightenment. He may shine as the leading light of surgery or transform a courtroom with his facile mastery.

Indeed, Mr. Genius' occupation can be almost anything. It isn't what he does that counts. It's how he struts it.

Whatever Mr. Genius' endeavor, and however he feigns humility, he's as grand as a mufti can be. He's forever a cut above regular. Heaven forbid he should be just any Joe who trucks along and does his job whether he's gifted or not. You see, Mr. Genius is convinced that some higher-up in the supernatural department thumped him with a magic wand and made him better. He's got something that belongs to very few. He's got bippety-boppety-boo. He believes he's more intelligent, talented, wise, saintly, or gifted than anyone else. The trouble is, whether he is or not, he claims to be. He doesn't necessarily prove it. He also reserves the right to be unruly because he is so special. And there's the rub. When a man finds it hard to accept his commonness, his mortality, life with him hardly verges on paradise. It's more like tyranny.

If he's the golden boy among men, his lady must be silver. Mr. Genius tends to pick sterling women. He likes beauty, but not in the form of a flashy bauble, more in the shape of a tea tray. He wants you noticeable but serviceable, comely but enduring, admirable but tractable, nice to demonstrate but easy to put in place. And it helps if you lack polish, i.e. if at least at first you're less worldly and knowledgeable than he.

Story

One woman I interviewed unfolded a perfect Mr. Genius tale. Her Mr. Genius happened to be an artist.

Patsy met Leo when she was an art student. So was Leo. But Leo was different, he claimed. He was destined to make waves and change styles. Or so he said, mainly by criticizing others. Leo loved to hang about the huge school studio with his cronies and followers. With jeans hanging low, sockless sneakers, splotched shirt, he would sip on a can of beer and crush it between his thumb and fingers. He would lean on a sculpture and disparage education ("Art is not for teaching. People have "it" or they don't."). He acted like a Baby Chaser around young craftswomen. But basically Leo was a settler, not a hustler. He needed a number-one follower, and Patsy looked like the prizewinner.

Patsy worked in ceramics, where she had incipient, yet-to-blossom talent. She wasn't unable; she was simply unsure. She needed time. All the better for Leo. In every one of Patsy's departments, Leo was quite superior. Patsy liked her art, but she wanted other things as well: love, work, creativeness, happiness, even a family. Not so for Leo. As far as he was concerned, there was only one nirvana and he was there already. He was a rarity, a truly great painter. All he needed was fame, money, and world recognition.

Leo impressed Patsy with *his* knowledge by making her feel she had none of her own. Every simple statement she offered he reduced with ridicule. He addled her with sarcasm, twisted her with teasing, heckled her into speechless adoration, and badgered her into bed. That was the beginning and the end of their courtship. After that, he latched onto her like glue and told her that she couldn't do better.

Leo's idea of sex was to have Patsy in, on, and out of bed and, in fact, all over the place. A lot. But Patsy found that sex with Leo was like a volcanic eruption (his) to which she was merely the audience. She wanted to tell him so, but the cat had her tongue. Besides, he convinced her that he was a perfect lover and she a mere novice. She decided to distrust her own feelings, or lack of them, and abide by him for some big happening later on. He told her it was coming, if she'd just relax and let it.

She also stayed for another reason – Leo's portrait of glory. He was big time, she was little. Only with him, and if she turned her art to domesticity "at least for the time being," could she see Paris, parties, and bejeweled high society. Meanwhile, living penniless in a garret would be "romantic." It all sounded pretty attractive to Patsy.

Soon Leo won a grant, Patsy got pregnant, and they were off to Italy. They lived in Florence in a miserable four-story walk-up. They stretched pennies with pasta. In four years they hatched three babies. While Patsy's belly occasionally deflated, Leo's ego didn't – it swelled and swelled. He grew even more despotic and grandiose, while Patsy got haggard. He refused to help her in any way or even show common courtesy. The domicile was her job, unworthy of His Eminence. He was certainly too dandy for the diapers. He came and went as he pleased. He drank a lot.

In response to Patsy's first few mild complaints, he broke dishes and smashed windowpanes. He trounced off day or night to his huge studio despite illness and infancy in the homestead. Patsy and the babies had two rooms and no running water. Though she rarely saw him, she never asked for help. She thought his genius gave him such allowances and that every artist's struggling years were like this. Still, she figured that if she really needed him he'd be there for her.

Then one week Patsy and the children fell sick. Soiled clothes lay everywhere and not a single grocery sat in the larder. Patsy had hit bottom; she finally asked for aid. Leo flew into a rage. How, he shouted, could she expect *him* to lower himself to household chores? He stomped off for two days. That was the end of Patsy's illusion.

Patsy wired home for money, packed, and left. But it wasn't over yet. No sooner did she arrive home than Leo came begging for forgiveness. But Patsy demanded promises first. She wanted decent habitation, equal freedom, space, and help. She got his agreement forthwith. But the instant she returned to Leo, he reneged on all the terms. He got a house, but he wouldn't let her have a room. He tore down walls to suit his fancy and never repaired them. He got a job, but he wouldn't give her enough to manage on. He overloaded her with chores and had fits if she failed to perform them. Soon she was worse off than when she started.

She left again. He followed. She went back. That happened *three* more times. Each time he reassumed his usual outrageousness. How could she expect to decorate their abode when *he* was the artist? How could she demand space when he required sanctuary? How could she ask for company when he was busy *creating*?

He also started having affairs. Or rather he started having them more obviously. That was the last straw; finally Patsy saw that Leo so feared being ordinary and meeting normal expectations that she would always be the victim of his self-importance. And she simply couldn't afford it. So, with regrets, she kept her little children and divorced her big one. It was rough. Leo refused to pay support; he stormed her home and tried to win over the children. But she held tight. She raised her family a while before she could return to art, but now she's doing fabulously. Her ceramic pieces have caught on nationally. And Leo? Leo is teaching at the old art college.

Some of the most glorious trees overshadow other plants, so they remain shrubbery forever. Mr. Genius can be magnificent – he's thrilling and dazzling. He can offer an unconventional life and alluring romance. But he can also obliterate sunshine. It's best to learn to identify him. Then if you decide to sit in his shade, you can figure out whether you can thrive in the light that's left.

How Can You Identify This Kind of Man?

When you ask a Mr. Genius what he does, he answers with his name. If you inquire who he is, he tells you what he does. The implication, of course, is that he's a one and only.

He's not unlike a Coke. He's got strong flavor, a lot of character, and is quite effervescent. And after he recites his commercial at you often enough, you're inclined to believe that he's not just any old cola – he's the Real Thing. If there were only some way to put him to the Pepsi challenge, perhaps he would be easier to spot. But to see that he's just one of many and not unique, you would need at least two Mr. Geniuses, a blindfold, and an outside observer. And that's nigh impossible. In the first place, Mr. Geniuses avoid each other like the plague, so it's hard to get two together. And second, they're too jealous to let you taste them both at once.

Mr. Genius is surprisingly hard to recognize. Not because he hides his iron-fisted ego, not because he changes his style from before to after, but because he's so *convincing*. After a short blast of his charisma, you no longer see the spots that reveal him. He turns you into a true believer. And once you acknowledge that he's extraordinary, you make your first mistake. You agree that regular rules don't apply to him. Then you're in trouble.

Mr. Genius tingles; everything about him vibrates with intensity even when he's quiet and soulful. If you don't think he's wired, just look at his hair – it almost stands up by itself. Sometimes it's kinky. And whatever the color, it's vivid, even when, as often, it's prematurely grey.

He's somewhere between the age of one and six. He doesn't know where his edges are, has no sense of boundary. He's afraid of his mortality. He believes in magic. And he thinks he can get away with anything. He fears that if he loses control, he just might collapse into a black void, so he demands to get his way in all matters, even the trivial – even if he has to throw a tantrum to get it. Then, to avoid the horror of nothingness, which uniformity, monotony, and regularity evoke for him, he's forever doing *something*. He's never inactive. If he's not doing his thing, he's thinking it, living it, or saying he *is* it. Any time you "bother" him, you're interfering with his *genius*. And he requires inordinate attention.

Outer Signs

Mr. Genius creates himself down to the very last detail. Even in casual disarray, his image bears a constructed precision. Though he may claim clothes are mere social drapery and disavow concern with them, he dresses for effect. He can range from sockless rebel leader to spotless head surgeon, but in any case he practically *paints* his look. In either a T-shirt or starched collar, he's in costume. He always knows exactly how in and how out his shirttail is.

His automobile (it's never a "car") is either spotlessly chromed and polished, humming along in awesome magnificence, or else it's disheveled just enough to throw a pie in society's eye. He prefers classic Jaguars or original Ramblers.

As far as his living quarters go, if anyone can find a hovel with cachet, he can. It may be tiny, always with the impeccably right atmosphere for his purposes, located in the midst of just the right area or just the right amount of ghetto. Or else it's cavernous, loft-like, with faultless northern exposure, in an old fire station complete with brass pole, or a converted cable-car rotunda. It brings to mind poverty, elegance, and/or madness. Every rug and tatter is precisely Mr. Genius. You always know you're in *his* place – even when you live there.

Often he has an office or studio as well. It always includes some sleeping arrangement. It might be an attic or garage, an old storefront, or it might have acres and acres of glass and ceiling. But never fear – he has his den or garret even if he claims your whole house for it.

Wherever he wanders, he pulls either a leader or anti-leader pose. Both bring followers, which he *loves*. Awestruck attendants confirm his uniqueness. He ambles to a corner, where he leans one shoulder on the wall. He picks his toes while he sits cross-legged or glares across his tripod, but somehow he always draws notice. Sometimes he discovers how to be intensely silent and use stillness like an electromagnet to scoop up the curious; other times he's extraordinarily talkative and does a monologue to proselytize his opinions.

He allows himself a full range of emotions. Since he won't be bound by convention, he becomes a constant potential explosion. Mr. Geniuses will do things in public and private that no one else would *dare*. He intimidates by embarrassment. He boils, fumes, or booms out his moments of anger and ecstasy. He might even go so far as to become destructive. While most people get tired of saying no and give in on some issues, not Mr. Genius. His refusals continue endlessly.

He treats himself pretty well. The extent to which he'll go to get his way is nothing short of amazing. But there's something about his self-adoration that constantly taxes him and becomes his tragic flaw. He so desperately wants immortality, he can never let himself relax. He lives as if the minute he lets his guard down, he'll keel over, that no one will notice quickly enough that he's a genius and save him. He brings upon himself false goals and shallow rewards: once he jumps the gun on history, not to mention the Almighty, and proclaims himself special during his own lifetime, nothing ever comes out good enough again. Some Mr. Geniuses get so stuck in this syndrome they can't produce a thing. Most are never satisfied with who they are.

Sex Signals

His lady certainly can't be perfect in his eyes. He wants you beautiful, talented, or notable, but only as a counterpoint to enrich him. He conjures the caretaker from your depths (he can take any Wonder Woman and turn her into Diana Prince – out of the sequins and back to the glasses – rapidly). Every now and then he wants you to take a spin and show you off to the crowd, but not for long. He only shares the spotlight for a second, and then it's back to the wings.

He's quick to move in on you, slow to give commitment. When it comes to steady, he always says, "Well, *maybe*." He expects bed immediately. He tests you for intimidation.

Sex with Mr. Genius has several twists. He's sure he's superb, but he still wants proof from you. He wants to *make* you come; the way you want to doesn't count. If you don't do what he desires, he accuses you of being hung up. He expects some sort of surrender, yet he's never sure he got enough of a surrender from you and always wants more. Ultimately he pays more attention to his own pleasure – forgoing your climax if he feels like it. He wants you excited and willing whenever he's hot but doesn't return such spontaneity. He gets the "too tired" or turns you down a lot. He also sometimes gets up first and leaves you lingering.

He considers himself, and is, a very sexual man. Sex is the first and foremost spice to his life. But he never does it quite with you, only to himself *and* you.

Money Markers

Money is on his mind a great deal of the time. Either he broods about it – how much he has or doesn't have, how to get more – or he cries about how other undeserving people somehow get the cash he doesn't. He usually works for his money. He's not the Idle Lord. He doesn't demand that others provide his lucre without anything in return. But he only does the work he wants. He can also go through quite a bit of cash to muster his image and he rarely makes as much as he thinks fitting.

Occasionally he can be honorable about your money, but if he *needs* your finances, he'll use them. He always uses more of your mutual funds than you do. Sometimes he hoards the treasury and won't let you have access, or he might allow you provisions but not luxury. Since money is an outward proof of his ability, he prefers you not to work or to work only for subsistence, certainly to have less prestigious employment than his.

Family Aspects

Mr. Genius doesn't see or deal with children (although he does want to pass his genes on). Children threaten him, and he'd rather avoid them. He simply can't stand the competition. He knows that in comparison to *real* kids he will suffer. It's less likely someone will say, "Aren't you acting like a child?" when none is present. But since Mr. Genius tends to have long-term unions, frequently women have children with him by accident or design, or he "allows" it in order to produce little duplicates.

He seldom helps with the child care, however, and he certainly doesn't let the little tykes interfere with him. He might grow closer to them when they grow older, but he won't do their laundry or keep them for a whole day and night. He ignores infants, and he treats their mother very badly, particularly during pregnancy and early infancy. Later he pressures the older children (and their mother) to make them become brilliant like himself. It's not unlikely that his children dislike him quite profoundly.

He has a great capacity for making his parents and yours feel out of place and uncomfortable. He gives them no grace. He won every battle growing up and, instead of letting go with age, he *still* has them squirming. He's abrasive with all elders and most relatives. He more or less ignores his brothers and sisters, who are often very angry with him, with long memories of everything he got away with.

That Mr. Genius ends up with pals at all seems a contradiction. After all, he's not good at sharing attention. He avoids other men and carries on an odd combativeness with them. Yet, after the initial sparring, he establishes a clique of equally powerful honchos. He rarely has friendships with women that aren't in some sense sexual. The pals you have together tend to be all his selections. He doesn't like your friends and slowly rids you of them.

The friendships he and you maintain aren't the usual, supportive, passionless sort. Mr. Genius' affairs, as well as yours, tend to happen within your circle of acquaintances. Mr. Genius often acts as if he could gain strength by claiming his rivals' possessions, so it's frequently his semi-friend's or quasi-competitor's lady that he beds. Sometimes an old group of Mr. Geniuses have been together and at each other so long that have virtually practiced sexual round robin, moving around to each other's partners. You may end up living with your ex-Genius' best friend.

Mr. Genius doesn't admit to his own fears, yet he does his best to terrify others. Since it's terribly important to him to surpass all other people and to make anyone and anything else dull, you lose the joy of just being average with him. What you can get is the dynamic dash of not living in a run-of-the-mill style – if you can handle the mania.

What Is in Store for You?

Whether your Mr. Genius is a microsculptor, a designer, a drummer, engineer, a psychologist or guru, you should inspect life with anarchy before you join the party.

Mr. Genius tends to be a ten-year disaster. Once devotion sets in, it takes longer than you think to come to an awakening – and then longer *again* to make up your mind which direction to move. Mr. Genius isn't so much "In for a dime, in for a dollar." He's "In for a day, in for a decade."

He has a credo that goes, "You have to take me exactly as I am and all the time and not interfere with me in any way because *I am so special!*" From that axiom he derives a lot of postulates for you to live with; combined, they make your happiness pretty hypothetical. One, he imposes a "take me or leave me" condition. Two, he gets to make the rules but he doesn't have to follow them – you do. Rules, you see, are for *un*special people to follow, for the special to break. Three, he gets all the attention.

So what looks like life in a glamorous bell jar with him all too often turns into a dust bowl. Obviously a lot depends on how he expresses his tyranny, how far you can stretch your stamina, and how much you think your union is worth. In his unawareness of limits, Mr. Genius goes as far as he can. He seems unable to stop himself or call upon his kindness. Once you settle down, you become the last person who can contain him. He likes to think you're more hooked on him than he on you. The more he pretends he's detached, the more he sows in you the seeds of apprehension. In reaction, you agree to less-than-satisfactory conditions, which get even worse.

While thumbing his nose at society is one thing, venting his spleen at you is another. It's hard to remain unaffected by his sharp tongue, pointed wit, temper tantrums, and refusal to help. When you take a stand against him, he gets better for a while, but when you shy away again, his gestures return. As time goes on, he expands his caustic vocabulary. While in the first stages of a relationship with him he seems just a difficult man whose habits you must learn, later it appears more as if he creates new turbulence to test your adjustment. Life with Mr. Genius proceeds like a croquet game in Wonderland: he changes the rules from post to post, it's always his turn, and he insists the wickets move to fit his whimsy. Meanwhile, your own mallet grows as ineffectual as the neck of a flamingo.

You do what he says. If he decides to work at night, you can expect sex only by day. If he needs the dining room for a study, you'll have to take the table elsewhere. If he suddenly seeks rest and peace, you'll sleep upstairs with all the kids. If he decides on a new place to live, you up and pack the boxes within forty-eight hours. He picks where you go and what decorations go on the walls. You wash clothes by hand because machines disrupt him. He claims the bath for a darkroom, so you use the kitchen sink. He deserts you with a day-old infant to take up residence in his office because he "can't stand crying." You hang about the streets for twelve hours because he can't work in your proximity. Pretty soon you wonder about yourself, "Just who *is* this Alice with no possessions or character?" Possibly he wonders, too. It's not out of the question for Mr. Genius to get possessed by someone else's arms.

Not all his disturbances are *simple* irritations. Involvements with a Mr. Genius have a built-in time limit. Since he continuously seeks homage, your applause can only gratify him for so long. Then he begins to feel dragged down. He seeks praise elsewhere – without giving you up. It's he who says, "My wife just doesn't understand me." He doesn't admit he's no longer happy with you or himself. And he's the kind who wants to try a trial separation or vacation but doesn't want a divorce.

If dwindling tribute doesn't cause him to panic, age certainly does. When the years grow upon Mr. Genius he worsens acutely. After all, age brings life's termination ever closer. Expect to find him using strange, as well as predictable, ways to cling to youth as time goes on. Mr. Genius is prone to a big mid-life crisis. He finds everything that reminds him of his age (that is, his whole life – plus you) very threatening.

Life with him makes *you* prone to a good crisis, too. About the time of the seven-year itch, disappointment in his affection, his glory, his wanderings, and his tyranny can clash mightily with your needs. You slam into a big brick wall. While his crisis becomes perpetual, however, yours only lasts five years. If you haven't rocked the boat before, you start to do so now. You have an affair with his pal or someone else, or maybe you toss him out. Perhaps you wander out one day and forget to take the babies with you. It's *your* turn for art and *his* for Pine Sol.

Usually with Mr. Genius you part and reunite a number of times. You alternate who wants and who doesn't want the union. Meanwhile you cross-inflict affairs and injure one another. Occasionally Mr. Genius couples pull through this stage to reach agreement and satisfaction once again. More often those who remain intact do so less than ecstatically and bear many scars. Many simply do not make it.

When a relationship with a Mr. Genius ends, it's surprising how much you *don't* end up with. Easy divorces and good settlements from him are rare. Prepare for rancor, bellowing, and custody threats. Once it's totally over, he might disappear and never make payments.

What Are the Telltale Signs of Trouble?

With the Mr. Genius (as with *all* types of men), you need a bit of skepticism. You *should* believe in your man, but you should also consider the conditions that come with him.

Consider the way Mr. Genius baits you as an omen, a bad one. It's first in jest, next in sobriety. He introduces you to his crowd, but is critical of yours. He takes you around as if either you're on a leash or you have "ring around the collar." When a man shows you off as *his* accomplishment or his hanger-on, you're destined to become old hat. Even in his first moves, Mr. Genius overshadows you and makes you feel like an undeveloped nation. All you're expected to do is adhere to his prowess, praise his honor, purchase his products, do the work that's beneath him, and never ask for autonomy. Right at this point you should consider action. Remember it takes ten years for the storm to turn critical unless you force the issue.

The dots and dashes signal disaster when he demands total determination over your circumstances because *he's* the sensitive one. That indicates you're not a citizen. Any time, in any relationship, when a man implies you don't quite deserve him, you've got a real problem to face. For whatever reason you originally latched on, once he treats you like a peasant, there's an uprising coming. Sooner or later you'll take up your scythe and march on the monarchy.

Stay mindful of the fact that when a person uses both outrage and rage to win, he'll use them anytime he chooses. You'll spend your life walking on needles and pins, never knowing what will cross him. When that begins to happen, it's time to consider getting another bed to lie on – this time not on nails.

If, despite all warnings, you decide to try a Mr. Genius, do yourself a favor: get a notebook and keep a record. On the chance that everything great does occur that he says will occur, you can sell his biography. And in case no kudos come to him, perhaps you can write a novel. At least that could make you *some* money if all else fails.

What Are Your Chances and What Should You Do?

My best advice is to avoid Mr. Genius. He's much like a cantankerous weed. He stays tenaciously rooted in his home ground even when he sends out runners into other gardens. Even after an apparently total extraction he tends to pop up again. So while he's in some senses dependable, you never know where he'll resurge or what thorns he'll sprout. Mr. Genius saps the energy from all but the hardiest women who have the most vital inner strength. He's a long termer but that doesn't mean he *ever* turns into a rose; some men aren't even *late* bloomers. Mr. Genius doesn't change; he's too freaked out by age and dying. The only women I think benefit from Mr. Genius are those hardy souls who get a kick out of irritating specimens like poison oak and don't get a rash in direct contact with them. Ladies with that immunity are rare.

If continuous uproar doesn't upset your equanimity, and saying "now, now" to Eric the Red is within your ability, Mr. Genius does satisfy a curious need for safety and perversity. Security exists in that you can probably remain in a Mr. Genius involvement permanently. Notice I say "involvement," not *union*. The perversity is in how much you're willing to put up with and still stay on. Some of your years with a Mr. Genius might be fulfilling but some might be close to a sickness or to suspended animation.

Women who get involved with him generally get wiped out. Ten years with a Mr. Genius can leave deleterious effects that take a good deal of recovery. But if you decide to tag along with a Mr. Genius anyway, try to approach him like a Girl Scout on the trail: be prepared. If you expect his cycles and crises, you won't feel cheated. You can keep an eye on yours as you fluctuate with his. You might have an intriguing life. I also suggest something else: cleaving to Caesar doesn't make you Cleopatra unless you *make one of yourself.* Try to stay in the style of a high-class courtesan as you live with him, or else present yourself as an *equal* Genius. Don't slide into a handmaiden role. That way you win more lasting respect from Mr. Genius, plus some attention of your own. But don't expect a simple life. Perhaps you should refuse to marry and you should keep your *own* studio. And don't forget, you'll have to *stay* purposely pretentious right to the Grande Dame age. I also counsel that you consider not having children in a Mr. Genius relationship.

If your present relationship is with a Mr. Genius, and is already well into deterioration, or you haven't the desire to play as if you're as extraordinary as he is and you just want to live, then it's time to pull up stakes. Prepare for two or three go-rounds, then untwine – for good. Despite temptations, you should try to limit repeating and starting over with this man. If after one or two changes it still hasn't improved, don't get yourself talked back into the go-round.

For Mr. Genius to give up his hold on special treatment means he has to face life, with all its drawbacks and benefits and impermanence. He has to make a very deep and personal change. If he does so, you'll find he's redefined himself so drastically he's hardly recognizable. He'll certainly no longer be a Mr. Genius.

Where Do You Fit In?

Usually it's not only a Mr. Genius who has a definite evaluation of himself. So does his lady.

All too often the woman who does the Mr. Genius believes she's *adequate*, but only adequate. Certainly not as adequate as he is. Such self-depreciation may show in such thoughts as "I hardly deserve him" or "he could always toss me over for another" or "women like me are a dime a dozen or maybe a nickel for three." Mr. Genius, in his mania, feeds upon such trepidation in his partner.

Feeling not as wise or worthwhile as the man you love is bad enough, but with Mr. Genius this tendency usually has another detrimental aspect. To live with him and take his tyranny, you almost have to be (consciously or unconsciously) a hassle avoider. Somewhere, somehow, you learned to live in fear. Perhaps your parents' tempers were so severe, or their discipline so costly in guilt or other ways, you began to tiptoe carefully around them. You discovered that submission was easier or cheaper. Or you simply grew afraid of what they could or might do. Perhaps you learned these traits not from your family but from the Mr. Genius himself. But *something* taught you intimidation. With Mr. Genius, apprehension lives in your back pocket.

Of course, with all kinds of men, a woman sometimes wants a union not only for love but because she feels that stardom isn't available to her alone. Due to her own mediocrity or lack of opportunities, she won't make it to the top of the hill. She sees a mate as offering advancement and glamor. And Mr. Genius is one of those fellows who seem to bear promise. He may obtain fame and the society to go with it. He may offer avenues to fabulous events and exotic places. But with Mr. Genius, since he declares himself the one and only in importance, there's no way you can ever be as good as he is in his eyes. To achieve equality you have to be fearlessly obstinate. If you have the least little vacillation he gains ascendancy, and the Mr. Genius can make anyone hesitate and back off.

Watch for any cowardly or demurring traits in yourself. Don't let yourself get put down or pushed around in public, private, by yourself or by any other. Stand up for your own authority over your life. You have a right to equivalence in your relationship even if what you do is less prestigious in society's eyes. And if you need help to conquer alarm and intimidation, *get it!*

Nothing is worth the price of living in timidity. Whatever you fear – desertion, pain, loneliness, or disregard – you'll find that if you evade it by shutting up and submitting, the price is just too high. Fear makes a bad self-image go into an ever-worsening tailspin. Fear is what makes you unable to end a deteriorating union, what makes you set a man up to desert *you* when you ought to leave *him*. Only you can paint your own life and feel satisfied about it. Since the best associations come from two free and independent people, why do anything that makes you feel chicken?

When the next arrogant man turns on you and tells you he's the one who is grand, don't be a shrinking violet. Stand up tall and come up roses.

Mr. Geniuses often have elements of Woman Haters and Male Supremacists about them, so you might want to check back to those chapters. They can also have traits of the Man Who Would Be Mogul in their drive for glory.

Worse, they can be related to a type of man who thinks he's *so* special he doesn't have to work. He's so great, the world owes him a living. Only it's generally you that ends up providing it. It's surprising how many women end up with men who refuse to work, men they have to support, or who have them living on handouts. You might have been with such a man, or are with one now. You might think he's good for you or you might not, but he probably isn't. I encourage you to learn to differentiate him. He's the next man I deal with.

10

The Idle Lord

Who Thinks the World, and You, Owe Him a Living

He leaps onto your stage like an outlaw or a trickster. He knows what's wrong with the whole wide world, or at least the half he's living in. He can show you that what others think is right is most definitely in error. He disdains compliance with the "normal" ways of acting, and especially with common toil. "Why work?" he says. Truth be told, the world owes *everyone* a living. He's just the first to collect.

Round and round goes the wheel of fortune. Where it stops, no one can tell. Some of us get diligent men and some of us get Idle Lords. The question is: when your needle stops at the Idle Lord, do you win or lose? The answer is neither and both. He's quite a confounding spin. In your twenties he seems like a gypsy or renegade, quite wonderful. In your thirties you see him as a bum. When you meet him, he's a rebel. When you leave him, he's a layabout. How can he make such a drastic switch? He doesn't. You do. You get older and suddenly you see that beneath his glib and facile exterior, his often boyish charm, he is thoroughly and totally *irresponsible*.

Of course, not all the other kinds of men labor relentlessly. Here and there some are always a little lazy. Others are content to live off the land or the cash at hand. Still, most pull their weight one way or another. They may get a little drunk or land in jail, but all in all they keep their upkeep up.

Not the Idle Lord, however. He refuses to stick with any occupation. Perhaps he makes up projects, deals, and ideas he then never produces. Maybe he just never works or claims he can't find work. Mostly what he does is play philosopher king. He talks about how the world should be. He blames other people, or harps upon the sins and errors of society. Meanwhile he commits himself to little that's useful and leans on other people.

But, ah, he can be entrancing. He's certainly not your everyday fellow. He has time for pleasure and a way of talking you into going along with his pleasure. The only misfortune is when you mistake him for a mate.

Then again, it's hard to tell a player from a partner when you're feeling mutinous yourself, and that's almost inevitably how a woman is feeling when she thinks an Idle Lord is great. The Idle Lord almost always heads toward women who recently asserted their independence or rebelliousness themselves. He's aware that when you think *you* can change the world, or *you* are going to be different, you're vulnerable, emotional, and ready for something unusual. There's nothing that seems quite as romantic as a free-thinking man. So, if you're presently being Mary, Mary, Quite Contrary (or were one before), watch out for the Idle Lord.

Story

In the many Idle Lord tales I've collected, the men range from do-gooders to drinkers to demons. Yvette's story is average. I think it's a good one to tell.

After going through teenage intractability, insurgence, and sexual rebellion, Yvette had finally just stepped out completely on her own – got into a state college, got her own place – when she met Phillip. Phillip was certainly different. He seemed free, charming, confident, and sexy. He had definite opinions. He sharply and acutely criticized the government, rules and regulations, society's obsolete constraints and ways of operating. He was a truant. But a most lordly one. He called himself a jack-of-all-trades and Yvette had never met one before.

Yvette felt she had to prove that she was daring too, so she went to bed with Phillip right away. That clinched her attraction to him. To say that Phillip was erotic would be an understatement. For the first time, Yvette felt knocked asunder by a man's sexual presence. He moved in with her practically the next day. After all, she already had a place.

Yvette told me that over the next few years she felt like a runaway gypsy. At first, Phillip came and went and lay around talking about his projects, but they never happened. Never mind, she still believed in them. Then he said it was the fault of the college and the place where they lived that no one recognized his value. So they moved. He took her to Oregon where, for a while, they lived out of a van.

But Phillip "couldn't find any work that was up to (his) qualifications" there, and besides, the people were "closed" and "snobbish." So, they moved again. Again the locals wouldn't offer him the right position or buy his ideas. Meanwhile, everywhere they went, Yvette had to scrape for a job – waitressing, cleaning, dog grooming. When she didn't work, it was she who had to go for unemployment, food stamps, and welfare in order for them to survive.

Although at first both Phillip and the different lifestyle captivated Yvette, she began slowly but surely to grow annoyed that she always had to take the jobs and buck the lines. She also noticed that any tidiness depended on her. Disarray was fine up to a point, and the laundry and dishes always ended up piled sky high unless she did them. Phillip simply claimed he'd just as soon wear dirty clothes or eat with his hands. He didn't care how high the piles grew. He left his tools and clothes everywhere. His scattered projects were never picked up or finished, and nothing was repaired.

Yvette also began to realize how greedy Phillip really was. His anti-money philosophy certainly didn't mean he didn't want his share, and more. He spent their funds – what she mostly earned – quite freely on himself. He wanted them to get married so they could cash in on the wedding gifts. They did. He resented it when Yvette used the car. He bellowed when her mother sent her a ticket for a visit home and he didn't get one. He wouldn't let her go unless someone sent him one, too. Ultimately, Yvette found herself pregnant. Phillip was happy. He thought the baby would prove a financial advantage to them despite the child's own costs. Now people would have to give them money. Who among grandparents or agencies would let a child starve?

Phillip managed to keep matters mentally, as well as physically, depressed. He had always stipulated an open marriage, but his most pointed and blatant affair was during Yvette's pregnancy. She had had her affairs, too, mostly in response to his, but she hadn't expected that. And after the child arrived, he not only brought in no money but was gone a lot and gave no help at all. He didn't alter his personal habits one bit.

Yvette began to want to live a little better. She wanted some ease, some time for herself, and some loving care. It wasn't just her labor or Phillip's selfishness taking their toll, though she was very, very tired. She simply changed. She started to assess Phillip very differently. What Yvette had not foreseen was that as years passed and circumstances changed, Phillip did not. His evasion of duty was permanent, no matter what their needs became, no matter how old they grew. In Phillip's eyes all his and Yvette's personal problems would remain someone else's fault and someone else's job to fix, mostly the person who tried to make a life with him. Pairing up with a rogue had been marvelously different and contrary at first, but as time altered Yvette's desires, the returns not only diminished, they almost disappeared.

When her second child was born disabled, the roof caved in. The situation finally and absolutely called for real responsibility. The child needed constant care. Phillip walked out. Luckily Yvette's family rushed in to help her. Having recognized Phillip for what he was instantly (but not being able to convince Yvette), they had always disliked him. Yvette had a life ahead that was what it is now, children, one handicapped, a hard row to hoe. But they would help her as best they could.

A lot of tongue-rolling words exist for the Idle Lord. So many, in fact, that only someone as compelling as he is annoying could attract so large a vocabulary. He's been called a "free spirit," "individualist," "libertarian," "maverick," "lazybones," "lounge-lizard," "laggard," "loafer," "shirker," and more. The words are different, but they all apply to the Idle Lord at one time or another.

How Can You Identify This Kind of Man?

The Idle Lord, when you meet him, emanates originality and nonconformity. But that doesn't mean he's actually uncommon. Idle Lords have been around since the days of the Scarlet Pimpernel. For all we know, there may have been moochers among Cro-Magnon man. The term "Idle Lord" used to refer to the son of a quality family who came to no good, caroused around, caused various fiascos, broke hearts, blew fortunes, sniffed the winds for his advantage and never made the most of it. And why should he have? He always had Mom, Pop, uncles, and cousins by the dozens to fall back on. He could stay well-heeled while living as a reprobate. He's much the same today. Only his relatives have changed. Nowadays the Idle Lord depends on Mother Earth and relies on Uncle Sam.

The Idle Lord has every reason, philosophical to religious to political to healthful, to explain the folly of hard work or diligence. He often claims he lacks ambition, but that isn't really so. He *longs* for power and glory. He just won't toil for them. So while he squelches major aspirations, he remains an opportunist. The Idle Lord doesn't hang loose just to hang loose. He does it to stay ready for whatever opportunity comes along. When one does come along, however, he can't hang onto it. He keeps all his options open: residential, financial, temporal, spatial, sexual, and occupational. He won't commit himself to Saturday Little League with Idle Junior or to your wedding day, because something better might come up. He expects success and notoriety to walk into his living room (like guests who don't have to telephone first). In fact, he generally acts as if they've already arrived.

Outer Signs

His dress is both a statement of policy and a description of his philosophy. He defiantly shows he's not run by society's usual rules. Sometimes he wears only things from Goodwill or a free box; sometimes he dons drawstring pants and Indian chintz holy-man pullovers. He may attire himself in such fashionable clothes that regular people dismiss him. He speaks loudly through his socks. He wears thick red ones, mismatched ones, green silk ones, or none at all.

His dress, uncommon or normal, is nonetheless always a bit provocative, sexual. It's hard, therefore, to tell how immature he remains because his appearance makes him such a bold announcement that he's anything but a child.

Oh, but he *hates* to be treated like a child. Early in his teens he declared he's adult and autonomous. To demonstrate, he becomes sexually active as soon as he's out of his Toughskins. His style continues to evoke his sexuality. He's sensitive, almost narcissistic, when it comes to his hair, which some say is a sexual symbol. He acts as if, Samson-style, his power lies in his silky strands, which he wears very long or very fluffy, waved, braided, beaded, styled. or slick. He carries combs or headbands and likes to have his locks touched. He frequently grows a full beard or a mustache.

If he has a car at all, it's more than likely an old heap. Well, maybe an old heap of a Cadillac, spiffed-up. He likes to sell and trade cars, which are the closest thing to money when he's down to zip. He carries no car insurance, but if anyone hits *him* he gets outraged and sues. The condition of his vehicle constitutes a highway menace. He's prone to getting tickets for parking, a faulty exhaust, and reckless driving. He spreads army blankets or fake fur over the car seats. Beads or amulets hang from the mirror, cans roll around on the floor. He converts the back seat into a bed or the whole rear end into a trailer.

The Idle Lord has an amazing capacity for picking rundown home surroundings. When on his own, he seeks free or dirt-cheap housing, rooms in shared houses, or other people's apartments. Or he inhabits the seemingly uninhabitable. He makes a home out of a Sears prefabricated tool shed, or he rents a garage and brings in a mattress. He house sits or shares a dilapidated mansion in a commune with numerous others, some of whom he has slept with. Sometimes he remains at home and irritates his parents.

When he hooks up, he quite likely moves into his lady's abode, or her family's if they're well off. When you get a place together, five will get you ten he picks decaying areas. Sometimes he heads for isolated rural acreage with hardly a path to drive on. Almost inevitably he settles on a place lacking at least one modern convenience. There may be no plumbing or no electricity. Perhaps the roof leaks. The place is dusty and hard to keep. There are no shelves or cabinets, only Sunkist orange crates. Legions of termites and cockroaches think they live in the Galapagos Islands instead of a house; they sit around and evolve new species while getting suntans.

The Idle Lord keeps unpacked baggage about or scatters belongings like Hansel leaving a trail to get back out of the woods. You can unravel events much like geological ages when you plow through the strata on his chairs and couches. If he decides to work on something, he selects the most inconvenient site possible and yells if anybody touches his tools.

The Idle Lord is surprisingly self-indulgent. Often he's just plain greedy. He's always watchful that he doesn't get the short end of the stick – in cash, clothes, food, or anything. He also cheats, but only when he can justify the cheating. If he doesn't pay taxes, it's because "the government is bad." If he shoplifts, it's because "stores are capitalistic." He claims a suitcase he didn't start with because "airlines are huge companies." He never gets caught without his American Express traveler's checks; he "loses" them to a friend who cashes them while he gets a brand new set. His blanket rationalization is that he deserves to live as well as anyone else.

While an occasional Idle Lord claims perpetual illness as a reason for his exemption from labor duty, most rarely get sick. He insists he need not exercise, he "stays fit naturally." While some Idle Lords are health nuts, many are heavily into drink and drugs; the Idle Lord is frequently an alcoholic or addict or both.

Sex Signals

He likes rebellious and independent women. But he doesn't go for the *long-term* individualist who's strong-willed and demanding. He goes for the lady with the learner's permit – one who just became rebellious or autonomous. She's the kind who thinks he's a rogue and who is willing to take second place.

His approach is a fast and very effective hustle. He pushes you farther in the direction you were heading anyway. You might have been dressing with less than ever before, but he'll say, "Do you always wear so many clothes?" You were becoming *very* erotic, but he'll ask, "Don't you ever do anything to men?" You were trying new things, but he'll come up with even more offbeat adventures. He'll offer a new drug, a whole day of street theater, or a whole day in bed – something that you've never done before.

Sexual power is his high card. He turns himself into a walking, talking aphrodisiac. Sex with him is more than lusty and passionate, it's sensuously carnal. He plunges in everywhere and likes a lot done to him as well. He often manages to lie back and get more than he gives. He turns you on to the point where you never say no. He likes devices, mirrors, odd places and positions. Your body seems to belong to him, and you aren't sure you want it back.

While on the one hand he renders you rapturous, he proposes a no-strings attitude. To him sex is just one of life's little pleasures that means nothing in itself. He claims sex has nothing to do with relationships, that it can't be controlled or limited by partners. And you know what that means.

He may even like two women in his bed.

Money Markers

While the Idle Lord purports to share money and support, he acts quite differently. He most likely contributes very little or no money, and when he does earn something, somehow it always slips away toward his own "development" before it hits the common depository. Either you become the financial mainstay or you manage to live on nothing. And when you're down to zero and someone must get money, you're nominated again. You work, get welfare, borrow money, use your inheritance, or beg.

He certainly uses any money that's about, no matter what he says about being "materialistic." And the nickels he doesn't spend directly on himself, you seem to end up spending his way anyhow. The Idle Lord is also a skinflint, you see. At least where living better or your wants are concerned. He has strong ideas on how money should be used – often for pleasure instead of needs (though he'll call such pleasures "needs"). If your ideas of how to spend your loot are different from his, he condemns yours until you agree with him. So, on top of obtaining the money, you'll also have to make the pennies stretch. Even if you have a dollar, you'll buy beans instead of bacon.

Family Aspects

Somehow the Idle Lord manages to leave any decisions about bearing children entirely in your lap. That way he can claim that any offspring belong to you, not him.

If you do have children with an Idle Lord, prepare to be the one and only parent. Financial support and child care rest with you. He may haphazardly help out, but he comes and goes when he wants to and never makes any payments. He may love his kids, but he doesn't want them to interfere with his options. And even when he does occasionally take over the care of the kids, he hauls them along on what he does instead of doing something with them. He'll shoot the breeze with strangers or fiddle with some project while they play around unattended.

He almost always claims detachment from his own parents and family, but in truth he harbors hostile sentiments toward them. He feels his parents did him wrong or didn't do enough. He blames them far longer than the normal rebellious stage most people go through. After a while, when he never steps into their shoes and sees their side, they finally give up on him and get angry back.

Probably he's closer to his brother than to any other man, but still the tie shows strain – they can't talk spontaneously but have to engage in discussion. If he has any intimate family bond at all, it's probably with his sister. She often adores and defends him, if not vice versa. He certainly spills a bitter version of past family history into her ear.

The Idle Lord often has a brusque attitude toward your own family. He seems to tell them, "Take me as I am and then like me if you can. But if you can't, too bad. You haven't got a choice." He likes to put himself between you and your parents, although he might demand you go to them for aid more often than he will go to his. In no time at all your parents most likely hate him.

The Idle Lord doesn't really seem to care for other men, perhaps because men more quickly than women spot him, dislike him, and dismiss him. And although he is definitely friendlier to women, he rarely has a female pal that isn't a sexual intimate at some point in his life. He often chooses women who are mated to other men. He seems to use other people more than he esteems them.

Still, he has his assets and they sure can hook you. He's complex and interesting. Like the Woman Hater, he's a verbal enchanter. Like Mr. Genius, he seems special. When the lights are out, he's a close encounter of a very alluring kind. So with him you can certainly collect on eroticism, if nothing else. That eroticism may be enough and well worth the price. But in the long run, most women with him realize he's a serious drain, a negative influence. He dwells on what's wrong with the world, not with what's right. While he may claim to offer a new vision, he's fatally short on action. And all told, while he sees himself as a bird of paradise, he actually is – a parasite.

What Is in Store for You?

There's hardly another relationship that so suffers from the ravages of time as that with the Idle Lord. More than any other twosome, it has foreboding age stages. A union with him may be appealing in your twenties because he seems like a change, but it becomes boring in your thirties because philosophical reward grows thin when faced with hundreds of dirty socks. Staying with him can easily turn you into a shrew in your forties and dry you up in your fifties and beyond.

But it's mighty hard to see the road ahead when you're having daily delights in the spring of your romance. Almost nothing feels as delicious as doing what you shouldn't. The Idle Lord tastes like thrillingly forbidden fruit. You're together a lot – after all, he doesn't depart to the tune of the old alarm clock. Everything you do together seems different from your previous life. He marks a turning point, and somehow that period will always remain very special to you, no matter what transpires.

But few flings last forever and, sad to say, the Idle Lord is no exception. As maturity means more responsibility, the Idle Lord becomes as burdensome as he once was liberating. For his upkeep he relies upon his Adam's Rib; he becomes your total dependent. And what few women consider until they're well into an Idle Lord relationship is that his ideas on survival tend to make *more* rather than less labor for his partner. It's well known that monetary stress makes more work and eats up a person's time. Cheap food requires lengthy preparation. Sewing, altering, and rummaging for used items takes hours. Lines take standing in.

Still, work and a meager existence can look like gold if your man plates them. If the Idle Lord appreciated what you did and praised you occasionally, you could certainly say, "What the hell?" But unfortunately the Idle Lord is not one to acclaim anyone but himself. He not only doesn't acknowledge your contribution, he thinks everything he does for you is utterly magnanimous of *him*. In his eyes, the favors he does for you eclipse anything you do for him. He's determined to have his way, and when you cross him he condemns with a razor-sharp tongue. He wins all the arguments because he overwhelms you with verbiage.

Since he perceives of himself as very much a Man, he demands all the privileges that presumably follow: by rights his feet are loose and his fancy free; he's surely his own boss. It's not that he *denies* you the same rights, but since his options come first and yours second, you have a harder time putting yours into action. He even gives you the same sexual freedom he claims for himself. But you get the feeling he does so in order to keep his own license clear. Besides, when can you exercise yours – on your trip to the grocery store?

It's no wonder that an Idle Lord's spouse often finds that in a few years she's fed up. All along he has taken your attempts at being sensible and mutual as a policy of resistance. Now you no longer attempt to be sensible. He treated you as an obstacle. Now he's the same to you. Your freedom gnawed away at his liberty. Now you turn the tables.

Unhappily, any measures you take to make him change his ways rarely work. He simply doesn't begin to face obligation. Instead matters grow even worse. The ultimate Idle Lord partnership is when he not only thwarts his own successes but spoils yours. Every time you work for a goal, your partner blows your savings. You have a child and he has an affair. You plan a holiday and he picks a quarrel. He makes sure you know of his brawls, his lost jobs, and his flirtations. He has a grand eye for messing things up.

A great deal depends at this point on how magnetic the bond between you is. Present circumstances give you every reason to leave, but memories of passion past provoke you to stay. And it's hard to see that the relationship may grow yet more barren.

Usually at this point you begin to retain your own money, form your own goals, and stop considering his. To stay with him means you begin to treat him worse and worse over the years. You oust him in almost every way but physical. You take over and become a matriarch. You strive for yourself and your children without any regard for him. You think you tell him to "take it or leave it," but he stays – and you still take it.

But to leave also has a strange aftermath. He bestows a bitter wariness on any woman who's been with him and supported him that can make you seem tough, stubborn, and anti-male. And while you may have some short romances, usually you don't trust love for quite a while.

What Are the Telltale Signs of Trouble?

If a man comes on sexy and bewitching, claims he's exempt from work but thinks that you should work – you might taste his tallow, but don't sell your soul for his candle, no matter *how* big it is.

A man who's dependent on women almost *always* has a woman around. The Idle Lord's relationships go back like a steady stream, starting in youth. He goes very quickly from one woman to another, sometimes within forty-eight hours, but certainly in no more than a few weeks. He also has a small collection of single lady friends, so some new nest is never far off. And if he has shirts made by one past lady friend, gifts from another, and a third's car, you know he picks caretakers every time.

Pay attention when the quality of your man shifts in your mind's eye. The very first time you mumble the term "good-for-nothing," it should ring like a five-alarm fire signal. You've begun to disrespect him, and when you disrespect anything about your man, it doesn't bode well. It's time to consider the decade ahead.

You get an especially loud signal of serious trouble with the Idle Lord that women in other types of relationships rarely get: you don't want him to leave, you want to get *him* out. You figure the place is yours. He earned little and deserves less. Whether you notice or not, your sense of injustice has grown ominous. All too often when you get in that position, where you want what you deserve, you hang on to win when you should simply end matters without more losses. Better stop and think, which do you want – your freedom from him or the house?

What Are Your Chances and What Should You Do?

When it comes to the Idle Lord, the chances are high that he won't change. What's more likely is that *you* will become different from what you were. In the first glow of an Idle Lord pairing, it's so hard to see the future that in all probability the only women who will recognize the truth of what I say will be those looking back. Considering that fact, my advice is this: do the Idle Lord if you will and must, but don't think in terms of forever and a day. Think of him as an event. When it's over, say "So long." Most likely you will start to take life seriously somewhere along the line, even if he won't.

The Idle Lord relationship will almost always cause an irreversible shift in you. It can happen in one of two ways. In the first kind, you stay close to your own life, your work, and whatever you would have had anyway, while you foot his bill. In this case your transformation is inward, not outward, but it changes your life anyway. You may continue to live mostly as you did, but your outlook turns pessimistic. Certainly you keep on working, but the combination of work and a gloomy outlook becomes poisonous. If you remain with the Idle Lord in this state, you suffer malcontent. If you leave him, all too often you become the type of woman who then seeks to find a man "who will support *me* this time." And that's bad. Such a bitter ambition not only goes against love but often works exactly contrary to your desire. Men recognize ulterior motives and quite rightly retreat very fast.

In the second kind of change, the Idle Lord causes you to stray very far from the way you would have lived otherwise. Perhaps you quit school, move, never pursue your career, drop out. Sometimes you can fight your way back to the kind of life you led before him, but often, whether the transformation suits you or not, you have to stay with it, even if you end up not staying with the Idle Lord.

Though Yvette's parents rescued her, her case was this latter one. She was a changed person. She now couldn't go back to school and a neat little life. Again, luckily for her, she decided that although she hadn't necessarily meant to live a non-conformist life when she started out, it now suited her. In certain communities the way she now lived was more the norm than the exception. She returned to one with her children. There she found support systems and a lot of caring people around. And she did get some new schooling and a steady job. But she also recognized that she had a long time before she would be ready for another relationship. When she met new men she acted like a black widow spider. She used them once, then chased them out before they had a chance to use her. All in all, therefore, when you meet an Idle Lord, my suggestion is *Look Ahead*. The fun and games of an irresponsible mate simply don't do with every stage of life. Also, if you find the break with an Idle Lord miserable and seemingly impossible, don't rush to the decision that you can't do it. Usually a split from him takes a long while, and during it other men don't seem to come up to the old one's snuff. After an Idle Lord, one of the healthiest things you might do for yourself is to withdraw from all sexual relations for a while. Once you distance yourself from passion, you can better return to a more caring love. *Then* you can retrieve the sex!

Where Do You Fit In?

Often when a woman chooses a man who's loose in every way, she's every which way *but loose*, only she doesn't know it. She seems free and easy, but deep down she isn't the totally unrestrained soul she aspires to be. Instead of being an escape from social constraints and upbringing, her fling with a ne'er-do-well is in part an escape from herself.

Many a rebellious earth mother is a dutiful caretaker. Sadly, the Idle Lord is often an attraction to your projected self and not a match for the real you. In time, when the real you crops up again, so do the irreconcilable differences between you and him.

If you are prone to the Idle Lord, you most likely have strong ideas on how life should be led. Chances are you're responsible, ethical, loyal, and honest. As your ideas lead you toward independence, you mistakenly believe that you aren't bound by rules, at least not the *old* ones, and that's where you go wrong.

For a clue to yourself, just examine the motivations you have for falling for the Idle Lord; I'll bet you find some righteous principles involved. Did you choose the union because of love? Well, after all, "for love" is a *very* principled reason for mating. Did you desire a new, more *real* kind of life? Are you stubborn? Then a commitment to duty and obligation probably isn't far behind. The trouble is, when you pick a man who lacks responsibility and you have it, you end up picking up his slack.

When you're with the Idle Lord, it's not that you can't change him, but that you can't always change *you* either. You may kid yourself for a while. You may reveal to yourself only slowly exactly what you are like. You may ignore the evidence that you and your mate differ greatly, but the ways in which he seems erring in your eyes reveals as much about what *you* are as they do about him.

When you select someone you'd like to be, only to find out that you can't be his way at all, it's hard to face. But you are not to blame for a lack of self-awareness – if you grow with your errors. You can only get knowledge by the process of life itself, and to do so you have to live it, miscalculations and all. You didn't make a *mistake*; you may have lacked insight and foresight, maybe at worst you held on too long. But you did try. You'd regret it more if you hadn't done it at all.

The Idle Lord is worse if he also bears characteristics of the Woman Hater or the Male Supremacist. And sometimes he can. He can pull a total switch on you and go from wonderful courtship to debilitating and destructive criticism. He can also ballyhoo about men's prerogatives and demand you stay in a woman's place whether you support him or not.

Of course, he clearly shares a pattern with Mr. Genius. They almost make a matched set, the one who works and the one who doesn't. Having completed that set, it's time to go on to a different kind of man. And believe me, the Disaster Broker is different. He's not quite as common as the Idle Lord, but he can be equally exhausting. How long, after all, can you thrive on danger?

11

The Disaster Broker

The Man Who Flirts with Danger, Disaster, Death, and Broken Bones

Death, doctors, injury, crimes, courts, the law. One more roll of the dice, on the brink of losing it all. One more try for the trophy. One more campaign trail. One more fire. One more war.

Imagine yourself attached to Sonny Crockett, Rico Tubbs, Batman, Napoleon, Sam Spade, Rocky, Rambo, Evel Kneivel, Mario Andretti, General Patton, Al Capone, Bruce Lee, or Indiana Jones. Maybe all of them rolled into one. Always high-pitched action. Always a crisis, an emergency, a big event. And the next. And the next. And the next.

The Disaster Broker runs on risk. Jeopardy is the breath of life to him. He's unable to survive without pitting himself against huge, unwavering outside forces – catastrophe, disability, stigma, bankruptcy, loss. He threatens himself with the heavies – hospitals, prisons, blacklists, and oblivion.

If the stakes aren't real, he can't feel.

Of course, he also can't be a Clyde without a Bonnie. Or a Julius without a Cleo. What would he be without a moll? So, the Disaster Broker likes to attach himself to a combination decorator piece, first lady, and fan. She should be someone who shines for an audience, stands with him against adversaries, works for him, cares for him, puts up with all his buddies and cronies. She should also have spunk. That way she herself becomes a trophy. He can lose her and try to win her back.

And rewinnable she is. For while the Disaster Broker's lady is outstanding and tempestuous, she also tends to be unflaggingly devoted and full of grit. So dedicated is she, she bends her every ultimatum and gives in to his every trip.

Story

Take the case of Sky. Sky grew up on a small ranch as a tomboy through and through. But fate played a trick on her. Tough as she was, she also took on good looks, feminine urges, and lots of natural class. By the time she was sixteen and eyeing the horses at the local rodeo, the horsemen were eyeing her.

Monty was one of them. Monty rode broncos and did stunts, but he already had his sights set higher – or faster. He had tired of horses. He now wanted speed vehicles; cars, motorcycles, and anything else that moved like white lightning, including ladies. At first, being charming and a little bit fatherly, Monty "let" Sky hang out with him. But he knew that as a conquest and sidekick she would be a feather in his cap. Pretty soon when he put his saddle into the back of the pickup, Sky was riding in the passenger seat, and they were sharing rooms in motels "by the month."

Sky heard all of Monty's plans. But she had no real idea what doubling up with a daredevil could turn into. In time they were no longer a couple; they were a caravan. As Monty struck out for ever more spectacular events, they needed trailers, more trucks, then more trailers again. Sky became ticket taker, second driver, hand shaker, errand runner, mopper upper, and mascot. They took on mechanics, agents, and managers. In addition, Monty added advisers, helpers, and hero worshippers. Soon they were never alone.

They also had another ever-present, invisible companion – danger. Monty not only flirted with disaster, he tempted the odds. He wasn't just after the win, speed, and prizes, he was after *peril*. He ran races in ticklish circumstances, added hazardous devices. He managed to crash one craft after another on a regular basis. Sky spent more hours than she could count escorting stretchers, following ambulances, and sitting in hospital corridors. She would nurse and feed Monty, then watch in dismay while he sawed off his casts three weeks early so he could ride again.

She also sat in jail houses and legal chambers. Since money was like the rest of their life – all or nothing – Monty had a sideline. Being into zip and excitement, he had gotten into drugs. And after getting into them, he quickly realized it was more thrilling to deal them. He could not only risk the money, he could risk the law. He claimed he needed just one big score with dope to get enough money to back his racing, but Sky suspected his motive was the risk and melodrama. Not satisfied with simple sales, Monty took to shipments from Lima and Thailand. He so feared a rip-off that their trailer looked like the Alamo and every stranger became a potential "Fed."

Everything Monty did had to have a critical edge. Even sex took on a frenzied aspect; with Sky and Monty, every amorous event became a marathon. They were on the bed, off the bed – all over the place. They were upside down, inside out, and halfway killing each other. They climaxed like trains crashing. They played at sex like a bomb team carrying TNT. Monty liked it best when he felt there was danger of getting caught. He would pounce on Sky just as people were coming over or a race was due to start; sometimes they would fight in a restaurant, then make love in their car in the alley behind. That is when he wasn't "jinxed," and couldn't do it at all.

Unfortunately, getting caught occasionally meant his getting caught by Sky. Once in the cycle rig (after a triumph) and once in her own bed (after a loss), Sky found Monty naked and entwined with someone else. Lord knows there was a reason to suspect other times. Sky flew into a fury and departed on both occasions, but Monty chased, charmed, and persuaded her on his knees to come back again. He also sent his friends to urge her home. Sky switched from beer to Seven and Seven.

They lived traveling, crashing, and racing for six years before Sky announced she was pregnant. But only when she was three days overdue did Monty drive her to a Justice of the Peace. She got married in her jeans, fly open, and with Monty's shirt as a maternity smock. They produced yet another baby ten months after. And still they trucked around from one race or stunt track to another.

Both kids were still preschoolers when Monty pulled his final crackup. He wasn't even racing. He was running a tryout lap. With his usual bravado, he refused to wear his fireproof garments. He burned to death before they could remove him from the wreck. Sky became a sudden widow and, although she was always aware of the possibility it might happen, her recovery took quite a while. Monty's death came at a strange and poignant time for her.

A few years before she might have gone on to another rash prodigal son, a politician or fireman. But Monty crashed just as Sky wanted out of the whole affair. On the one hand, Monty left her alone a lot and ignored her on the sidelines. On the other, they had so many fights to clear the air, the air was as pure as a bottle of Canada Dry Club Soda. Sky could no longer stand the pace. It had gotten so she scarcely spent a day without a Valium or a drink – or several. She wanted to enjoy the children. She was intrigued with real responsibility. She wanted occasional peace and quiet, relief from constant worry. She didn't like the liquor and drugs. But no matter what she said or did, Monty would not quit. At least not for long. On the day

Monty died, Sky had been examining her wrinkles and telling herself it was time to call it quits. It was hard to accept the truth as a widow, but Sky knew her feeling for Monty had died before his crash.

Not all racers, sportsmen, gamblers, warriors, or politicians are Disaster Brokers. Only the particular sort who seem to goad disaster. With such men, kicks come from playing brinkmanship, not from loving and living. There's no doubt they kindle constant excitement, but the price accumulates. You suffer wear and tear. Your emotions and your body play tit for tat. When you don't leave, your sacroiliac does. When you watch him lose, you start to drink. The trouble is the Disaster Broker can be so intriguing that he becomes just as addicting as the habits he leads to. That's why it's not spotting him that's difficult, it's trying to quit.

How Can You Identify This Kind of Man?

Instead of tinker, tailor, soldier, sailor, the Disaster Broker is burglar, stuntman, gambler. They're also foreign correspondents, doctors (emergency or surgery), lawyers (defending against a lynching), or truck drivers (of big rigs going breakneck). Also C.P.A.s who fake tax returns. Then there's the man who is so trouble-ridden or accident prone you *know* something is going on. You just don't know what it is.

Sometimes the Disaster Broker only dabbles a bit in the game that attracts him. Sometimes he's a full-blown pro. But whatever peril he prefers – war, arrest, or high steel – and to whatever degree he pursues it, one fact remains: what he has going makes him an ultimate escape artist as opposed to a quick one. He's so preoccupied with crises, he obliterates almost everything else there is to feel.

Often the Disaster Broker not only turns his life into a cliff-hanger, he sets things up so he's sure to lose. He's never satisfied, and no one event is ever good enough. So he has to keep keeping on, do what he did one more time, only bigger. Eventually he pushes it so far he fails, or gets killed, or ages beyond his capacity to win and goes into a tailspin. When he fails, he then launches himself back to start all over again. When he ages, he hangs around talking of new tries. Of course, some Disaster Brokers manage to stay just on the winning side of victory the whole way, but even they push their luck over and over again.

The Disaster Broker even whips normal daily events into critical ones. He can't participate in any situation unless it practically screams with tension. He frets, strategizes, analyzes, prepares for "contingencies," hones equipment, and spends hours talking about what might or might not happen. He lives in the not-here, not-now until either triumph or disaster smacks him with the present. Even then the effect is short-lived. Sometimes his surface is seemingly serene, but behind his eyes he operates on a constant red alert. Sometimes his whole demeanor is agitated. Whichever, he has trouble with the fact that he's alive. He tests his existence with peak experiences simply to prove to himself that he's real. The trouble is that as long as he *stays* alive, his testing has no end.

Outer Signs

The Disaster Broker either dresses to be the center of attention or else in such a way as to dispel suspicion. That's because notoriety is his enchantress. Notoriety – in either the positive form (becoming known) or the negative (escaping from becoming known) – confirms his existence. His dress follows. He either seeks public recognition with it, or else he plays the game of getting away without being discovered. His actions follow also. The Disaster Broker likes to celebrate. He'll celebrate a public win in public, and a private "getting away" with something in secret. He celebrates a lot.

Those Disaster Brokers who go for public notice might don studded show-stoppers, satin jump suits, or jackets sequined with stars. Or he'll wear such expensive, impeccable business suits they almost twinkle like stars. He's very blatant, hard to miss. Something about his garb is a dead giveaway. He's also the kind of guy that's liable to appear in a uniform. Sometimes he wears a sloping helmet and red suspenders, big high boots and a yellow slicker. Sometimes he wears blue with a badge on his chest and a big brown holster. Sometimes his outfit is striped and has his lockup number on the pocket. Or he wears a black body stocking and face mask. Or it's racing skins, diving tanks, epaulets, or riding chaps.

The more hidden sort of Disaster Broker wears clothes so perfectly suited to his job that he fades into the wall: the perfect accountant's garb as he defrauds the account or grey flannel as he runs his stocks and bonds over the top. Or he dresses so ragtag casual that he defies distinction from the surrounding populace. (Who'd have ever thought he dealt dope or ran brinksmanship wheels and deals?) But almost every Disaster Broker – hiding or shining – has some little personal touch in his dress that becomes his trademark. It might be a scarf, a cat's-eye signet ring, a special jacket, or an eye patch. He has some kind of lucky piece he carries everywhere – a worn out dollar, a rabbit's foot. Or he absolutely always wears some particular color – say blue, or never, never wears or drives anything green.

He tends to go for large cars, swanky cars, sports cars, motorcycles, monster pick-up trucks, limousines, or very special cars. He owns a rare type of Lotus of which the factory only made three, or he alters his vehicle so that its maker would never recognize it. When he's a policeman or fireman or hot-rod trucker or general speed demon, he adds some individual attachment to his dashboard. His vehicle always makes an impact. It has speed, or luxury, or hidden but mighty power. He may well own a boat or plane in addition to a car. He gives all his vehicles names and often puts on his monograms or has them painted with unique designs.

His home can be anything from a hotel room to a mansion. It doesn't seem to matter that much to him. He has his own housing wherever he is. Everything he needs goes with him. He can turn any room or wagon into his own the minute he occupies it, because he doesn't really have a home –he has a hub of activity. He has a crisis central. Even when he gets a house, he alters the space until the rooms don't make sense. Parlors become conference centers. Bedrooms turn into supply cabinets and offices. Kitchens get reorganized into switchboards and E.R.'s. Private life and business are for him forever jumbled. Try as you might for separate space, you and your room are just part of the mixture. He doesn't give a hang about decor as long as there are plenty of chairs and ashtrays around. Mind you, his home is also like a guarded lair – the CIA, NATO, a fortress. What's talked about inside is a secret. Strangers are kept out or rebuffed.

The Disaster Broker thrives on interruptions. His concentration span, although intense, lasts only two minutes before he needs new input. He loves to handle about fifteen actions and conversations – some overt, some covert – all at once. Voices in his head are always talking to him; one is ever mindful of the next scheme he's planning. The only time he's totally present and focused is when he's just lost, just said "Fire," just realized he's escaped, just tossed in the towel, or just proclaimed a win. Meanwhile the attention he gives people is permanently superficial because only *events* really capture his imagination.

Bodily, he wears himself ragged. He doesn't always know it, but the dark areas under his eyes definitely show it. Sometimes he breaks his bones or overuses his adrenaline. Sometimes he gets thrombosis, strokes, and tics. Sometimes he finally kills himself. Often he uses drugs, smokes, drinks like a fish, and womanizes mindlessly – he plays his body out to the limits.

Sex Signals

But the Disaster Broker usually has a very good eye for women. Although he has a fixed idea of the type he likes and tends to pursue duplicates, what wakes him up is when he gets a snappy, sassy response along with a pretty face. And he knows when a woman has heart and stamina underneath. Often he goes for the lady with more quality or looks than he has – in other words, a *prize*. And he recognizes those who find his circus exciting. When he spots a woman he likes, he moves in on her pretty fast. He picks you out in an offhand manner, as if he weren't looking. Then he scoops you up, "whirlwinds" you, and sometimes scares you. At first you're liable to stay up all night and be spontaneous to the point of wildness. Often he brings all his male helpers so you're the only woman and it flatters you. Later, you become his aide. You carry his silks and files, put on bandages, and brew coffee during long nights. You become one of the guys, with a special distinction and an occasional kiss – you're a mascot.

Sex is like a version of life against death or a race against great odds. He makes love as if you're climbing over rocks, cliffs, and glaciers, maniacs are chasing you, and there's no way back. He drags you along, eggs you on and on. He won't let you get stuck on the ice, and he'll be damned if he'll let you fall behind. He'll go on forever until you get to the top – so you either climax or fake it.

He seeks these arduous adventures at strange hours, on the spur of the moment. He also has a penchant for public places and unprotected situations. He'll try it standing up in the airplane toilet or on a theater stage before the crew arrives. At home he goes for bathroom floors and kitchen tables. He enjoys a chase and being a little too noisy; he likes guests to guess that they just interrupted something. Sometimes he does it while talking on the telephone. You don't exactly get a regular sex life with him. You get it anywhere, anytime, five times a night five nights in a row – and then get abstinence while he's off on devious doings.

You get hooked on sex, but *he* says when it happens. And sometimes – often for a long time – it doesn't happen. He doesn't want to. He's busy, obsessed with other things, scared, jinxed, unsexual, or unable. He can get you very frustrated.

On the other hand, he likes to play the flower to which the honeybees flock, and he also likes to play the bee. He's extremely aware of all women and likes "groupies." But at the same time he prefers to have an official consort. He doesn't necessarily want to officially marry you, although he will. But he does maintain a permanent alliance, after his own fashion. He may well have one-night stands or short affairs with others, especially when all else is quiet – he usually does them just messily enough for you to find out. Still, he tosses you just enough exhilarating moments to keep you attached, and in the meantime, gives you the company of all his pals, so you're never exactly *lonely*.

Money Markers

To the Disaster Broker, money, like everything else, represents a means to create hazard. He uses it to promote risky ventures, or he merely risks the money away. He's a real spender. When he has it, he burns it. When he runs out, it's down to the very last dime – and lower. He borrows. He can run through cash so fast he doesn't even know where it went. He feasts (which to him is either health food or a huge steak), or he starves (which to him is a vitamin pill, upper and/or downer, and/or drink), but he rarely saves. And if he has a family inheritance, he probably goes through it.

But *your* cash hardly seems to enter his mind. Financial advantage is not what he seeks in a female. He may eat in your kitchen when he's down and out or he may take some of your bucks in need, but mostly you both ride along on what he's got. Like the Male Supremacist, when he's flush he loves to toss you a big bill and tell you to spend it. He rarely minds your expenses. In fact, he uses paying for you as another excuse for his dangerous risks.

Family Aspects

If he collects anything, it's people. He keeps a troupe. The Disaster Broker allows his friends constant access to himself. Those who abet him or hang out with him have open channels to his attention anytime – even before you. He relies on constant intrusions to bring him new and crucial data. "What's up?" is the first thing he says to chums. They tell him the bad news. Sometimes they invent it or whip it up just to help keep things hopping.

His legions are mostly men. The one or two women he befriends are separate from the crowd and are probably on their way to a potential affair with him. He is brotherly to, and basically ignores, your one or two women friends and the wives of his pals. In some ways his buddies, especially his best one, and maybe his brother, will always be closer to him than you. He calls *them* when he's injured, lost, or arrested. They break the news to you. You stay by his side till he's over the crisis; then they come back when he starts up again.

He wants you to have children. (To keep him busy?) Once they're born, he treats his offspring like trophies on a shelf. He coos at and glows over them from across the room. He shows them off as if they just got polished, but when it comes to real care they're *yours*. Later, his version of fathering will include putting toddlers on his lap behind the wheel and letting them steer, plunking them on a pony and slapping the horse's behind, or letting them hide under his podium and calling over the cameraman. When they're older, he tries to make them equals, friends, to get them to follow his calling. Parenting is foreign to him. After all, he's still playing hide and seek himself. But if you break up, suddenly the loss of his children becomes a drastic event. He'll try almost anything to get them back, especially cross-country kidnappings.

He has a powerful attachment to his blood kin. Sometimes it's loving, sometimes bitter, sometimes open, sometimes secret, but family ties bind him one way or another. He may distance himself from his relatives and try to forget them, but more frequently he incorporates his parents, siblings, and cousins into his keeping. He does favors for all the relatives he can, as long as they come to him. Even when he rejects his family, he allows them strange ways to find him. He uses his feelings of guilt, responsibility, or anger toward them as another reason to take chances.

He can lose his name, his fame, his life, and his money. He can go to prison and take you with him. He makes ordinary satisfaction impossible for you. But if you like drama, the Disaster Broker is everything you ever wanted. He's as close as you'll ever get to making life into a movie screen. He's a thriller, an adventure, a living, walking chase scene. You don't have to sit on a seat in the dark to watch him – he's there in Sensurround and you can join him. But you better have nerves of steel.

What Is in Store for You?

Did you ever want to run away and join a circus, not to become a juggler, nor even a clown, but to wear a little tutu, climb up a rope ladder, and hold the trapeze for some daring young man? (In tights!) Somewhere during his act you would get to take a swing into his muscular arms. When you told your mother, she clucked her tongue and said, "Darling, what looks like fun when you're young isn't so enjoyable as time goes on." Somehow you knew she was telling the truth.

Everyone likes an occasional crisis, a little touch of danger. They add zest to your life and take top billing in the stories you collect about yourself. But a steady diet of them is liable to do to your psyche what three meals a day of Godiva chocolates is liable to do to your body. When all your hours are zero hours you wind up badly undernourished in spirit, with cavities in your self-control.

With a Disaster Broker, unlike with most men, the transformations and stages you go through as a couple largely emanate from *you*, not from him. The man who plays footsie with fatality can rarely hide himself for long. He's not one of the obscure sorts who seems one way during courtship and then changes when all is said and done. Nor does he often change his ways. That's the trouble. If the Disaster Broker is anything, he's perpetual. He may shift the kind of peril he pursues. He may go from firefighter to financial phantom or free-fall parachutist. But he hardly ever gives up *all* temptation for calamity.

At first you get to play moll and adjunct thrill-seeker. You meet adulthood in a captivating manner; all they ever said about being young and free seems true. Without set schedules and regular expectations, you cut yourself loose, throw yourself into life, and enjoy an exciting man.

But even in the first stages of a Disaster Broker affair some less-than-pleasant aspects start to appear. Like it or not, you become part of his act. In some cases your role is to stand just outside the spotlight, show a lot of leg, or wear a perfect pillbox. In other cases you're less obvious. You may even be in the dark about his doings. But mostly you serve as the net when he takes a spill. And you worry, fix up, and clean up the mess.

Sooner or later, three things happen. First, you realize that to entertain himself he needs external excitement provided by someone or something else, not himself or you. When the two of you are alone, without a sexual episode or quarrel, you can hardly keep him amused. In fact there's nothing much at all to your relationship except for the times you play to an audience. You must have somebody else to see you, check on you (and maybe not discover you), know about you (or get fooled by you), for you to have togetherness. Part of the reason he always has his pals around is to take up the slack of what he hasn't got going with you.

Second, you get tired of the hollowness of the thrills. When he's around, he's exhausting. When he meanders off, you get the emptiness and the hole he leaves behind. Soon your energy runs out. You lead a draining life on every level. You never know when disaster will occur. Even quiet spells are ominous, because they might be the prelude to twisters. Tension comes and goes in waves. You get weak. You spend a lot of time in places with pumped air and Muzak (like in hospitals). You sit on a lot of benches (like in court). You reverberate around another person's actions. His dealings may cause drastic events to happen to you as well – you could end up anywhere from the White House to San Quentin to the grave. And when you seek some nurturing from him to compensate for the strain, it just isn't there.

Everyone knows that when you're under a lot of pressure something's got to give. It does. Enter stage three. You begin to fall apart. You increase your cigarette consumption from ten to sixty-four per day. You get virus-prone and go from colds to double pneumonia. Your bones get brittle, your muscles grab. Pills get handy and so does wine or pre-mixed Tequila Sunrise. You get cut off from other people. With the Disaster Broker, most often you talk in codes, have insignias for friends and strangers, use cryptics for telephone calls and hand signals for commands in public. You talk to those that know your language and cut off outsiders. Every person you meet is an "in" person (in on what you're doing) or an "out" person. All emotions are black and white to the Disaster Broker. *You* may feel grays and in-betweens, but you can't tell that to your man. He assumes you're loyal. Quibbling puts to question your faith. Outright fights are allowed (and you have a lot) because he thinks you're just letting off steam and afterwards you'll comply. With your devotion so expected, you just go ahead and give it. To leave would be to become a bad guy. Soon you get so removed from reality you seem a little crackers.

He's always doing things to push you away and then reclaim you again. And you let it happen rather than leave the strange and marginal world you know. You're afraid that there's nothing left for you anywhere once you've gotten used to his extremes.

What tends to happen when you stay is that you add to the action. You have crises of your own, stamp your feet, break glasses, and throw tantrums. You get sick, weird, and drunk. You almost leave – but not quite. That always kicks up dust. You become a semi-invalid with chronic problems.

Fun in your twenties, dreary in your thirties, weary and withdrawn from forty and on. That's the program unless something happens: one is an actual disaster, an event that alters your life and relationship conclusively. The other is that one day life just gets more precious to you. You decide to stop playing "let's run the gauntlet together," leave the ranks of the super, and join the ordinary crowd.

What Are the Telltale Signs of Trouble?

The Disaster Broker doesn't have telltale signs – he has air raid sirens and seismic warnings. The trouble is, you're probably the kind who hears the rumbling and says, "Gee, an earthquake! I'd like to try that once!"

If a man comes around who's got on a costume, perhaps you should stay behind closed doors, or at least think twice. Also, reconsider if the man you meet slips in the door in the middle of the night and the first thing he says is, "pull down the shades," then peeks out the window to see who's watching; he builds smuggling holes in his hang glider; he adds fourteen gas tanks to his overloaded racer; he keeps dangerous trinkets, like submachine guns, plastic explosives, high-octane fuel, blackmail evidence, heroin, and spying devices; he doesn't tell you his name at first, or he tells you one but turns out to have six others, all with different mail drops; he sands his fingertips; or he has a permit for a regulation gun but carries a snub nose in his boot.

Once you have a union with him, the storm warnings for trouble come in two big ways. The first is when he reveals a tendency to lose instead of win. *Professional* gamblers, soldiers, and climbers – the ones who succeed – like as little messy action as possible. They keep their situations simple and tidy; compulsion, complications, and carelessness spell risk to them. So when your mate goes after too many wins, take heed. When he shows he's accident-prone or when two out of three times he comes home with losses or injuries, you'd better realize he's aiming for peril despite what he says.

You're at a critical point with the Disaster Broker whenever the stakes get too high for *you*, regardless of him. It also comes when it becomes obvious that he's slowly committing suicide, when he's on drugs, rides too dangerously, does stunts too precariously, deals with assassins and killers, or runs into the line of fire. But his obsession holds you to him and so do his injuries. If you feel compelled to watch him fall, perhaps it's time for you to consider that your presence *abets* his flirtation with death. Your presence makes him do it more, not less.

Certainly if and when what a Disaster Broker does endangers you bodily, financially, or otherwise – STOP! You might become responsible for his disasters in ways you hadn't even considered. If you like a dangerous aspect in life, why not at least pay for your *own* actions? Become a fireperson, policeperson, detective, or stuntwoman yourself. Get the benefits, a support system for yourself, not through someone else.

What Are Your Chances and What Should You Do?

Can you stay with the Disaster Broker? With no other kind of man is that question as hard to answer. Luck plays such a heavy hand in the Disaster Broker's future. It is almost more his mate than you are. You have to consider it a silent partner that can keep you together or interrupt you forever.

Can you change him? No, you can't. The Disaster Broker could be likened to a hurricane. Once he's started, nothing can turn him back, unless another extreme front comes along and blasts out all his punch. When he comes your way, you can either weather him, ride him out a while, stay on his edges, shelter yourself as he passes, or just get out of his way. It's up to you. Once he's sucked you in, he may toss you about, but he rarely spits you out, so what to do about him is in your hands. A lot of women leave as soon as they see the storm ahead with him or go through some of his episodes.

My advice concerning the Disaster Broker is multiple choice. If his scene is very dire, if he indulges in truly dangerous drugs for use or sale, practices serious crime for fun or profit, gambles with heavy losses, or does life-endangering stunts, I strongly suggest that you stay far, far removed. You may need a lot of things in life, but those are items you definitely can do without.

On the other hand, if he seeks thrilling action and perilous challenges with some sense and precaution, and you like him and find him exciting, why not join in while you're young and free? But just for a spell. Then when you desire more substance in your life, make like Wendy: leave Peter Pan to the pirates and crocodiles, fly home, and grow up. If you follow this course, do it with honesty and heart. Make the terms of your commitment clear to him up front. Most likely you can see the future well enough to know that he won't change and you will. Say at the beginning that you will stay until the time you want something else. You don't mean to alter him, pressure him, or torment him. You merely mean to be true to yourself.

If you *don't* think you can enjoy him for a while and take off with a fond farewell, I advise that you don't do him at all. The conditions that come with him are hazardous to the health. I'd certainly shun the game of leaving and getting re-won. As long as you stay on a Disaster Broker's invisible tether, you never become free.

If you remain with a Disaster Broker, it's very important for you to create an eye in his storm where you can rest and gather a calm center within yourself. In order to maintain your mental and physical well-being, insist on your own space where trespassers are prohibited. Then – and I can't stress this enough – - learn techniques for inner peace. Try meditation, self-dialogue, or prayer until you find that very quite place within you where you can gain repose and strength. Make rules about how you will live, who can come and go and when. Then keep the rules despite what's going on. You may even consciously choose to remain ignorant of his actions. Since you are his number-one sidekick, he probably respects you more than you think. He'll heed your conditions if you insist.

In order to weather him, you will need not only to keep up the spunk and ability you started with, but to learn not to overload, to limit yourself. Perhaps you should relinquish the thought of having children. Possibly you should only take on certain well-defined tasks with him, or none at all. Maybe you should develop a career attached to, but different from, his, then stick to it and nothing else.

Whatever way you choose, when you link up with a daredevil it's bound to be tough. You're probably more of a survivor than he is – he knew that instinctively the minute he met you – so trust yourself, whatever happens to him. If you end up alone or with a disabled companion, you will manage. Instead of fretting, believe in yourself and cross bridges when you come to them. Never forget one thing: you can always decide you've had enough and get out, at any point. With the Disaster Broker, quitting isn't necessarily losing, it's staying well. You don't have to carry through with everything you start just because you handled it once. Whenever the costs mount up beyond your scope or the peril is more than you're willing to risk, cut your losses and part. Throw loving kisses, cry if you must, but don't end up in some dire place or condition just for the sake of sticking it out.

Where Do You Fit In?

So you want to be a pistol-packing mama? Lois Lane? Marie Antoinette? The smuggler's moll?

Usually that means one of two things. It may mean you're from down-home, nothing-happening land. With him you tasted your first thrill. Now you love it and don't want out. You have an addictive streak, and you found your drug in an exhilarating life. Maybe you also discovered booze, cigarettes, the roar of the crowds, an occasional toke, hit, or snort? And maybe those habits are growing.

Or it may mean you too are a crisis-monger. You like zero hours yourself, and if you don't get them from him, you create your own. He's just an easy way to have them without doing your own inventing.

Ask yourself how many walks you've taken, only to come back. How many threats and scenes have been replayed? How many fights? How often do you get ill? How much do you really like it when he gets busted and you have to bail him out? How exciting do you find it when you have to hide from the law, trick opponents, set up a con, call ambulances, use codes, keep score, and destroy evidence? If this comes too close for comfort, maybe you yourself are afraid of an ordinary life.

It's true that routine life can appear quite appalling. To some it's like an endless living death, so rather than face it, they manufacture extremes or develop addictions to keep their lives different from routine nothingness. Do you so dislike silence you play the radio from dawn to dusk? Do you feel nothing when nothing's happening?

If plain life seems too dreary or if you show escapist patterns, you might want to explore the subject with outside counsel. Self-recognition is a big step. These are the sorts of issues that counseling really helps, if not to alter them, at least to understand them. Such aid is available almost everywhere. But if you're on a race circuit or in the underworld where help is hard to get, at least keep a notebook in which you religiously jot down your habits – when they happen and how. Note everything: cigarettes, the radio, drinks, mad expenditures, gambles, headaches, broken bones. How frequent are the flirtations with danger? When you read your notebook, you'll see predictable patterns you never knew existed, and with that knowledge often you can call a halt.

Sometimes, however, the Disaster Broker doesn't match your own tendencies. You just thought his craziness was a phase of his youth. But he kept on doing it and never grew up. Or the adventure he offered looked exciting to start with, but very quickly turned old. Then you need to examine what continues to hold you to him. You fell for something that was in your imagination – a man you thought would change and didn't, a life you thought was fun and wasn't – not something real. If your illusion has long since passed but you're still hanging on, you'd better ask why. I'll bet you find that, if you didn't to start with, now you do fear a routine life. Like an addict or a mother facing the empty nest, you no longer know how you'd go on without his crises.

Of course you may fit in with him simply by choice. You don't desire crises yourself, you just prefer verve. I once heard the story of a woman who died very young. Everyone grieved her passing, for she had marvelous wit and charm. Yet she had often said she would rather have a short, bright life than a long, dull one. She acted on choice, though unconsciously. The people who really loved her knew she would not have wanted them to mourn.

Every human being has the right to decide how to utilize his or her energy. Some go for low, steady, and long. Some want to be like fires that consume every coal. They prefer to burst forth and kindle fast even though they know they may quickly die out. If that's the way you want to burn, the Disaster Broker may be good fuel for you. But then don't complain. And if he isn't good for you, if he's too hot to handle and you don't want to burn out young, learn to tell the difference. Avoid him or leave him.

The Disaster Broker often resembles the Compellingly Intense (But Crazy) Man. He can be magnetic. At the beginning he, too, can seem like the most intimate man you've ever met, but only for a short span and until his next event. He also doesn't fixate on you as one of his intensities. If he does fixate on you as something he must have and know and devour, read back to the Compellingly Intense chapter.

The Disaster Broker is also not unlike the Man Who Would Be Mogul, my next subject. The Man Who Would Be Mogul is, however, if not more ordinary, at least more common. He's not so much after acclaim and excitement, as just getting. Getting things. Getting to the top. Still, he often is a big risk taker and he's certainly about as driven as the Disaster Broker. If you lead a rather normal life, it's much more likely you'll meet – or already be with – the Man Who Would Be Mogul. He's hard to spot up front (until you discover just how lonely you are). Reading about him will help you learn to identify him and know you're not alone. You meet the Man Who Would

Be Mogul in many walks of life – your boss, your partner, selling you your car, as your neighbor, or your brother – and he can be bad or good for you in a number of circumstances, business as well as romance. I consider his a highly important chapter. You probably will too.

The Man Who Would Be Mogul

Who Intends to Be Top Lawyer, Doctor, King, President, CEO, Construction Czar and That's All He Pays Attention To

He is (or will be) famous. He is (or will be) wealthy. He is (or will be) president, senator, producer, director, general, magistrate, or potentate. The Man Who Would Be Mogul has career madness.

He seems smooth and suave on the outside. But inside he's the engine on the Rock Island Line – a nonstop express that moves a mile a minute. They named a dance after him: the Hustle. He was too busy to learn it, but he sure can talk it. It's his native tongue.

He's hooked on *getting*, not being, so there's no end of the line. As soon as the last deal is sealed, he moves on once again – often to the neglect of what he just accomplished. Many times he has a hidden self-destruct button to make sure the ultimate coup always eludes him. (Only a few become *real* moguls. The rest remain ever would-be moguls). But even when he fails, he always fails upward. And he never quits. On his way up to Mikado, he becomes Lord High Executioner. He axes associates and even mates. He also acts like Lord High Everything Else. He overrides contributors, helpers, family, and staff members.

First in his life is Ma Bell. Nothing is as important to him as the telephone. When he enters the door, he never fails to walk directly to the nearest Touch Tone and ring his answering service. And always just as you're about to leave for somewhere he says, "Wait a minute while I make one more call." He lives solely for business. All other things – women, children, friends, ambulances, fire trucks, paddy wagons, floods, hurricanes, holocausts, baptisms, bar mitzvahs, and funerals – simply come second.

Since he always makes deals, you might be one, too. He goes for several different kinds of women. Ones who are largely domestic, who will keep up his home and family. Ones with minor careers that will grace him. (Only even when you're free, he isn't). Ones with work or businesses he can enter from the side line and try to push to become moguls, also. Whoever she is, his woman is a benefit to him, an asset he acquires and ties down. All three types must be presentable, sociable, good hostesses. What he wants is an attractive, indefatigable keeper-upper (socially and otherwise), a backdrop and buttress – installed somewhere or other (preferably other). If he thinks a woman's not quite smart enough, couth enough, or solid enough, he'll have an affair with her, but not a relationship. And since she always is less important to him than any business at the moment, once he takes her as a consort, he turns her into a lady in waiting.

Story

When my sister's school chum Marlene wed Jack, she also married a master plan – Jack's. He aimed to ascend a conglomerate tower by way of Babel – he could talk anyone into anything.

Jack's father had a small air-freight service. But Jack wasn't content to glide. He wanted to fly high, world wide. Nothing short of tycoon would do. From the minute Jack took over, he was wheeling and dealing, dividing and diversifying.

Marlene never knew whether she had a silent partner or was one – Jack was always conversing, but to somebody else. He considered her perhaps his only transaction that was totally signed, sealed, and delivered. Not that Marlene wasn't ambitious and competent herself; she was. She had an interior decorating business that was doing well. She wanted to expand it, but only so much. She had decided she wanted to stay "feminine," as well as working. She only wanted a modicum of success and a small business. (Jack would have the "big" business.) She had their lives to run, to keep up socially. She liked to dress well, be a good hostess, and she wanted to be a man's partner, a "good" and valued partner. Jack looked like the perfect mate to her. He proudly showed all the ambition she closeted. She was sure they'd make a good combo – like Batman and Robin. She'd be equal to him, just as active, only smaller in stature.

But Jack didn't see it that way. It's not that he judged all women's talents as sardine sized in his world of "big fish eat little fish." (Some women were "big fish," but he didn't want to be in the shadow of one of them.) He just didn't have time to care about Marlene's ideas. The Man Who Would Be Mogul swims upstream for himself. And Jack didn't particularly want Marlene leaping in with him. Jack decided things so quickly, gave his opinion so bluntly, and was in and out the door so fast, Marlene found there was little dialogue between them. At one point she mentioned joining with him more. But he didn't seem to hear her. Taking another tack, she asked for advice on her business, but he simply launched a megaplan at her that had nothing to do with her desires, then turned to make a telephone call. Never getting any interest from him, she began to lose what dreams and ambition she first had about their union.

Bit by bit an originally self-assured woman turned into a tortoise. She began to act more and more domestic and wifely, a way she'd never been before. She falsified a sense of family around an absentee husband by getting new furniture, talking about children. Despite her own work and clients, and while she professed contentment, she suffered constant, nagging boredom. No matter how busy she was it seemed she waited endlessly for Jack. He was always at an appointment or in a meeting. At the last minute he'd shuttle the vacation dates she had long since planned. On Sunday, supposedly his day at home, he inevitably had to go out "for just an hour or so." She got virtually no companionship, and never any intimacy. She bided her time and hoped for her turn, but it never came. Other, more "important," people always had priority.

When Jack did spend time with Marlene, everything they did was business related and had business people around. They gave no dinners except for clients. They took no trips except to inspect facilities, and his company paid. They attended no party without potential business partners present (and then not even Hurricane Helen, not to mention Marlene's dislike of parties, could keep them away). Sometimes Jack went alone, telling Marlene it was just business, she didn't fit. Back at home, they lived beyond their means, causing Marlene acute discomfort. Jack considered their lifestyle an investment. It had to be highfalutin and look rich. Marlene lived it even though it went against her needs for security.

Sex came and went on a pretty steady basis. It was reasonably well accomplished, but it just wasn't Jack's preferred intercourse. Often he was too busy or tired. At first Marlene asked for sex a lot more than she got it. Then she grew tired of asking, and became increasingly withdrawn. She got so she turned him down. She no longer cared. Quite secretly she began having some affairs. As for Jack, he had always been faithful before, but as his corporate power really began to swing and he grew bored with Marlene, Jack began to wonder if he shouldn't swing also. He was away a lot and met many people, women included. In his constant search for advantage, he wondered if perhaps another woman might pay off better than Marlene. Jack wasn't the fling type. He liked settled deals, so what he did after a try or two was take a permanent mistress, another committed woman who had her own career, was a complement to him, and thought she'd share his life.

After a time, Jack dropped on Marlene the news that he had another woman. He wanted out, or at least a separation. Marlene countered that she'd had affairs too, long before him, and as far as his separation, he could bloody well have a divorce. She'd had enough. She'd just take half their goods. But suddenly that rang like a five alarm fire to Jack. Take the goods? Jack busily set about hiding all their assets, what few were left. It turned out much of what they had he'd leased or borrowed against. He closed off his business records to Marlene, and all their – his – client "friends" withdrew from her. From "lovely" wife, she went to "nasty, suing" wife. She got her lawyer. He got his. Words like community property, alimony, deposition, took over her life.

The divorce took a tremendously long time in court, more in emotional impact. Marlene thought she was quite prepared to be rid of Jack, but it didn't work that way. She got the house to start with, then found it too expensive to keep. Finding little capital left and not being able to get a full half of his endeavors, she had to start working much harder. He also sued for her business and she had to buy him out. Her life was turned inside out as Jack, armed with lawyers and protectors, moved in with his mistress and the mistress began to move in Marlene's former circle. She also ended up much more alone than she had anticipated, especially since she wanted to find a man who was "good or better" than Jack just to show him, and all the men like Jack were already attached.

It took time, but Marlene recovered. She had to get far more in touch with what she wanted out of life and how she wanted to live. She made friends. She put her energy back into her business. But it took her a full six or seven years, and left her a decade older. Jack never calls her.

Not all unions with the Man Who Would Be Mogul break up. Some continue, but the women remain lonely. Marlene knew a lot of Mogul mates. Some lived very separate lives from their men. They were seen together only on required occasions. It was hard to tell if they ever had sex. Some saw the writing on the wall early, wrote down every asset and tax number, and left their husbands first. Others ended up forty-five years old and dumped. Others like Marlene left their mates, but were not quite prepared for the loss they'd suffer.

The Man Who Would Be Mogul looks like fame and fortune. Sometimes he can make life Wonderland. His life moves as fast as a game of craps. In the meantime, you stand by and breathe on *his* dice – not taking a chance on your own. And since he gambles on roll after roll after roll, any jackpot he wins is always in his control.

How Can You Identify This Kind of Man?

With the Man Who Would Be Mogul, what looks temporary is permanent: the way he is now is the way he will always be, how he acts about business is how he acts about life, and how he treats others is how he'll treat you. He's not hard to spot. He stands out like a Porsche on a Nicaraguan freeway, madly accelerating, endlessly passing.

He believes in Time. He thinks you can waste it, kill it, lose it, stretch it, and certainly use it, but not put it aside until later. He's more than prompt – he's four minutes early. He yells at you to get ready, makes you wait for a call, and still you arrive too soon.

He has faith in space and substance. He likes things massive, talks big, things big, and chooses big. For him, bulk means he can back up what he says; so he likes huge homes, large cars, grand music, king-sized beds, and enormous desks. Naturally he subscribes to the theory that might makes right, although he doesn't necessarily say it. He sees people in two categories: winners and losers. He deals with the one and discards the other. He judges the successful not by their feelings of personal achievement but by public image – money, power, and fame. He equates talent with "getting it on." If it's manifest, it's real. If it's latent, it's of no account. He hates muddles and speaks his mind in direct speech. For him it's "I don't like it." You never hear an "I don't really care for this, do you?" out of The Man Who Would Be Mogul. He doesn't elicit your response or tell how he really feels. He just makes lightning judgments.

He's as sure of things that flop as he is of his brilliant success. Just because he *would* be mogul doesn't mean he gets there or always makes good moves. It's his *style* that makes him his type, not fault-less achievements.

Outer Signs

He's just aggressive and dominant enough to be taken for a king-pin. He dresses in a look of *slightly* conspicuous consumption – a look of substance, not quite ostentation. He's not fashionable as much as comfortably expensive. Quality is his style. His suits, jeans, or shirts are exactly right; his one or two pieces of gold jewelry (not to mention his flash) are subtle; his shoes look hard to find; his scent whispers "Men's Boutique."

He drives a sleek, heavy, often spacious automobile; the older he is, the larger or more costly it is. It's dark grey, dark maroon, or dark *something*, usually. It has automatic transmission and power steering. Sometimes the windows are ever so slightly tinted. Smoky, austere, significant. Low level or high level, it's a luxury car.

He likes bricks and rocks, especially in walls and fireplaces. He wants his abode to be back from the street, sheltered by some expanse of greenery and with a solid front – traditional English, brownstone, modern mansion, or high steel and marble. He longs to cross thick, endless carpets. His black leather chairs turn into lounges and outweigh the Washington Monument. His couch looks like the Great Wall of China. He wants his own private den. Young, he'll have an apartment but never be there. It barely has a bed, no pots or pans, but lots of packages from the cleaners. But even when he has a big estate he's not there much, or at least not involved with it. He leaves running the house to you, no matter how busy you are or if you have a career also. Of course, he claims he could run the house better than you, he just has more important things to do. (So, line up those cleaning people.) And he sure can complain if the running isn't meticulous. (He'll also fire lots of the help you hire.)

He doesn't like to eat at home. He prefers to eat out, it's so much faster. And he wants you free to do so. (So line up those baby sitters and live-ins.) When eating out, he never likes the table he's given at a restaurant. He always picks a better one. Or else he establishes himself with the maitre d' at one special place.

He's inordinately fond of communications equipment – ham radios, Betamaxes, T.V.s, Stock Quotation Video – but especially the gadgets of A.T.&T. and Western Electric. He wants *all* their latest goodies. He likes his extension cords long and his wall jacks frequent. He has an in line and an out line, two or more numbers, and phones of all shapes and sizes – in numerous places. He prefers buttons to dials – they connect faster. He has (or is about to get) a car phone; he's thinking about one for his briefcase. He uses the operator a lot, and he's a regular on information. He hooks his T.V. to a cable. And he can open a lovely folder of colorful credit cards: the gold ones for special privileges show above the others ever so slightly.

The cards and equipment aren't for display alone. He's a frenetic user and doer. He acts like a man on the edge of starvation. He develops long, sensitive antennae directed toward a man's world. He derives his packages and prizes from other men's kingdoms, so he aims his ears for men's talk. He goes to all-male lunches, or hovers in the men's circle at parties. The social affairs he attends resemble solar systems: big moguls stand stationary like suns while little moguls circle them like planets.

The Man Who Would Be Mogul treats himself to lots of things, but not to leisure. He gets no relaxation. He creates no privacy away from his employment. Wheelers and dealers call him at home, during meals, and in the bathroom. A last-minute phone call, no matter how vague, can scuttle six months of your arrangements.

He overuses his engine. And while he makes sure he has nice things, he may not have a very good heart, brain, liver, or bladder. He exercises irregularly, though he may join a men's club. His stomach gets upset and he has headaches. He's prone to a huge mid-life crisis. Failure to him is like death. Often he's afraid of airplanes. He's sure the next crash is bound to be the flight he's on. He studies the odds. Some Men Who Would Be Moguls carry guns – from the paranoia bred of self-importance.

Sex Signals.

In a woman, The Man Who Would Be Mogul seeks either a supporter and social secretary (who is also a good piece of scenery), or a woman who looks like she was a major deal to have acquired (as well as being a good piece of scenery), and he won her.

He sets his sights on a female Sherpa fairly early in his career. (The Sherpas are the bearers that go along carrying the load for men who climb the Himalayas. Most people don't know that it was really a Sherpa, Tenzing, climbed Everest first, with Hillary – similarly, it may be some Moguls' women who make the accomplishments, but only the Moguls get credit for it.) He'll have some long affairs early on in his careers, if not a full scale union. He could hardly conquer Everest without a bearer. As usual, he doesn't want to fuss around when he spots a likely woman. He zeroes in and courts you with intensity. He paints a picture of gains and glory, takes you to some fabulous restaurants and some gatherings of bigwigs. He pays attention to you – until you sign a merger.

And he merges very well in the beginning. At first, sex is abundant and sexy. Then it becomes sufficient. Finally it gets scarce. It has to slip between the schedules, not just the sheets.

Yet he thinks of himself as a sexual man. Probably he began having sex early. He knows some razzle-dazzle techniques. But lovemaking with him is rarely leisurely after the first thrilling months. Certainly it takes place late, late at night, after all the business is over. In time you realize it's more surgical than cozy. Sometimes he goes for a spontaneous quickie (that's all you get in the morning). Mostly, he's as functional as a sleeping pill; bed, sex, slumber.

The Man Who Would Be Mogul likes control in sex as in everything else. When you're aroused and interested, he often says "not now." He makes you want it when he wants it, but doesn't return the favor. He's also happy when he gets something for nothing. He nudges you into a variety of positions. He'd almost rather win a contortion contest than achieve an orgasm.

He *does* relax with women, whereas he can't with men. Since he doesn't really view females as competitors in his economic war, he can almost let go in their company. At least for three minutes or so, and after the switchboard's closed. And he only lets himself relax and get tired at home. It's the only place he can. Perhaps that's why you often sympathize with his plight and feel close to him.

Money Markers

You would think money is property to the Man Who Would Be Mogul. It's not. It's *proof*. He doesn't judge himself by how much he has, but by how much he can "swing." He might stockpile a little money he isn't using, in order to attract more, but most of all he plays with his currency. To him coins are simply chips to risk and flirt with. He skirts the edge of financial ruin. And he'll use your money without a second thought, forget what he borrowed, and try for even more.

The Man Who Would Be Mogul is related to the type I call the "You Send Me To Medical School" Status Seeker. The "You Send Me To Medical School" Status Seeker uses a woman's contribution to aid his own progression. In fact, one woman after another. One woman may put him through school only to be dropped later. Another may labor like a silent partner to get him business connections or clientele. After a certain point, he may seek yet another woman whose gentility offers him pure status.

Each woman expects some reward to come later, perhaps her turn at advancement. But the "You Send Me To Medical School" Status Seeker leaves her behind and doesn't pay her back. He tends to desert a partner at life-transition points, just as he has achieved a goal that they worked for together. She's not good enough to move him to the next level, so he goes on alone.

Beware of the "You Send Me To Medical School" Status Seeker in the same way as the Man Who Would Be Mogul: don't support them or give them money. They could happen to anyone. They seem to be "all for one and one for all." You trust their words and good intentions. Don't. Don't assume anything that isn't specified and don't take turns – *without a written agreement.*

Family Aspects

The Man Who Would Be Mogul usually doesn't have children for a long, long while. Most expect to have two quickly and get it over with. Maybe two with each wife. A few want to bear a platoon of progeny. Among his offspring, he prefers the verbal tykes with congenital con artistry. He doesn't participate much in their raising although he thinks he does. Children are for lower members of the staff – such as mothers, sitters, and live-ins – to oversee. He insists on keeping his freedom from them. Either you have plenty of substitutes available or you stay in alone with them. He must get to those appointments.

Some Moguls view their families as dynasties. Some cast off all their blood ties. The dynastic ones get patripotestal. They try to incorporate parents, children, nieces, and nephews into their company. Other Moguls treat all relatives so offhandedly they soon dismiss him as a distant acquaintance.

As for friends, he negotiates contracts, but he exchanges little in human relationships. As a result, he rarely cultivates, much less keeps, any friends. He judges people as winners or losers so harshly and quickly, he excludes many who would honestly help him. He ends up surrounded by those he deals with and who don't care a hoot how he feels. And since he moves through collaborators along with collaborations, he rarely has any partner of long standing.

Obviously, behind that drive, the Man Who Would Be Mogul hides some serious liabilities. He intends to rise at any cost. He uses people and sees you as a silent constituency, not a partner. His vibrancy never reflects on the moment he's living but rather feeds on what's coming; while he's seemingly after booty, he never stops to enjoy it.

But he has his pluses: he provides you with a glittering vision that makes life seem exciting. He's quick to sweep you off your feet. It's attractive to see yourself as his lady, especially if you can cohabit the heights he wants to reach and cavort with the funds he aims to throw around. There's always the chance he might make it.

What Is in Store for You?

What's it like to live with high rolling and hot talking? To consolidate with Trans General National Universal Incorporated?

With The Man Who Would Be Mogul, his dream has to mean a lot to you because his presence is scarce. He means long spans of little affection and short spans of irresistible magnetism – just enough to keep you hanging on. Some are basically affable men who are simply so obsessed with personal progress they battle onward, oblivious to your needs – with them, you face a future with lots of time on your hands, but no malice. Others build their kingdoms in a more cold and driven manner, kicking whatever gets in their way and leaving behind what doesn't, even their lady friends. Each kind thinks the grass is greener somewhere else.

Once the Mogul sets the wheels in motion, he generally wants a permanent alliance. The steps ahead are pretty predictable. The thrilling preliminary trance passes in a whirlwind. Then, very quickly, he makes it clear that he does his business alone. What he defines as "business" grows and grows. He finally comes to the realization that some honors come more quickly to the loner than they do to the family man. So he develops two profiles; one single, one paired. Soon the occasions for which he wants to show he's mated happen far less often than those where he wishes to appear alone. He starts to exclude you; first by day, then by night, for weekends, and on trips. He goes lots of places; you stay home. Even when he promotes the reputation that he's a solid spouse, you're heard about but rarely shown. You become a mystery woman about whom people say, "Have you ever met her?" Others don't know that you exist.

That doesn't mean you never join him or help him. You do, but within limits. Most likely you serve as a memory bank and computer. You record dates and places, do books, groom appearances, eye the winds for coming trends, put on dinner parties for close associates. He expects you to be as silent and regular as a monthly bill from the gas and electric company.

When you do escort him in his paired manifestation, he talks only to men. You sit silently or chat with other moguls' abandoned paramours. He gives you instructions on how to behave and what to talk about. Any role other than that of unwavering cheerleader is definitely out.

It doesn't take long to realize that your Man Who Would Be Mogul is a gambler, and a compulsive one at that. You have to tighten your seat belt and pretend the ground beneath you won't suddenly disappear. If he's not incessantly putting all your cash on the line, he risks other tangibles and intangibles that have to do with your security. Naturally the subject of money looms more than merely prominently in your daily dealings – it takes over. The getting and keeping of money becomes a leitmotif weaving its way into every concern. Almost all conversations and quarrels soon wind around to the topic of cash. You could write a *book* on the subject. And your children turn out to be very materialistic little creatures.

Your man also turns out to be a fighter, a dirty one. He has to win just for the sake of winning, even when his opponent is you. He pulls out all the heavy guns, no matter how petty the argument. He holds an ancient, ever-ready list of sins and errors and uses them as evidence, whether they're relevant or not. He may even lay the groundwork for imagined future battles – he may leave you out of titles or get your signature on obscure documents that forfeit all your claims.

From moment one, he wonders if perhaps he couldn't have found a better sex partner. No matter how hard he worked to get you, from the instant you say "I'm yours," he begins to view your union as somehow not all it could be. The thought that there must be more to this relationship business, that maybe he cheated himself, gradually nags him to death. Occasionally you find him scrutinizing you; then he'll sigh and carry on. He ponders whether his associates get something he doesn't from *their* mates. He envies single men and those with new, young wives. He treats you more with toleration than with affection as time goes on. And he starts to look around.

Aging (both yours and his) becomes your nemesis. Most Men Who Would Be Moguls try to counteract decades with affairs. Quite often they go baby chasing, turning back to younger bodies. They start to claim that men under as much stress as they need a less complex relationship in which they can get some peace and rest.

You *can* enjoy the way he keeps things hopping. Yet, your belief in his golden achievements *has* to dwindle sooner or later. No one knows what didn't happen and what deals haven't come through as well as you. Any consort of the Man Who Would Be Mogul lives with his past all through her present. If you're his first round, there are all the things he does on his way up. If you're a later mate, part of your fare is the paperwork, lawyers, and half-truths about the first. And don't neglect another fact. With this man you run a high chance of widowhood.

What Are the Telltale Signs of Trouble?

Even if you can't see the Man Who Would Be Mogul from up front, you can certainly hear him. He sounds like an airport control tower. All day long he radios in and out, issues takeoff orders, gives landing instructions, and radars new sightings. He's always checking his messages – he's crushed when he has none. And he tells people where he is now, and where to find him for the next five hours.

The more he leads a separate life, the more you're heading for troubled times. As soon as you notice you're left out in the cold more than your liking, you should call his secretary and make an appointment, then lay what you expect in a relationship on his table. Unwanted isolation has a way of breeding stopped- up feelings. You pretend all is well while you grow bitter. With the Man Who Would Be Mogul, you shouldn't let the topic of what *you* need slide away beneath his other conversations.

You might ask him about the reasons he gives for your lack of attendance at his happenings, and wonder what they show about his intentions. Consider the age-old signs of affairs: late appointments, frequent business trips, odd Visa charges, and a toothbrush kept in the trunk of his car. He doesn't answer the phone where he said he'd be (how *unlike* him!), and his address book lists certain last names without any first name.

With the Mogul, the more you don't know, the more critical the situation. What you know can make life stormy, but what you ignore can spell impending disaster. It's probably better to keep things turbulent and alive than to make like the *Titantic* on its way to an iceberg.

What Are Your Chances and What Should You Do?

There's no way to have a close relationship with the Man Who Would Be Mogul, and the chance of change is slim. If he does change, either he modifies his ways so late that the onus of irretrievable neglect is far too weighty to overcome, or else he changes for the worse.

I suggest you pass over the Mogul and seek a fellow with better balance. Even when drive and ambition attract you mightily, try to find the achiever who has another side to him. Many men who constantly strive for further accomplishments combine their pursuits with warmth and attention toward their loved ones. With the Mogul, even though you double up, you still live alone. In such circumstances most living beasts, especially female ones, tend to shrivel up. Far too many Mogul spouses substitute material goods for lack of companionship; but when baubles, bangles, minks, and Mercedes take over the soul, little spiritual development takes place. In the end, you cut off all avenues to emotional rewards. The only things left are visions of bigger and better Moguls.

If you are already with the Man Who Would Be Mogul, or see him on your horizon and can't stop yourself, I wouldn't say you should necessarily flee forthwith. You might approach him with an attitude of caution, mixed with common sense and a good sense of timing. And I recommend you begin, without fail, a program of self-reliance. Quietly and independently fill your life with your private joys. You'll be taking the risk that he might fault you for lack of support, but at least you won't spend your days shelved and suspended – the worst state to be in. Try to size up just how much intimacy you require. If you find closeness crucial, don't do the Mogul. But if your need to relate to your man is moderately low, then you can try to approximate a Loving Limited Partner setup, at least from your end of things. Then you can see what you can of your Mogul between both your doings.

If you want him with you and don't want autonomy, be warned: very few devices will attract him or reverse a growing rift. There's not much use in getting sick, causing scandals, or throwing fits to get him home. Of course, if you enjoy such things, you might as well go ahead. Just don't expect results. It's also not a good idea to try to get involved in his work, to try to compete with him in his field using his associates, connections, or companies. Better to develop your own standards than try to buck his.

You might consider dwelling with the Man Who Would Be Mogul only on a temporary basis. When the fascination ends, you can prepare for a civilized end. Even in the midst of a total involvement, you should try to keep track of when the returns you get from him diminish beyond a point you can tolerate and not hang on past a point of detriment. Everybody has a certain tolerance quotient: so much neglect, so many affairs, so little time, a mistress, or bad partners' underhanded business practices, may eventually top yours. You don't have to live with him, you *do* have to live with you. When your self-respect and your Mogul no longer mix, it's time to call it quits.

If you stay for better or worse, stay for love and no other reason. And then, for the love of him, remember this: try to get him to live for now. Don't wait for retirement or some far-off finish line. In the first place, he never retires! In the second, his super tension leaves him prone to heart attacks, strokes, and other catastrophes. Enjoy him while you can.

Where Do You Fit In?

A woman afflicted with a case of the Man Who Would Be Mogul – even once is suspicious – should examine herself carefully for "vicaria." "Vicaria" isn't exactly a virus or bacteria, but it's a malady just the same. "Vicaria" is the desire to achieve your ambitions through somebody else.

"Vicaria" tends to derive from fear. It's not just that you hide your desires for a more prestigious and affluent life. Often that's part of it and that's bad enough. The real cause of the Man Who Would Be Mogul affliction is the secret apprehension that you can't achieve great heights on your own. So you deposit yourself with an acquisitive partner who goes on to do some or all of your succeeding for you. And "vicaria" can even occur in career women who *show* some of their ambition.

Your secret apprehension about trying for greatness on your own may or may not be justified. Almost certainly it's learned. Until recently woman have had little access to games of power and position.

What's more, they've been generally taught to assume personal status from men rather than to achieve their own. Besides, if the difficulties alone of becoming a lady mogul aren't enough to fill your heart with trepidation, the negative connotations ambitious women face can give anyone qualms. To call a man "tough" or "hard as nails" is somehow a compliment, but when such appellations apply to a woman, everybody's nose curls up. (If that worries you, don't forget that sticks and stones may break your bones, but names can never hurt you.)

Most women have not only learned to fear going for the top on their own, they have even learned to deny that they are afraid. "I wouldn't join that rat race for anything," they say. Or, "Small time is good enough for me." But when you refute that you have ambition, or hide just how big your ambition really is, the age-old formula looks twice as good. Hitch yourself onto some man's wagon, then claim you have no such aspirations as his. You're just going along.

But there's a catch. When you latch on to a partner you're using to fill your own cravings, almost inevitably he becomes the center of your existence – work or no work of your own. In the meantime, although he occupies the most important spot in your life, the kind of man who seeks to conquer rarely considers *you* his central focus. So you end up with problems he simply doesn't have. Everything he does pleases or hurts you in some way. Meanwhile, he hardly notices you.

A vicarious vision that once seemed attractive can turn disastrous. The mates of the Man Who Would Be Mogul tend to hang on for dear life because he means so much to them. That gives him time to play you out until he's ready to leave. Then the material goods acquired in the relationship start to become substitutes for him. Property, homes, shares, potted plants, vases, paintings, and ornaments take on life-and-death consequences. Things get very messy when the relationship ends. The breakup is awful, goes on too long, becomes rancorous, and stays that way. Sometimes the defunct bunkmate of the Mogul jumps acrimoniously into an aggressive career – often the same one he has – just to show him what he lost. Others suffer such loss that their depression never ends.

All too often, as the mate of a Mogul, you put your own care second to his. You devote yourself to waiting, while he lives actively. With the limited amount of time we all have to live, there's *nothing* as wasteful as suspending your own animation. Then you get hooked on judging yourself by externals just the way your Mogul does. You size up your worth by what you possess. You begin to cling desperately to your high cards: your beauty, youth, figure, or zest, and forget to develop others. When your trump card is played and starts to fade, a big crisis is in the making. You shred yourself up inside hoping for his sign that you're still O.K.

If you're dwelling with a Man Who Would Be Mogul, try honestly to figure out if you have a case of "vicaria", no matter how ambitious you think you're being on your own. Then try to cure your "vicaria" before it gets critical. It's far better to work on your own ambitions and achievements (so that your mate can constitute a blessing to you, not a possession).

Men Who Would Be Moguls can often also be Short Affair and Quick Escape Artists. They only stay a short while and never get too involved with a woman. They can also be Disaster Brokers, risking, losing and playing brinkmanship, rather than really trying for success. Sometimes they also share traits with Mr. Genius. They think they are more talented than everyone else and deserve all the privileges.

Sometimes Moguls are gay. But if so, they are usually Gay Man Two (a man who doesn't have much to do with women) rather than Gay Man One (who can be warm, involved, and a good friend to a woman). The next two sections cover these kinds of men. Many of us know gay men, have relationships with them, love them or hate them. And as with any other man, those relationships take consideration.

13

Gay Man One

Everything Except For. . .

Oh, the wheels are ever turning. What was out is now in. What was pariah is now persona. What was outcast is now typecast. He's gay. And he's everywhere.

So many men now dare to be homosexual they've achieved the respectability of becoming ho hum. They may think they're unusual, but as eccentricities go, theirs is mighty conventional. Still, gay men are men, and they're often good ones.

Accepting that you'll never be his number one chum, why not make the best of him? The Gay Man offers plenty of the best. When he likes women, he's a great pal. Perhaps his situation sensitized him. His childhood probably wasn't all easy, nor is his current life. It also seems his psyche propels him to another wavelength. At any rate, he's often closer than a heterosexual to the middle of that strange emotional spectrum between men and women. That means better contact for you, and less misconception. Often he is miles ahead on empathy and three fathoms deeper on sympathy. He makes an easy, warm, and intimate friend – a companion when you are alone, an enthusiast when you want to talk about opera, a gourmet when you want to try new food, a peaceful presence when you want to sit around silently. Sometimes he is more like you than you are. And he has one other advantage – he knows what it's like to deal with men. But, as for a paramour, he doesn't come up to requisite snuff. So there's one key to a relationship with your local gay – look for a friend, cultivate not a mate.

Story

I have known some women so taken with the companionship of Gay Man Ones that they overplayed their hands. They accentuated the negative, eliminated the positive, and came out with nothing in between. For example, take Vivian.

Vivian met Chris while visiting Paris. Talk about a born companion! They instantly formed a club, the membership limited to two. Together they toured the city, thriving on the joy of their fraternity. But with a certain limit. Chris was homosexual. Vivian was not. Nonetheless, when Vivian returned to San Francisco, Chris soon followed.

Vivian was a native San Franciscan. She grew up the only child of a well-established family. Her impressive father ran his clan as he ran his business. Vivian never felt she came up to her father's fierce expectations. Without her knowing it, he scared her off. As an adult, she leaned toward men of a totally different nature.

Chris was not the first gay man Vivian had found attractive. As a teenager, she got a crush on a young man in her father's office. When he confessed just exactly *how* he "roomed" with his roommate, she covered her shock (and disappointment) with a sophisticated approach – she attempted to rise above prejudice about people's sexual preference. In no time at all she discovered a lot more homosexual men than she ever knew existed. In fact, she seemed to attract them. She lived among the wealthy and stylish, had lots of social connections in the art and theater world where gay men flourish. She forever attended openings, parties, and events with a clique of similar celebrants. And she was great at witty repartee.

But sexually she was thoroughly straight arrow, or so she thought. Behind those opera glasses lurked one conventional lady. Still, despite auspicious beginnings, few men pursued her or they only stayed for short affairs and quickly departed. In response, she developed protection. She covered her anguish with good one-liners, a worldly flair, and a phalanx of pals of both sexes, the males largely preferring other males. She may have wanted, but managed not to need, a lover of her own.

Chris was her most constant squire. He was always available (at least after noon and until midnight). He willingly ran about town as her escort and confidant. He knew her and her friends so well they could gossip like jaybirds or say nothing at all. They shared continuing sagas of his latest fiasco in the gay restaurant where he worked, or of her latest mad artist who had stopped calling. They hugged a lot, held hands, and even slept in the same bed upon occasion after bumming around town.

They were so close and cozily flirtatious, such *good* pals, Chris had openly hinted every now and then that they should just get it over with and be lovers, have intercourse. But he only hinted it when Vivian was safely involved in a solidly heterosexual infatuation. Chris encouraged the sensual aura between them, and clearly enjoyed a quasi-Romeo role. So one day Vivian decided to bridge the one remaining gap. She took him up on his hints and proposed they have sex.

Chris was instantly taken aback. After all, she *knew* he only slept with men. He liked cruising, even "safe" cruising, and he was really looking for a mate, a male mate of his own. While he often complained, he actually cherished his late-hours life and the encounters he had. Vivian was just a confidant, a sister, and fellow traveler, never a potential lover. He just liked to add a dash of flirtation for effect and thought she understood.

Vivian felt rejected, dismayed, and worst of all, foolish. Chris drew back, feeling threatened. Their friendship foundered. Each had breached a tacit agreement – Chris when he proposed a playful idea he never really intended to carry through, Vivian when she tried to alter a condition she pretended hadn't mattered.

A cold, awkward separation resulted. Suddenly left without her main man, Vivian saw the light. For a constant companion she had chosen a man with whom the ultimate intimacy was never forthcoming. She was spending almost all her time with a person who couldn't meet all her needs. She had smoothly avoided the hard times of a full-blown male-and-female relationship, the commitments, the struggles, the compromises. But she had also avoided the benefits. Vivian decided that her actions were not coordinated to her true desires. If she didn't want a total male-and-female union, she was O.K. doing as she was. But if she wanted a sexual partner and full-blown mate, she would have to make herself available for one. Either was acceptable. She came to grips with the fact that she was a very sexual person. She started to travel alone. Suddenly, opportunities blossomed. She no longer put men off with her gay bodyguard.

Meanwhile, Chris did some honest thinking, too. He learned to accept his own homosexuality without heterosexual titillations. Vivian and Chris reestablished their fine friendship. But as back-pocket pals and not social shields.

Obviously, nonhappenings as well as happenings indicate when Gay Man Ones are on the scene. Expected advances, even innuendos and "looks," don't occur. When you meet a Gay Man One, you have the choice of making friends or not. If whether a person is gay or not makes no difference to you, you can have, if you want, the best of both worlds – the cake of homosexual friends and the eats of heterosexual ones, too.

How Can You Identify This Kind of Man?

Spotting the Gay Man One isn't hard. Just use geography, topography, and choreography. Just as birds of a feather stick together, so do Gay Men. They often wear the same plumage, share the same habits, and frequent the same establishments. It's a better mating game for him when all the fellows show the same tail feather. (And the size and shape of that tail hold a lot of significance.)

Gay Man Ones even share one key characteristic. They're all preoccupied with their personal life. Romance, relationships, and encounters take up much of their time, most of their energy, and most of their happiness. It's not that they don't have other interests. They do, but their private life is primary.

A Gay Man One's life often wears him thin (a trait he considers absolutely essential). He tends towards dissipation, he smokes and drinks too much. He's low on energy, and he gets sick often. He's a bit fickle. Since he follows his own individual path, subjective experience, exactly what he wants in life defies pinning down. His goals are cloudy. He samples from life and moves on, he wants to see and relish diverse places and things. He nestles down only to fly the coop, that is, his unions may last a night, a month, or often a number of years, but they rarely last forever.

Outer Signs

Right now you can find the Gay Man One appearing in one of two types. In one, he leans toward continental. He's a city bird. You find him wearing tight European cut pants (with aubergine bikini shorts beneath). His shirts are white. Often they are sheer and silky, or very crisp cotton. They're cut to hug his body down to the ribs. He saunters about in soft cordovan loafers without socks, sports a bracelet or necklace. His hair is scissor cut and fluffs about the ears. "A friend of a friend" styles it. At least once in his life he tries altering his hair color. But his skin tone tells all. It looks a little dissipated.

The continental type moves in fast circles. He's into what's hip, who's in *Who's Who*, and what art form is in now. He's a social climber, a people collector, and sometimes a name dropper. He knows the pecking order of fame and class in any particular territory, sometimes in French and Italian. He cruises world capitals if he can.

The other type of Gay Man One lives and looks more woodsy. He wears button-down blue denim Levi's with white jockey shorts. He alternates Pendleton plaid flannel shirts with sweatshirts and T-shirts. He sports square-toed cowboy working boots, or hiking boots with hooks for lacing. His hair is very short and trimmed like a hedge. He's more prone to stay home than the continental city sort. He takes it pretty easy, a lot of naps. He'd rather receive visitors than go out, and then it's to a good but quiet restaurant, or just a movie. He's a little softer, cuddlier, less high flying.

Both types are very affectionate. Both are *very, very* tidy. One style or the other, the Gay Man One loves his home. He fills it with bits and pieces of things that delight his fancy, bric-a-brac or heirlooms, till his home looks like a display case. And all the things are kept perfectly positioned. He also likes his things exotic (often from his far away travels) and expensive. He prefers oriental rugs, old brass, antique furniture, or the very best designer leather and modern pieces. (He cultivates good taste and likes to be known for it.) He also likes his place light and airy. He enjoys high ceilings and lots of Boston ferns and philodendrons. He possesses a green thumb that works like magic, so his houseplants exude utter ecstasy and grow like crazy. He's domestic, no doubt about it. Even when he's renting a room, Gay Man One decorates it. And can he cook! He also often shares his housing arrangements with a roommate or several of them. The Gay Man One usually likes company.

But however he shares his space, he still tends to abide in an eco-zone of his own kind. Where the town turns gay, that's where he's gathered. His section is almost rundown, almost old, and almost historical – Deteriorated Ritzy. But gay men give the neighborhoods a special renaissance. They cause a mushrooming of cafes and activity – starting from brunch on, but not breakfast. In such places, you'll find the crowd rather homogeneous.

While his nest is important to the Gay Man One, his wheels are not. Most don't much care what kind of car they have, though they do tend to like them small. They might switch according to who has what for sale, from a small Toyota to a Renault to a Ford Fiesta to a Hyundai to a Yugo. Others with more money like small, conservative, and clean cars. They might drive a BMW 320i or a well-kept Rabbit. Cars seem like so much trouble, often the Gay Man One would rather walk or take the bus. Or better yet, get someone to pick him up. Someone cute, hopefully.

He loves restaurants, art galleries, concerts, and operas. He likes saunas, swimming pools, and the gym. (Those that don't go to the gym chin themselves on a bar in the doorway, or do ten minutes of yoga stretches. They don't jog and tennis is not their favorite kind of ball.) Still, Gay Man One is always obsessed with weight, no matter what he does. He tries to stay boyishly thin as long as possible. When that thirties "fill-in" begins he's anguished, and suddenly the diet begins. But not a consistent one, and rarely one excluding liquid libation of the spirit persuasion. Any temptation, and he's all too eager to roll off the wagon. He loves wine, a good scotch, and often drugs. In fact, what's truly erratic about the Gay Man One is his self-care. He can be stringent yet also go on binges. He can work hard and still go out all night. He can do nothing and still get weary. In seconds, he can swing from immobility to peak activity. He can overdo and overdose, undereat and underachieve. He gets hepatitis and multiple colds (plus other communicable diseases, now dangerous ones). But none of this really makes him lead a more regular life (more careful maybe). It just leads him to try mysticism, health foods, hot toddies, just necking, or to grow a little more fussy.

The Gay Man One prefers women along the same lines as his choice in theater: he likes women who have an interesting act that gives him stories to tell. He leans toward the lively, the witty, the jaded, the crazy; to the lady marked by elegance or oddity, depth or brassiness. Usually, if he hits it off with you, he does so instantly, then loves you for life. By the second meeting his relationship with you becomes a movable feast of fun, food, companionship and commiseration, symphony and sympathy. It seems he's known you for a thousand years.

You'll treat each other like kindred spirits, a little like blood kin – kissing cousins. The friendship is charged with a certain sexuality; you both act as if incest would be interesting but never quite broach the subject. There's an invisible line, approached and avoided, between you. While physical affections abound, gestures stop short of carnality. You can bill and coo together, but you can never lay an egg. You can flirt and flatter but can't probe or penetrate. If you ever cross the line and the touch becomes too much, a shock wave usually repels one party or the other.

Money Markers

It's easy so see how the Gay Man One spends his money – for personal indulgence. And that's also how he pursues his education – to make life more pleasurable. Some Gay Men One live on inheritances, aid, or unemployment. Some have moderate to fabulous incomes from jobs in education, industry, entertainment, fashion, real estate, graphics, or publishing. Certain members rule the art world, some live off others. But wherever it comes from, money usually runs through the Gay Man One's hands faster than he ever expects. He so incessantly spends on little luxuries he finds himself short for the big ones, though he usually manages to hustle up the cash for them somehow. He spends for his senses, his entertainment, and his friends. Funds flow so rapidly in his community it's hard to tell who's buying and who's selling. Never has a group of people been more ready to utilize each other's money. If you can get an income without much labor or from freelance esoterics, you're a much admired member of the clan.

To insure the money doesn't stop, though, the Gay Man One gets – or gets worried about – investments. And he thinks the best investment is real estate. He loves real estate. He definitely likes to buy his own house or condo. Maybe a small income yielding property. Maybe a country home. Maybe is a key word. Some Gay Men One are successful at parlaying real estate, but a surprising number buy at the wrong time, sell in the wrong way, and lose.

With women and money he gives and takes hospitality with no tabs kept. Every now and then you split the bill, or bring the wine to each other's dinner parties. Also every now and then, when he's flush, he pays for you. Still, if you have the money and feel unconcerned about paying for someone else, and he's rather a poor Gay Man One, he'll happily use your capital. When he's in your company, that is, not usually when you're apart.

Family Aspects

The ties that hold the Gay Man One to his family are strange and strong. Sometimes his parents and siblings know his romantic preference; sometimes they don't. In either case he's extremely protective of them. He even safeguards the way he makes them face the truth about him. He considers himself enough of an outlaw in his choice of mates he's usually willing to be a good boy for others. He idolizes his sister, tolerates his brother (although if there's anyone he's totally estranged from, it's his brother), thinks of his father as sweet, his mother as complex. He forgives them, even if they don't always quite forgive him.

Usually (but not always) he loves children. He's happy to play uncle. He'll even live in homes with children, especially with single mothers. Still, he's glad the children are yours. He'll keep them company and relieve you of them, but he's also happy when they're gone. He has the qualities that make a wonderful teacher, which he often is. And a Gay Man One would never hurt a hair of a child's head. He'd never hurt anyone, in fact. Those who do, gay or straight, are another kind of man.

He's an ideal man in many ways, the Gay Man One, except for that one drawback. His relationship with you will never include sexual intimacy. And that drawback can be a large one. Whatever is the secret of sexual intimacy, most women prefer it over just about any other kind. And most women want to have it. Of course, if you don't, then perhaps a Gay Man One could be good for you.

He does have all the assets of a fantastic friend. He's there when it counts. He listens to what you're thinking and feeling. He's more interested in people than things and he truly likes women. But remember, often he'd rather be with someone else than you. He's looking for love, too, and not with you.

What Is in Store for You?

The real issue with a Gay Man One is not what's in store for you, it's what's not in store. In short, a relationship with the Gay Man One is a bit like a Steady-State Universe – beginning, middle, and end about the same. No big bang at the start. No violent finale at the end. At most, an exhaustion of energy. When you take male and female and remove the tension, the wire goes from tight to slack. Compared to heterosexual types of men (the ones that serve up all the courses, from soup to nuts, for you) a gay man who likes women is a veritable Rolaid and perhaps should be used as such. He spells r-e-l-i-e-f; he soothes. But he's no final remedy. Removing symptoms rarely cures. What you probably need is some of him and some of someone else. For the very best of prescriptions, take a Gay Man One and a heterosexual union as well.

A good Gay Man One relationship provides a deep friendship in which both of you lead very separate lives. Once you establish a link, the only alteration comes from what your other involvements bring. The long-term Gay Man One pairing generally lacks distinct stages. Rather, it bears a lethargic drift. While the quantity of company may diminish over time, the quality remains the same.

And yet special problems do set in with a Gay Man One after a while. For one, it's hard to think up something new to do. When you feel like soul mates right from the beginning (added to the knowledge of where things will never lead), it's sometimes easier to shut down rather than add stimulation. Since you do things with and not to one another, you can slide into doing nothing or spending a lot of time thinking up what to do. One says, "What do you want to do?" – until it's your ritual. Or you collapse on old standbys – like eating, drinking, going to old movies, or to the same old gatherings.

Even the whole reliance can bear a one-sided nature. More often than not, you two use your acquaintance to cheer each other up, not to grow maudlin. There seems to be a rule against acting agonized in unison. But while good cheer can be comforting, it can also cover up avoiding the issues. Be wary of excessive dependence on your gay friend. As much as you love him, he can impede your progress and you his. Sooner or later, due to your romances or his, your new curiosities or his, you might drift apart, but not forever: call out his name, and he'll be there. You've got a friend.

What Are the Telltale Signs of Trouble?

No matter which way you're going, the Gay Man One gives you ready warning. In certain places, it's become the practice to consider any well-groomed man gay until he proves otherwise. You don't need binoculars to tell the Gay Man One by dress and habits. You can certainly decipher his coming-and-going patterns – usually with a number of the same gender. He frequents places where the female half of the population is scarcely represented, spends an inordinate amount of time with his "roommate" and male buddies. Sometimes they wear each other's clothing. They seem all to wear the same size.

Of course, there's another way to peg him. You could call it the "gestures in absentia" method. Usually there's little doubt when a man desires women sexually. You can hear, see, and feel him telling and asking. With the Gay Man One, the onslaught never happens. He's close, but not *too* close. His kisses are self-conscious. If you touch him by surprise, he jumps back.

Sometimes the identification problems don't exist – he tells you before you guess. Ultra-modern gay men often detail not only that they're homosexual but when and how and why it happened. When you're out together his eyes move around the same half of the crowd that yours do – the half that's got pants on and shaves. Only you eyeball from top down, and he goes from bottom up, lingering at a certain point halfway up.

Though misreading him may bring disappointment or exasperation, the real warnings you need to heed are not what the relationship is, but how you are using it. Beware of crossing that line where both he and you need each other too much. Keep uses and abuses straight from the beginning. The Gay Man One is very aware of energy drain. He's a little selfish and fearful of attachments even in his love affairs, so when a woman soaks up time, he tends to run and hide. And if he's leading you to think options are open when they really aren't, he's setting you up for fall person. He may be proving to himself once more that he's gay, or he may need a cover story. I'd call him on it.

And note still other points. Sometimes the continental Gay Man One might be seeking you out for social position or money. You should be wary of him. All friendship has some use involved. Some kinds may be all right by you, some may not. And it's equally problematic when you use him. You may desperately need entree, frivolity, or someone to hang on. And his closeness leads you to lean his way. If you're keeping company to the detriment of a more satisfactory relationship, you're working at your own self-defeat.

What Are Your Chances and What Should You Do?

Very occasionally a Gay Man One turns heterosexual, but only *very* occasionally. When it comes to sex, people usually have a favorite flavor and they stick to it. That's not to say that homosexuals haven't tried the opposite sex, or heterosexuals haven't tried out their own, or that some people are just plain bisexual. But most individuals show a strong inclination one way or the other.

If you are with a man who has affairs with men, exclusively or with you also, you'd better decide if his activities are within your emotional toleration. You can bury your agitation and feign approval, but if you find yourself saying your relationship is wonderful when it isn't, you'd better cancel your endorsement and close your account. Everybody deserves the whole works – love, attention, *and* sex, if they want it. And being shunned sexually in favor of someone else of either sex is just too painful.

When a man is solely gay and you are solely straight, I advise you need neither fight nor flee; just keep your fingers out of the ointment. Look for a best friend, not a lover. Rather than refuse the relationship, use it. But use it properly. The Gay Man One is an elective, not a requirement. He's best as an enhancement to your other essentials. His material is delicate, so don't abuse it. Apply yourself carefully. Hang loose to hold the most. Let your gay friend lead his own life. You get the best of it if you don't ask for too much time, attention, or sexual interaction. Prize your intimacy with him. Don't overburden his natural sympathy. If you unload problems too much, he'll need to cut free.

Some women flee from gay men or pay them little heed, feeling homosexual men divert them from their own potential coupling. Some working women prefer gay men because love affairs cause too much interference on the job or because they want companions but not sex. Some mated women find gay men the best males to befriend. Each of these reasons is fine, if it suits your needs. Probably no other relationship with a man offers such flexibility in matching what you need from it, except for the carnal coupling.

If you seek a heterosexual mate and haven't got one, keeping to a low quota of Gay Man One is simply pragmatic, but don't totally dismiss homosexuals. Killing off one kind of male/female pairing doesn't promote the growth of others. Shunning any variety of friend can take away from your own scope and potential. You *can* play all possibilities if you keep the forms in balance.

Where Do You Fit In?

So what happened? You look around and discover that you've culled more than two or three or four homosexual friends. You've signed on a regular bevy! Or maybe you've surrounded yourself with just one who's so intense he *seems* like a swarm. In the meantime, your nest is empty.

Sometimes the Gay Man One can become an albatross. In his company, you parody male/female harmonies, but never sing the Song of Solomon. You're due to examine yourself if for one reason or another you're avoiding a serious link-up with a man. Perhaps you're a Short Affair and Quick Escape Artist yourself. Behind an abundance of Gay Men One in your life may lie fear of sex, fear of tyranny, or fear of another broken heart. Sure, it's entirely possible for you to discover that any permanent romance would mean forfeit, or that you find one experience with love more than enough forever. That's fine. But if the cause is indeed fear, perhaps you might want to consider conquering it and taking new steps.

If you want to like sex and can't, many avenues for help exist. If you open up to some expertise, you'll find others have worked through similar problems. Sex *can* often seem like an ordeal by fire; you worry so much if the ice maiden will ever come that facing even the possibility of bed becomes torture. What you may not know is that sexual confidence takes *years* to gain, a fact that most sexual propaganda neglects to state. You have a right to give yourself plenty of time and seek out the right situations, no matter how many turndowns it takes.

The compromises involved in permanent relationships seem like surrender to many. Indeed, many men are petty despots towards their mates, but a union doesn't *have* to be that way. To assume so is flagrant overgeneralization. Usually when you see any alliance with a man as slavery, the real tyrant is in your head. He's twisted from some male figure in your past, or he stems from a family where the men were always dominant and the women submissive. Rather than live a life haunted by old ghosts, try to be here and now and construct something different. Purge the bogeyman within to find a better man outside.

If you had a broken love experience in the past, realize that, especially with present odds, a broken relationship may be a lost battle, but it's certainly not the whole war. It's nice to have wanted one man to love forever, but very few people achieve that any more. And maybe some of the ones who do shouldn't have. Rather than hide, muster your courage and try, try again.

If a chaste life holds little reward for you, don't be a dodo: remember a cock in the hand is worth two in the bath, and you *may* become one of the fortunate ladies who can enjoy *men* – both gay and straight!

Now on to Gay Man Two!

14

Gay Man Two

You Won't Meet One Anyway...

Y ou won't find a relationship here and you shouldn't, not in
any sense even close to intimate. Not even if he was married
once and changed in later life. This man simply excludes women
from his world.

You can't scale a sheer cliff or swim a whole ocean.
You're excused.

15

The Father Knows Best

The Man Who Treats You
Like a Child Forever

But you're not excused from the Father Knows Best. Or rather, like a school teacher who never stops admonishing, he won't excuse you. And you meet him everywhere. Men who will try to control women by fathering them appear as employers, ticket takers, accountants, parking lot attendants, doctors, counselors, lawyers, contractors, mechanics, repairmen, but especially as boyfriends, husbands, and fathers. (How many times has one of these men tried to tell you what was best for you, or just to let him take care of it?) His technique for control is very effective and very insidious. We fall for it *a lot* because it seems so protective and caring. But it's also very debilitating. It can take the pegs right out from under you, rob you of command and independence.

But there are ways to recognize it.

I now start on a set of men who can devastate women not by their arrogance, demands, or bravado, but by smothering, over loving, manipulating you. I start with the Father Knows Best.

How do you spot him? Well, think about what daddies do. They protect you and provide for you. If you make a dodo of yourself, they fix it all up while saying, "tsk, tsk." They know everything *so* much better than you. They tell you where to go and *just* what to do. And they like their little girl. So much so, in fact, they don't let her grow up.

The Father Knows Best relates to women only as a parent to a child. He never acts as if you were an adult. He refuses mature communication with you. With an unwavering belief that he's so much older than you, whatever his age and experience, he turns into an imperturbable despot. After all, everybody knows that fatherly authority is as close to unassailable as authority can get. Upset your father and you're bound to lose. You can also get in big trouble. By inherent rights, no matter what transpires – father knows best.

In particular as a lover or mate, the Father Knows Best takes his part so to heart that he turns himself into your benevolent protector. You can't question his opinion without his getting stuffy. He treats any refusal on your part as a rebuff, confrontations as contradiction, till pretty soon you're left with little choice. You turn your relationship into a game of Daddy, May I? You sugar and spice your way to rewards and pout over punishments. You plead and wheedle, cajole and manipulate.

The Father Knows Best is smart enough to head for certain women when he forms his unions. He finds some women aren't malleable to him, so why attempt the impossible? He looks not so much for young women, as for women who continue to stretch a girlish demeanor beyond the girlhood stage. He notes un-chaperoned ladies who still act skittish, those who hesitate to relinquish a precious kind of charm, and those lazy about self-maintenance who would rather lean on a maintenance man. He very often meets his mates just as they are facing a big transition from family, home, or school into the outer world. Such transitions tend to heighten both damsel-like distress and the desire for feathered nests.

Story

I once had a student named Ruth who was a number of years older than her fellow classmates in my introductory class. Ruth was a returnee to college who had recently emerged from a long-term co-coon into a new life and new wings. It was quite a difference from her previous existence as perennial princess in training.

Ruth grew up as one of four daughters, all doted upon and all owning every kind of stuffed animal, canopy bed, and dust ruffle possible. Her father so adored them, he acted as if his wife and daughters were a personal treasure. He could only let each daughter go by throwing a spectacular wedding in which he zealously gave her away.

In her last year in high school, Ruth started going with Lester, a man six years her senior. She didn't question the fact that, rather than go with a college woman, he preferred the company of a high school girl. Ruth's father sent her away to an out-of-state university, but she transferred right back to attend the local college. She dated other men. She even broke up with Lester. But as her program neared its end, she decided to marry him. She spent her last semester majoring in engagement and showers. She never even finished her last Incomplete. Lester didn't see why she should.

Despite his youth, Lester made life anything but unfettered. He knew the only "right" way to do everything, and told her how to do every chore. He directed Ruth's shopping, didn't approve of her cleaning, patronized her cooking failures with an "I told you so." He only wanted Thanksgiving stuffing the way his mother did it. He insisted the Fourth of July always be spent at the lake, as in his childhood. He didn't like anything *new*. He turned into a grumpy monster when he got sick. And he would get in such a huff when Ruth tried to fight with him, she found she was better off wheedling.

Ruth worked on and off as a receptionist in a doctor's office, something "girls" did – not too serious and where women were still called "girls." With little else to do, Ruth became thoroughly preoccupied with what Lester would like her to do, what was for dinner, and what they needed next. She got into spending money. She bought clothes (lots of them), picked new dishes, and planned shopping expeditions. Lester would hesitate, talk budget, and refuse. Ruth would beg. Then he would go ahead and get her what she had her eyes on as he patted her on the head. He led Ruth to believe that "no" meant "yes, but plead first." Soon, "Oh *pleeeese*, Lester," was part of her every sentence.

Lester never told her the limits of his salary or the meaning of his budget, so she never knew whether funds were tight or loose. He always said things like, "We'll find a way" or "I'll manage it somehow." On every level he treated Ruth as an unreal and ineffectual being. He acted as if, other than providing entertainment and decoration, she had few capabilities and even less consequence. He often said "she would never learn," so she had to follow his more knowledgeable and more rational instructions.

Except when it came to sex. Ruth kept waiting for tutelage, but it never came. He was *more* than gentlemanly about sex. He was bafflingly restrained. He used her naivete, her hesitations, even a yawn, to "free" her from sexual obligation. And when she clearly wanted sex, he would indulge in only a little cuddling and then turn over to sleep. They had intercourse, but what was satisfactory to Lester was utterly empty to Ruth.

In a few short years, Ruth found herself disappointed, frustrated, and out of love with Lester. But meanwhile she had grown up so little that her attempt to end the union came out like a thwarted child's. Rather than formulate clear actions, she began to flirt with other men. One was particularly consoling. He sympathized with her and offered her shelter. He had a home and a salary all ready, so one bright day Ruth sashayed away from Lester and over to Wayne.

It was out of the frying pan and into the fire. Ruth went right to another all-caring, all-capable, all-controlling parent. Wayne was so composed and complacent that despite her attempt at scandalous behavior, Ruth reverted to an innocent child-bride. Wayne acted more like a school principal than a mate, so Ruth acted like a buoyant bubblehead who needed remedial reading. Meanwhile, their erotic life became almost as dull as that with Lester. Wayne seemed to get aroused only when Ruth played babyish, sat on his lap, and called him "naughty."

Years went by as Ruth puttered around her new doll's house. Wayne was growing ever more fussy. Ruth felt cut off. Women friends lost patience with her. She grew lonely and bored. She felt pointless. She began to have problems with envy. She either loved or hated every woman on soap operas or in *Ladies' Home Journal*. She ate and ate and became very overweight. A depression set in that seemed so close to a breakdown that a friend suggested Ruth seek therapy. When the vacation Wayne proposed instead didn't work to cheer her up, he grudgingly agreed to let her go. He didn't want her unhappy but felt threatened by her change.

Ruth found therapy uncomfortable and distressing, but she wanted to keep it up. Something was happening to her. She was clamoring for an adult demeanor and liked the way it felt. She started doing things her own way. She demanded to see the bills and began to tell Wayne off. But the more she changed, the more Wayne resisted. When he didn't bend as she had hoped, she realized she didn't have the strength to fight both for herself and for him. She had a difficult choice. She could remain a partial child in the guise of a wife forever, just as her mother had, or she could leave and try to stand on her own. Ruth decided to separate. She was afraid, but she felt if she didn't make a break she would stay under someone else's care for the rest of her life. That's when she went back to school. Soon she got an apartment far from Wayne (her first one had been close), and drifted away from him until she no longer saw him.

The Father Knows Best is usually a good and well-intentioned man. Unfortunately, he knows no other way to love than to emulate a parent. Many women hate him. But to those he attracts, his bearing seems so natural they glide right under his wing without a second thought. A relationship with a Father Knows Best is a two-way street. When you check his signs, check yours, too. If yours are the opposite of his, if you're still not taking responsibility for yourself, while he does for you both, take heed. You might *think* you're heading for romance and end up with adoption!

How Can You Identify This Kind of Man?

Dos and do nots, how and how nots, shoulds and oughts, right ways and wrong – somebody has to know just how things are done. And the Father Knows Best thinks he is the one.

When he was very young, someone or something got into his central computer and tried to make him perfectly socialized. He got programmed with responsibilities and regulations, systems and means. He was told the *one* right way to celebrate a holiday, the *one* proper hour for supper, the *one* efficient method to mow the lawn, the *one* sensible approach to buying a car. He learned that you don't jaywalk, wear shoes without socks, forget clean underpants, close the window when you sleep, that rarely should you weep. And while you claim you aren't prudish, you believe in modesty. He found he got approval when he followed all the rules like a little man. Since then, he's equated affection with regimentation. Now he does the same to you.

The Father Knows Best is a kindly man, but his kindness comes out as concern for your welfare. He's giving, but his giving is like philanthropy to a helpless charity – you. Much of any parenting is in the pose. And the Father Knows Best has the pose down pat. Even when he doesn't quite tell you what to do, he always acts as if he knows. Even when he doesn't say that he is right and you are wrong, he seems to convey that he's sensible and you're silly. Then he hands out rewards and administers punishments.

Outer Signs

His entire carriage implies he was grown-up the day he was born. There's hardly a snip, snail, or puppy-dog tail left in him. You, on the other hand, have a little curl right in the middle of your forehead. The Father Knows Best tries for the look of years, steadfastness, reliability, and experience. He likes venerated apparel, utterly conventional and unflamboyant, as well as the clothes that he bought ten years ago, from which nothing can separate him. His look is not unlike that of a bride at a wedding. He wears something old, something new, perhaps something borrowed, but *always* something blue. If he hasn't got a penny in his shoe, you can bet he's got one somewhere. He always carries a pen, maybe two or three; sometimes he has a pocket guard to protect his clothes from ink stains. His shirts are Van Heusen or the cheaper versions of Izod (like Le Tigre, Sears, or he orders them from Land's End). He wears a belt, or his pants are elasticized in back. He's clean and clean shaven, with short hair. His socks are blue or black, his shoes Florsheim – laced and resoled – and four years old, or else dark blue Adidas. He also has bedroom slippers. All of these things have a closeted, unaired (but not necessarily unpleasant) smell about them.

As he grows old, he's terrible to buy for. His needs are few, and he's got them covered with items from his past. Besides, his taste is fussy, and you can't find what he wants because they don't make them any more.

He likes his car stodgy. He takes factory regular (blue, green, or tan) right from the showroom. One color and no extras is good enough for him. Unleaded gas appeals to him. He uses S.T.P. and any other additives that makes his auto run better and last longer. He keeps his car for at least four years, usually close to ten. He doesn't play the radio when he drives around.

Before he hooks up with a daughter figure, he takes care of himself for a while. He lives in some very compartmentalized apartment. He cooks on a hot plate or small stove or goes to some nearby inexpensive restaurant. He works part- or full-time even when in school. He launders and irons his clothes himself. His lifestyle isn't expansive or exuberant; he likes the standard provisions.

He likes to do what he thinks is sensible and reasonable. Later, when you pick a residence as a couple, he goes not so much for design as for affordability. He prefers conventional, conservative, and smallish shelters, and he heads either for moderately nice residential areas where one house is pretty much like the others or else for huge, square apartment buildings where the flats are endless, square repetitions of each other.

Though some Father Knows Bests are quite worldly and like formal gourmet dinners, others get testy about garlic, onions, and vinegar. They claim to have sensitive noses and stomachs and like their cooking plain, their lettuce iceberg and their pie apple. They fuss over your cooking enough to make you feel that you're Holly Hobbie at a baby Betty Crocker Mini-Wave Oven. Under such scrutiny, you start to burn things. All the more reason for him to take you out.

He watches sports but rarely plays them. He tends to get thick and lose body tone. He's more and more inert as time goes on. His skin gets soft, and he starts to go for cardio-cholesterol checkups. He turns into a terrible baby whenever he gets sick.

He's very, very cautious about what he does. He says "don't," "watch out," and "be careful" a lot. He aims them at you but lives them himself as well. Occasionally he says "I forbid," but he's aware that he steps pretty well out on a limb when he goes that far. His first response to anything is more than likely "no." Then, with time, prodding, and careful examination he grudgingly allows what he once rejected. If you go through channels, plead, reapply, meet certain conditions, and wait ninety days, you can get a charge card for Dress for Less.

He carries on like a living bank. He watches his input, output, and rate of flow. He says he needs his sleep; he believes one can have too much sex. Sometimes he's a hypochondriac and thinks of drafts and germs.

He follows an internal rulebook for all his actions – as if he might get a bad check mark from the boss, the neighbors, or Big Brother. Then he treats you as if you were an extension of him, as if you reflected on his record. If you don't behave well, others will think it's his fault.

Sex Signals

The Father Knows Best heads for hesitant women or fledglings – or better, both. His opening approach comes in the guise of help. He takes care of a mess or a problem that you've been having trouble with. Then he offers more assistance, then some more. Pretty soon, he's lifting lots of weights off your back and becomes a necessary resource – and an easy way out. He pampers you in a way that makes you almost indolent. He encourages you to be superfluous but decorous. He makes it seem you can have an existence almost like a vacation if only you stay with him for good.

He paves his way to bed with small maneuvers. He adds food, care, and nice events. He seems to be the better judge of the two of you of when the time is right, so you don't have to decide. But once the union is established he's so cautious and so diplomatic about sex, you wonder who really didn't want it. You realize his courtesy may well cover his own lack of interest. The edge of rejection makes you all the more childlike. He makes you feel modest. He almost always waits until you're in bed before anything starts. He approaches under the sheets and often in night clothes. But sometimes he has a totally unexpected weird streak: he might like to spank, get spanked, or wear strange clothes. Even so, his rate of intercourse is slow, his desire low, and his performance short. Somehow you end up frustrated, and you don't know why.

He's not one to carry on affairs. After all, he doesn't encourage one whole, grown woman, so why two? And he thinks you won't fool around either. But he may well be wrong.

Money Markers

He holds the purse strings, that's for sure. The Father Knows Best always works and almost always saves. At least he uses savings as an argument. He applies his earnings to both of you, but since he expends funds less than moderately on himself, he puts you in the position of being the money spender. He allows you to purchase, but he makes your access to cash seem like a weekly budget you always run over. He doesn't give you an actual allowance, doesn't tell you the limits. He wants you to ask for money so he can give it.

Even though he both earns and pays for your living expenses, it's uncanny how often he marries a woman with at least some money. The Father Knows Best partner often has steady family handouts, trusts, or an inheritance, and frequently your family has a higher status than his. Since you live on his cash, he expects to supervise yours. He doesn't let you spend your money, but he feels he has to let you run through his.

Family Aspects

It may seem paradoxical, but the Father Knows Best hesitates when it comes to being an actual parent. He puts off having a family as long as he can and permanently if possible. He has all sorts of reasons. He may use what he considers your frivolities – "You're not grown up yourself yet" – to prove that you're not ready. The other reason he cites is that you need to wait till you can afford a baby. When he does finally have progeny, he often allows only one or two children, who are very carefully brought up. As a father he lacks the necessary sense of fun. He dislikes play and over likes instruction – through words, not demonstrations. He rarely lets the kid in him shine for his own child.

Perhaps his attitude toward parenthood comes from the fact that not many Father Knows Bests look back on their own childhoods as happy times. They have a few delightful memories, but the rest seem to fade into a sense of oppression. Often, one relationship was particularly difficult for them. Someone required the young Father Knows Best to mind his p's and q's too much. As an adult he remains attached to his family but not in an expressive way. They love him as he does them, but no one ever quite says so. A degree of disapproval always seems close at hand between him and his parents. As his mate, don't expect his family to adore you. Meanwhile, his feelings for his brothers and sisters combine a protective desire and a wish that they were really better friends. They are never as friendly as they try to be.

Although the Father Knows Best had several long-term friends in his youth, once he hooks up those friendships fade away. Once mated, he no longer has individual friends. Rather you two pair up with couples. He occasionally meets the man from the opposite twosome alone, and you see the woman, but mostly you do a lot together as a foursome. Within your whole social circle, with the Father Knows Best you have few unattached persons around.

The Father Knows Best has many great qualities, both obvious and buried: he means well and has good motives. He loves you. He also tries to love himself, but he tries to love himself through *you* and that never works. He doesn't know any other way to care for the child part in him but to turn you into it. And that's bad for you. If you can ever get beyond his patripotestal armory, there may well be a delightful man in there, though maybe never a lighthearted sprite.

What Is in Store for You?

Instead of well-defined stages, a slow but steady process of involution takes place in a Father Knows Best relationship. The pattern is most likely set early on in the romance. It just gets deeper.

When the Father Knows Best begins to take care of you, what usually happens is you fall into being taken care of. As he grows custodial, adult, and proud, you get giddy, silly, and young. Rather than having an equal-partner stance, the cute game between you develops into a tie of utter dependence.

Three insidious things happen to you when a Father Knows Best plops you into a permanent playpen. He removes you from serious activity or meaningful consequences in life. Having freed you to play, he feels it's part of his job to oversee and guide your amusements. And he makes the games hard for you to win.

Like a toddler stuck forever in a cell with only a Fisher-Price Busy Box, in a partnership with a Father Knows Best you become totally involved with the intricacies of getting along with him, getting a response from him, and getting what you want. As a consequence, you steadily get out of tune with the outer world. You get very good at games that only two can play, and some for only one. You turn into his "good girl." The Father Knows Best is not like the heavily adult and masculine Baby Chaser or the seemingly equal Secret Manipulator, against whom you can rebel. Nor is he the utterly compliant Sugar Pie Honey who somehow turns you into the Wicked Witch of the West. Instead the benign, always "for your sake" control of a fatherly type evokes too deep a memory and seems too hard to buck. So you take the opposite tack. You go so far as to believe that he dominates you *more than he actually does.* You lead yourself and others to think that you need his permission to go to the drinking fountain. You ask him for your allowance and request him to limit your Pepsi's.

Soon he acts as if no matter how much advice he gives you, you never profit from it. And you agree. You come on like a novice who will never get promoted. Everybody knows that you lack gray matter. When he gives you *some* information, duties, and understanding, but never *all,* you assume that total accomplishment is simply beyond your ken. He enacts a reward and punishment plan, and you try to test but not break it. He becomes a benevolent missionary who nurtures the savage. To get in good with him, you seemingly follow his good book, of which he owns the only copy, since it isn't translated into Girlish. When you go wrong, he holds back on goodies, mildly reproaches you, and takes it personally. If you are really bad, his reaction can be very frightening. He asks you that since you can't take care of yourself, what would happen if he deserts you? They don't have orphanages for full-grown waifs.

You find that you start to use the age-old tactics of disenfranchised, powerless, and half-grown people. You get petulant, you deal in manipulation, and you start to use sex for favors. You flirt, with him at first and maybe others later. You get secretive. You do things behind his back. You store chocolates under the bed or bury a bottle of bourbon in the oatmeal. You make purchases and then subtract twenty dollars so he won't know the price.

When you directly confront a Father Knows Best or your cunning gets too obvious, he has a way to tie you into a permanent knot. He fights resistance with instant role reversal: he becomes the baby and brings out the mother in you. If nothing else gets you stuck, a surge of maternal control over him almost always does.

Boxed in, the mate of a Father Knows Best tends to take a much more dangerous kind of escape than actual flight, one that removes her from the external world even more. Quite likely you start to dwell in a fantasy world. Daydreams, like soap operas, start to take over your mind. You conjure up dramas and disasters. You begin to take too seriously the things people nonchalantly do. Perhaps you disappear into magazines, paperback romances, scandal sheets, and T.V. You become idolatrous and envious of people you don't even know. You imagine utterly ridiculous ways to gain approval: you dream you will walk up to someone's Steinway, sit down, and play Chopin's First Concerto. No one ever *knew* you could play piano so magnificently.

It's likely that you drift away on the wings of sexual fantasy, too. Since your mate doesn't surprise you in bed, perhaps some superstar will see you and do it for him. Or maybe a swashbuckler will kidnap you and whisk you off to his seraglio. He's nameless and faceless and incredibly erotic. He never hurts and he does just what you want, even though you protest.

You can glide through years with a Father Knows Best. Then with age, two changes head your way. Both are part of your process of involution and isolation. You reach a time when you begin to feel the loss of your most important assets: youth and attractiveness, both necessary for the ingenue act. The more your behavior contradicts your decade, the deeper the crisis gets. You become prone to more than one mid-life crisis. As you age, even fantasy offers little solution; divorce certainly does not. Quite the opposite – you feel you have nowhere to go where you can still be babied.

Meanwhile, rather than having a crisis, your partner reveals more and more of what used to show only occasionally – he demands more and more care. Instead of being an imperturbable despot, he becomes an incapacitated one. He gets needy and testy. He took care of *you* when you needed him; now, like a well-raised offspring, you should take care of *him*. And he *still* wants you to do it his way.

In some extreme cases of the Father Knows Best, the childlike mate finally gets even in older age. She uses the money, deserts him at home, bosses him around, even abuses her man like Buñuel's Tristana.

What Are the Telltale Signs of Trouble?

There are a number of signs that can alert you to a Father Knows Best early. When a fatherly hand always extends from a man to save you, watch out. When a male deals with romance as if it puts him in an advisory capacity, beware. If he pulls you into his lap and it seems as if you've sat there before, caution yourself. Otherwise you may be the owner of a proud new parent.

Take heed if your mate keeps his head and face somehow above direct eye level, so when you approach him it's always an interruption; he's behind a book or a newspaper plus maybe glasses. He's always preoccupied. True, he puts down what he's doing and turns to respond to you, but he acts a little put out, shows a bit of noblesse oblige, and he sighs before he speaks. He also expects to deliver full speeches and expositions without disruptive queries. If you have anything to say, you must save it to the end. Of course by then the plans you offer tend to look silly, because (he'll point out) he covered that ground before. If you had only been listening! If you dare to inquire why this way and not some other, he gets annoyed that you should contradict him.

The other storm warning comes in you. You suffer repeat adolescent growing pains, petulance, pouting, pimples (yes, you can even get pimples again), only they're worse the second time around. You slip back to even more immaturity. You start to lose self-esteem. You start self-destructive habits, drinking, eating. With the Father Knows Best, the storm warnings mean you're off the changing table and into the crib. They should make you sit up, clang on the bars, and realize this is *not* the start of something good.

Unfortunately, all too often these warnings come so slowly and evenly that you never notice them. You may also think your union is loving and wonderful when they appear, so you dismiss them as trifles. But later, one of two types of telltale signs often occurs.

The first big sign is when suddenly, without knowing quite why, you bolt from your relationship. You run away. Perhaps at first you start sneaking to some silly activities. Then you allow yourself to meet another man, perhaps have an affair. Finally you cut out, but only into someone else's arms. You felt growing exasperation in your relationship. You seemed stunted and stifled, and you knew something had to give. But instead of fixing your pattern, you fixate on merely changing houses and mates. Doing so, you set yourself up for the same thing happening to you all over again.

The other, less drastic, warning is when along with feeling exasperated, you start to resist. And the resistance grows and grows. You begin to see your situation, how you are treated like a child. You can alter yourself, but you can't necessarily change your partner. That means you're at a turning point. You either have to figure out a way to make him treat you as an equal, or you must leave him.

What Are Your Chances and What Should You Do?

Back in the days of yore when most unions lasted for better or for worse, when women had less freedom to exercise options, and when parents heavily influenced choices, Father Knows Bests were legion. Now, Fathers (or partial Fathers), while still common, hold a less popular slot. It seems many women who meet parental men simply don't stay for long.

I rather agree with the modern trend, despite the fact that the Father Knows Best is a long-distance runner who loves, cares, provides, and stays forever. I don't feel he provides what's right or beneficial – not for today and maybe not ever for yesteryear. After all, even then Nora had to leave the Doll's House, and, because she lacked a sense of her own significance, Emma Bovary created quite a mess for herself. My general advice for most women is not to tarry with a Father Knows Best. I also advise that you *tell him why*. If he's going to change, he has a far better chance to do so if he has strong evidence that a parental approach is counterproductive.

Once paired, the Father Knows Best allows for little development. Stalemate is in his interest, change is not. Just watch his reaction to the idea of therapy or even transcendental meditation. Especially when it's you who wants to try such things.

Occasionally a woman spots the potential assets of a particular Father Knows Best, stalwartly refuses his parenting, and still manages a relationship with him. But it requires a great deal of effort. He instinctively avoids adult women, and he's resistant and tenacious. The best guarantee you have of a perpetual relationship with a Father Knows Best is to remain in the same parent-child framework.

If that's all right with you, well and good. If not, the odds for permanence dwindle fast.

If you become intent on change in this relationship, a lot depends on whether you desire to modify *yourself*. There's no denying the most expeditious way to alter your own condition is to go out the exit door. If that's your goal, remember there's an easy and a hard way out. I suggest the hard. As difficult and uncomfortable as it may seem, *don't slide from one man to another*, don't take family housing or handouts, don't even take helpful but obligatory favors. Get professional aid if you can, definitely get work, make your own decisions, and pay for all the aid you get with cash. Then spend a good stretch taking care of yourself before you form an attachment again. Don't be one of those for whom once is not enough. Repetition costs time and energy. Also remember the longer you're with the Father Knows Best, the harder it is to leave. You lose your spirit to change, especially if you coupled your habit to him with food, alcohol, or anything else.

If you have it in mind to grow up and at the same time shrink your present partner down until you end up on an equal plane, you'd better get some protein powder and build up your strength. You're going to have to be the adult for the two of you. In order to rearrange a Father Knows Best while staying together, you have to be utterly determined to stick to the change and stick to him, and you have to let him know it. The shock of that is about the only thing to get him moving. Don't make threats with a Father Knows Best. Threatening to leave is bad strategy with him. For one thing, threats are childlike and assure him that you're still his little girl. And he takes menace badly. He'll retrench more firmly than ever.

He needs love and affection, but he fears his need. To give him alternating childish and motherly attention you may meet his desire, but you perpetuate his fear. You can make a healthy turnabout only if you take a steady, mature stance. Give him concern without dependence; constant but objective compassion. If all goes well you might get . . . say, a Loving Traditional Man?

Where Do You Fit In?

It's even played out in a ceremony: a man passes one of his ladies to another caretaker in front of the altar. One man asks for your hand, another gives you away. So you're never unprotected. As much as we *think* we base our unions on love, the old pattern of being exchanged from one man to another hangs on more than you think. In a study I once conducted, none of the women interviewed said she established her permanent partnership because of love. Rather the women had three other main reasons. One, some inner sense told them it was time to couple up, so they picked a likely mate and settled down. Often that was toward the end of high school or college or after one year of work. The inner sense seemed to indicate they couldn't make it without marriage. So no matter what their supposed career plans, they dropped everything else and did it. Two, they wanted to move somewhere or travel away. But they couldn't fathom moving without a male protector managing it for them. So they zeroed in on a suitable relocator. And, three – the most startling, poignant reason – was that they married because their father had just died!

Obviously a couple of decades of social change doesn't automatically wipe out several millenniums' worth of deeply ingrained patterns. Even today, fears of growing up can make many a woman find a Father Knows Best attractive. He fits an age-old stereotype for men, and we have been inculcated with the age-old imagery for women which relegate us to permanent juvenility. Consider even some of the rather contemporary images: they still make us juveniles. "Chicks" are baby fowl, "dolls" are fake babies, and "babes" are infants.

We still have automatic time buttons that tell us we ought to couple up. We have trouble making our own space without a man. Like the women in the study, all of us are prone to old beliefs, expectations, and behaviors. For some of us at all times, and all of us at some times, the pressure to fall into ready-made grooves is particularly strong. It can seem more than handy to go from father, home, or institution (such as school) right to the shelter some male will provide us.

There's nothing wrong in picking a traditional union or even a fatherly mate when you do so consciously and choose the life ahead, but to do so *unconsciously* is called leaping before you look. All too often it ends you up where you don't want to be. Stop and consider any union carefully. To remain a colleen with a parental mate may look like an easy path and in many ways it is, but it's like being given a bicycle and never being allowed to ride it without training wheels.

Here you are with a *life*, a *mind*, and a *body*. If someone comes along to hold you up every time you use them, in the long run, the results can be catastrophic: you just stop using them at all.

Obviously there's a lot of resemblance between the Father Knows Best and the Baby Chaser, but the Father Knows Best is less of a heavily male maverick, and the Baby Chaser isn't necessarily fatherly at all. More than the Baby Chaser, the Father Knows Best actually shares traits with the Secret Manipulator. In fact, when he's seemingly letting you have your own way for a change, he can often act exactly like the Manipulator. I strongly recommend to any woman who is dealing with a Father Knows Best in any capacity, whether mate, boss, or father, that she read carefully the chapter on the Secret Manipulator.

On our way to the Manipulator some other types occur. Again they deal with "softer," but not necessarily better, kinds of men, and "softer," but not necessarily better, relationships. One of the worst of them, the Sugar Pie Honey, follows. He seems like a sweet, sweet man. But sweet as he is, you should definitely beware of him.

16

The Sugar Pie Honey

The Man Who Smothers You
in Endless Kindness

Think of marshmallow syrup, or creamy nougat. Now lead your thoughts to more sublime tastes. Imagine chocolate-covered care, sugar coated sensitivity, all pouring forth from a man, the Sugar Pie Honey. He's a sweet, sweet guy. But take too much of him and he becomes a Cool-Whip nightmare, endlessly giving way. You gobble away at him, searching for his substance, the shortcake, at least the strawberry. Something. *Anything!* But dig as you might, you can't find it. He never offers any resistance. He's so endlessly sweet, so constantly devoted, so perpetually giving, somehow it never tastes quite *real*.

The Sugar Pie Honey thinks his chances of winning love are so small he has to be extra good to get any. So he devises a plan, the way cereal companies do to get kids hooked on oat flakes. He adds an addictive ingredient – sweetness. The cavities follow.

He always understands. He forever forgives. (Or at least he *seems* to.) He wraps you in a coat of gentle, smothers you with nice, kills you with kindness. Terrible at measuring cupfuls, he glazes you over with sweetness in abandon, figuring if a little T.L.C. is good, a lot must be even better. Shades of a little boy told too often to behave, he comes on like a blessed archangel.

But since he restricts himself so obsessively only to being nice, nice, nice and understanding, you begin to wonder if he really loves, or if he resents, the object of his saccharine attentions, namely you. The answer becomes apparent, but backwards. What happens is eventually he turns you into the mouthpiece of all his repressed ire. He stays nice, but you grow awful. The more honeyed he, the more spleenful you. He wears the halo, you the devil's cloven hooves. And although he never asks for it, he takes hidden offense that you don't treat him better.

Who does he pick among women? It's obvious. He goes for women who are looking for a port in the storm. He likes ladies who are fighting some inner war, who are in crisis and constant distress. Who, rather than shore themselves up from the inside, succumb to an outside buttress. He heads for anything wearing a fragile, handle-with-care, or just-came-out-of-a-horrible-home, terrible-divorce, crime-victim, awful-situation, everything's-too-hard label. He offers a hand hold, a pat dry, a place in which to break away safely, and he'll hold you together.

Story

For a long time, my colleague Brian was the Sugar Pie Honey to end them all. He was a little short, definitely not built like a male model, and wore heavy glasses. His hair had a mind of its own. Too shy and too unnoticed for anything except answers to exam questions, he didn't even attempt dating till he was almost through college.

Secretly, he thought that the only way he could gain his own woman was to compensate for all his failings, so he used his keen mind to discover just what women were looking for. He hit upon all the things he assumed jocks were not – sensitive, gentle, and attentive – and turned himself into the deal you couldn't refuse. At first, he gained a lot of lady friends, yet none wanted to be his lover. But sooner or later he knew he'd score.

Enter Martine, an actress. Basically well intentioned, she was unable to face her own character. Her family, which acknowledged only saintliness, was austere, troubled, and very much into guilt, so she couldn't admit to aspects of herself that weren't nice. She was very confused. Martine was having trouble facing a cold, harsh world. She was caught between lack of money, lack of friends, acting aspirations, the competition her career involved (for which she was ill-equipped), and family duties, which were laden with false responsibilities.

Along came Brian, a human fur coat. Small wonder he looked like a little log cabin, complete with pancakes and hot maple syrup. She fell for the someone-to-watch-over-me aspect of him and ignored the instinct that told her that on a diet of permissiveness she might go sour.

For while Martine wanted to be Extra Select, it turns out she was just regular – sometimes nice, sometimes not so nice. She had a streak, perfectly normal but repressed, that made her want to kick up dust, be free, and be mean when she felt like it. With Brian, she opted for safety but he offered no restraints. He offered money to ease her existence, sympathy for her problems, and a business sense for her ambitions. He gave massages, foot baths, and hair brushings. And he *never* got angry, not even when he should have. He never said no and never even showed annoyance. Martine had free rein. With every liberty to be nasty, she couldn't find her own control. The devil within her got out of hand.

She began to provoke Brian, to get a reaction from him that wasn't nice. She became quarrelsome and critical. She was stubborn and willful. She didn't show up when she should, broke promises, refused to do any of their shared work, didn't join him for social obligations. But no matter what she did, he'd only be sympathetic and comfort her. So she got worse. She yelled at him and picked fights. She broke dishes and demanded her way. And he became even more understanding. She soon realized he was withholding any response other than acquiescence. He was showing one side of himself and keeping the other side hidden with a vengeance.

He even held back sex. Not that he didn't make love to her. He did. He just came so fast that she couldn't. And while he tried to please her in other ways, if she caressed him back, he'd go limp. That's when she *really* became difficult and irascible, and in fact, angry with him. Her behavior went beyond insult and zoomed into injury. She started keeping a lot of company with another man, an actor "friend." He was always over. Then she started going to parties and events with her friend, not Brian. Finally she stayed out all night. Brian just grew sweeter and sweeter. He greeted her home with orange juice. Finally she left for a week, leaving Brian with the child he'd pleaded for and she'd allowed (but only one). He took her back.

But behind her awful behavior, the truth was Martine couldn't bear how horrible she'd become. She acted cold, but she felt guilty. Brian continued to smile like sunshine, but inside he was fermenting and keeping a long, long list of her sins and errors. And he was withholding his real feelings from her now in an even more calculated manner, augmenting her bad actions. The diet of Sugar Pie was killing them both. Martine decided to move out, although she didn't move far. She started up a relationship with yet another man, and when it fell apart, she came back. She hit at Brian's soft spots and he let her, and their pattern started up again. Soon she took off again, this time for an acting job. Again she came back, looking for a shelter when things got hard. She did this several times, until at last Brian said no. Martine wanted to stay at least Brian's "friend," and for a long time he allowed that. But finally, slowly he eased her out of his life. Their break up was long and clingy, but together they had compiled too long a list of hurts to overcome. Meanwhile, Brian fought for the child, and won.

You've heard of a blessing in disguise. Well, the Sugar Pie Honey is the opposite. In his case, what seems like a blessing is a curse. What seems like sugar is poison. He's a good man, but he plants the seeds of his own disrespect. You simply become the one to act it out. And the person you end up hurting is yourself.

How Can You Identify This Kind of Man?

It's easy to see that a man might be a Sugar Pie Honey, he comes on so nice. But it's hard to see that he'll be the kind that goes too far and will never be anything but suffocatingly, self-effacingly sweet, a martyr. It's clear he's a nice man, so caring, so marvelous to women. But he actually knows how to make women care for *him*. More importantly, he doesn't know how to take good care of himself. He's usually a smart man, often very smart. He got the way he is by analyzing things and coming up with a strategy. After sizing up the data and his observations, he discovered that goodness endeared people to others. That it especially worked on women. So he made it his modus operandi.

His thinking was fallacious, of course. He wasn't as objective as he thought. But it's not so much the plan as his faulty execution of it that really gets him into trouble. Being nice is fine, to a degree. But he makes two errors. He does his kindness to excess, and he ignores and represses his own anger. He lives in terror of his temper, so he never tries it out. He doesn't know how to be grouchy and still have friends, and he never learns that you'll both survive it if he gets mad.

This combination of errors makes a messy mixture. His plan backfires. For his own rage is there, all right. He says everything is okey-dokey, but it *isn't*. He says he wants to be "real" – he thinks he is "real" – but he won't give you any response other than comforting. Meanwhile he's mild-mannered and unpretentious. He's bright and makes good conversation, but one of his give-aways is that he pours forth an endless stream of queries and it all centers around you. Where do you come from? What do you do? And especially, how do you *feel*?

Outer Signs

The Sugar Pie Honey is not very interested in clothes; he doesn't buy them often. He claims he's concerned with people, not trappings. He likes handmade, well used, or ethnic items, huggable textures and soft weaves, suede shoes and Hawaiian shirts. He likes rather long, unfussed-with hair, and beards. He's not flashy. On the other hand, he's not staid either. He's comfortable looking.

The same goes for his car. At first he's not very interested, then he works up more involvement, and each model gets a little more attention. Still, nothing with spectacular value. Always a common car, good and functional or old and funky: a Chevy, a Dodge, an old Toyota, or a Volvo, or maybe the kind of car his father had, with terry cloth seat covers.

He heads for vintage houses in folksy neighborhoods where old and young both live, with community centers, hangouts, little grocery stores. Certainly not a rich area, but a place where he can be just one of the locals, a routine, acknowledged presence, a good Joe. Sometimes he shares his house or apartment with another man, very much of his same type. His place is partly clean and partly not, partly decorated and partly not. He prefers photographs to prints or paintings and doesn't get around to rearranging furniture. His idea of warming up is lots of color, whole rooms of yellow, blue, or red.

His concern for human beings manifests itself in a modest political stance. He's for cheaper bread, medical clinics, more jobs, parks and libraries. He supports local campaigns like Stop the Freeway, Open the Bikeways, and the bottle bill. He may volunteer his labor for these organizations, or he may only chip in some money, and he drops dollars into the hat of the street corner fiddler.

He likes animals, music (especially guitar music), and has one favorite sport, usually basketball. He doesn't like to stand out in a crowd, but he's not the type that likes to fade completely away either. He wants to engage people on deeper levels, to elicit personal problems and talk about feelings. He isn't devoid of pride. He admires his own brains, his sensitivity, and how much niceness he's achieved. He treats himself all right. But just . . . *all right*. It's part of how he semi-devalues himself. He goes to no great lengths for delight. He will buy something that he really, really wants, but only after a great deal of deliberation, and he hesitates on items he would only *kind of* like to have. It's the same treatment he gives his emotions. He'll recognize the one he thinks he *ought to* – love, sympathy – but will sweep away the others – greed, lust, revenge. He thinks too much about how he should feel, about how he can make *you* feel. He lives in his head. It takes him a long while to disconnect his overactive frontal lobes enough to have fun. Drugs and alcohol often scare him because they short-circuit his synapses.

While the voices in his head talk too much, the muscles in his legs don't run enough; he exercises irregularly and inadequately. Yet surprisingly, he is not a bad athlete; he just looks more awkward and clumsy than he is. Perhaps his lack of grace is a way to get sympathy.

Sex Signals

He's not sure what he thinks about women. He wants to trust them, but unfortunately for him, he doesn't quite. He heads after women he views as more interesting and less stable than he. It's their fragility that attracts him. These women may cover fissures with an ambitious facade, but with his seismograph, he knows the fissures are there. The Sugar Pie Honey's woman is always under strain and close to cracking.

He approaches her through conversation. He spots a loner who's doing something a little unusual and seeks out the details of her life. Not shy about meeting and greeting, he knows he's good with words. Quickly he nice-talks and nice-times a woman into dependence. He becomes a special pal. The theme is "What difficulties did you go through today?" Despite resistance (which he gets because the ladies he chooses love his sympathy but not his physique), he eventually gets them into bed.

Sex is a giveaway clue of his slumbering emotions. Though some are sweet – frequently too sweet – lovers, often the Sugar Pie Honey has a hard time staying hard. Or else he climaxes very quickly, almost before anything had begun. In either case, too sweet or somewhat incapable, he continues the same pattern he finds operative socially. He is so solicitous, you feel like the guest on *I've Got a Secret*. Lovemaking with him is a cross between an amorous quiz show and a checkup. He asks, "How do you like this? And that? What do you want done? Which side do you want up? Does it hurt?" And (especially), "Did you come?" He elicits your verbal response to ensure that he's getting your other one – your physical one. It calms his nerves. Under his seeming curiosity about your orgasmic aptitude, he's very anxious to make up for his lack of one. He would love to become a better lover. But he's not, so anxiety grows. So does your disappointment. You talk over your "problems" in bed, seek books and techniques. Beyond that, no one rocks the boat. You don't discuss anger and resentment: there's too much to lose. Day by day, he's still a sweetheart. Massages, hot chicken soup, an ever-ready ear for your troubles. They make up for a lot, or so you both pretend.

The Sugar Pie Honey bears some resemblance to a type of man I call the Entrapper, but the Entrapper has a far more extreme method of approach. First he offers you wonderful evenings that are hard to resist. Then he starts bringing gifts, each one more desirable than the last and hard to refuse, so you accept them. Finally, he adds a third ingredient to the evenings and goods, he switches into guilt. He pleads that after the dates and gifts, and your involvement with him, you can't possibly leave him because he loves you so. He threatens suicide until you agree to stay. Using greed (yours) and implying your responsibility as well, he traps you. Entrappers will even get a woman pregnant on purpose. (Yes, it's true and it can happen. I know a number of cases.)

Don't get caught by the Entrapper! Remember, gifts and goodies don't magically appear without a price tag. Another person's proclaimed agony doesn't make you obligated to him. And above all else, protect your *own* body.

Now back to the Sugar Pie Honey.

Money Markers

The Sugar Pie Honey is sweet with money. In fact, it's part of his sugar coating. Usually his mate isn't quite as capable of earning a living as he is, or she doesn't want to earn one full time, day in and day out. But the Sugar Pie Honey is a worker; financial support, all or partial, is part of his package. (Occasionally, but only rarely, he's the houseboy, you the major earner). It's not that he won't use your money or combine it with his, but *his* is primary. To keep your finances on a par, you always borrow a cup of the old granulated from him, never he from you. Quite secretly, he keeps track of whose, and how much, went where.

Family Aspects

The Sugar Pie Honey wants children, but usually has to cajole one out of the union, as his co-generator wants motherhood less than he wants fatherhood. He likes to raise the children, be there for their wants and needs, be sweet to them. He'll fight for custody.

He's heedful of his family, kind to his parents. He sees his mother as cordial, his father as bittersweet. (His father is, or was, often a difficult, irascible man.) He does what his parents want him to do most of the time. Those times when he doesn't act like a good son occur away from home, and then he presents his deeds to his parents in the most palatable way. He doesn't use their money even when they have lots. He's a good boy. Often, he has only a brother. He's never learned to squabble with a sister.

As for friends, just-plain-friend isn't his style, *super*-best-friend is. He's very close to one or two men and spends a long time on the phone with them, or they watch hockey together on T.V.

Obviously, he's an over zealous friend to you, almost parasitic. But *any* woman in his life, past or present, lover or not, is earmarked as a pal. When he's not attached, lots of women call him to commiserate. Not too many want to hitch up.

The Sugar Pie Honey's liabilities aren't multiple, as with some kinds of men. The main one is that he can't see why anyone gets angry with him. But you do get angry with him (so do others) because he hides his real emotions. His one-sided presentation causes distrust. Few people can believe all white with no black. Certainly he has assets. In a generally crass world, he shimmers with positivity. Over-sincerity is a relatively minor sin, even when you suffer the consequences of it. Certainly, he's real nice. If only he knew it was nice to be real.

What Is in Store for You?

Too much sweetness isn't healthy for anybody. It certainly isn't nourishing. What lies ahead with the Sugar Pie Honey is a steady process in which satisfaction lessens and maladies grow. Three major troubles occur with the Sugar Pie Honey. First, he makes you the source of all negative emotion. Second, you're cut off from loving yourself. He's too fast at doing it for you. And third, you fight off what seems to be the obstacle between yourself and you, namely him. He's a false enemy perhaps, but too good a target to pass up. As a result, a spiteful and divisive side of yourself, which you repress and he encourages, arrives to stay.

It begins with growing grumpiness. Then you develop a "So What" syndrome, usually to cover the fact that you're beginning to feel bad for being so misbehaved. A Little Hitler is in the making, and he's living inside you. You push your little experiment farther. You get more and more obnoxious, hoping for a result. Will he ever get angry? Will he protect himself? Will he finally say, "Now you've gone too far?" But he continues to fall back and redefine what's acceptable to him, while you go ape and get zapped with guilt. The Sugar Pie Honey stays just nice enough to make you ashamed. A serious bad guy/good guy situation sets in. Only instead of you, he's the Shirley Temple and you're the Jack Palance. The worse you abuse his curly little head, the more you confirm your creeping fear that you're not a good person. Fairly early on in the relationship, he begins to withhold in subtle ways, mostly sexually. But then so do you! It's fair play to get cold, then frigid, along with everything else. Later, you can give your orgasms to someone mean instead of someone kind.

Under that saccharine skin of your Sugar Pie Honey, though, there's a record keeper who's making a list of your every sin and injury. Eventually, he lets you know your marks. You and he both establish together how no good you are, but he'll forgive you one more time, maybe two, maybe nauseatingly ad infinitum. His forgiveness has a condition though. You're supposed to act better. Now he has an excuse to watch you and keep track more openly. Finally under his sweetness, and now constant scrutiny, you snap. You leave, come back, leave again. Eventually you may leave for good, but surprisingly often, he's the one who finally calls the halt.

Leaving the Sugar Pie Honey almost always involves a long and arduous recuperation. It's hard to get over sugar poisoning. You had to have a need for sweetness to want him in the first place, so it's tempting to turn back to him again and again for quick calories. You two can stick together long after the breakup, intertwined in dependency. But you won't get on with your life and cure yourself till you wash your hands of him completely.

What Are the Telltale Signs of Trouble?

With any man, when you hear no no's, you should perk up your ears. Notice if there are no fights to clear the air, if he thinks out catastrophes instead of yells about them. If he coos at your disasters without an occasional "Well, it serves you right." These signs mean you're heading for gumdrop land.

When a man sighs but doesn't say what's wrong, gives poignant looks then only grows more distant, it's a sign that his resentment is growing. He's waiting to unload his grievances and ask for your contrition.

When you *take* kindness but react to it as if it's disgusting, as if you think he's weak, you're in for trouble. If you ignore your reaction and still accept more kindness from him, things are going to get worse. It's a discomforting indication. If he doesn't think he deserves better treatment, why should you?

Take a hard look at what constitutes a healthy, happy atmosphere. When you feel disrespect because he's too nice, but you stay because of guilt, right then you should question your relationship no matter how cozy it is. Maybe you should scoot yourself to a counselor. Why is sweetness a sign of wimpiness to you?

When you begin to perceive that his constant approval of you is a lie, it's time for you both to run for help. Nothing good ever comes of being false in a relationship.

What Are Your Chances and What Should You Do?

Only rarely can you and the Sugar Pie Honey eradicate the history you stack up between you. The sins you commit against one another result in the kind of hurt that never goes away. They also provide an endless source of reproach that can only lead to your needing a fresh start. An end is almost inevitable with a Sugar Pie Honey. My feeling is that it *should* end, and the sooner the better. The Sugar Pie Honey provides a self-defeating system – a tailspin of diminishing self-esteem. With him you may grow fat, but you don't grow tall. In other words, you may get cared for, but you begin to hate yourself.

However, while the relationship is rarely salvageable, you can have a good aftermath with him. The Sugar Pie Honey makes a great ex. He can stay sweet enough and involved enough to be more than civil, even more than fair in the financial settlement and childcare.

Besides, another thing happens in the aftermath. The Sugar Pie Honey relationship, once you've had it, changes you both. The Sugar Pie Honey's smarts ultimately save him. Generally he oversweetens a relationship just once. When he sees it doesn't work, he does some quick recalculations. He adjusts the seasoning, and tries a little ginger next time around. As for you, only a few women are willing to repeat their part of a Sugar Pie Honey twosome. They may head for the same sort of man, but they break up quickly when they see where it's going. You will probably go through a number of short relationships after a Sugar Pie Honey, until you grow nicer and learn to like yourself again. But they'll keep getting better.

Meanwhile, you'll treat your old Sugar Pie Honey better as time goes on, and he you. But as long as you remain friends, he will never quite understand why you got angry with him (he can't figure out what *he* did wrong), and he will never quite forgive you.

If you *do* attempt to rescue and stay in a Sugar Pie relationship, I suggest you first start working on yourself, then go on to him. Set your own limits. Gear your behavior to how you know you'll feel after the fact. Don't do what makes you feel bad afterwards. Also don't allow what makes you feel bad to be done to you, like accepting too many attentions. Remember to return your man's considerations equally. Then help him learn that love does come, even to those with tempers.

Where Do You Fit In?

Do you need outlandish support? A living crutch? Do you choose men who give these to you, but think less of them for it?

When you're hooked on the Sugar Pie Honey, you're often not looking to find out *who* you are. You are only telling yourself what you think you *should* be. Or maybe what you *shouldn't* be. You're asking, "Am I good or bad?" Then to make sure you are good, you settle for someone who gives you such constant approval he confirms for you what you hope to believe. You really are O.K.

But there's a problem. Actually there are two. When you settle for perpetual approval, you end up not knowing what you're made of at all. Secondly, if you confirm to yourself that you're good from outside opinion only, you'll begin inwardly to prove to yourself that you're bad.

To grow, like it or not, you need hearty victuals from the people around you and from yourself. You need a mix in what you nourish yourself with. You need criticism along with compliments, anger with the joy. You need to be taken care of and left to take care of yourself. True, such things as criticism, anger, and finding yourself responsible for yourself can be hard to accept in the short run, but if combined with the good stuff, like praise and well deserved compliments, they're good for you in the long run.

You have to let your friends – including your mate – be true and tell you what they really think, to take their bitter with their mellow. If you have trouble accepting their bad opinions, you may be missing out on their real affection. If you're battling with guilt, and you select a situation in which you can behave without reproach, you lose their affection and your own. Don't pick the perfect spot to wallow in self-condemnation. Wallowing rarely helps you win. Stop relying on indiscriminate acceptance and unending support. Clinging to the Sugar Pie Honey is almost like saying, "It takes somebody extra good to love me." Then, since he never seems to see how awful you really are, it follows you can't like him and you come to believe that you're bad.

But there's a secret to your being "bad." The secret is not that you have a deeply hidden wicked core, but that you don't. You're normal! Every person has a wide range of emotions and responses. You can be special and rotten at the same time, good and bad, nice, mean, and everything in between. There is no such thing as a consistently good or consistently rational person. All you can do is try to strike a balance, like and forgive yourself.

To say the Sugar Pie Honey is related to the Father Knows Best is not quite accurate. What happens is the longer you stay with a Sugar Pie Honey the more he becomes a Father Knows Best. After all, you keep proving you can't take care of yourself, you're silly, and a bad little girl. And he keeps taking care of you. Sugar Pie Honey can also be quite manipulative. In fact, the first stage a Sugar Pie Honey goes through in changing himself to a different man with women is to become a Secret Manipulator.

Courtiers can also be Sugar Pie Honeys. At least those Courtiers who only stay for a short while, or only want what you have. They can be super sweet till they're off. The long term, good Courtiers are too straightforward to be everlastingly sweet. Courtiers are men who go after older women, or women who have things they haven't and would like – money, status, power. They can be good and they can be bad. Any of us might find herself approached by one, now that women have more power, more position. And there's less and less stigma attached to having a younger man. So it's good to learn to tell the ones (and ways) who might benefit you, from the ones (and ways) of those who might not!

The description follows.

17

The Courtier

A Younger Man Who Likes Your Money,
Your Status, Your Good Life

Once it was just a dream carried on between *The Days of Our Lives* and dinner, or between three P.M. break and five o'clock quitting. You're queenly; you catch some young man's fancy; he eyes you in your ripened glory and comes courting. Previously it stopped there, with an accept-flattery-but-hands-off policy. Now the idea is no longer a fantasy lacking carnal knowledge. The Courtier isn't new under the sun; he's coming out from behind the clouds. Hallelujah!

There are plenty of reasons for a younger man to seek an older woman. Or a man with less to attach to a woman with more. You see, the Courtier is not necessarily younger in years. He comes in two styles. In one, age and experience count: he is younger and has less, you are older and have more. In the other, status and money figure: he has neither, you have both. But in either case, the primary item to remember is this: when it comes to the Courtier, some are good guys, some are not.

Sometimes the Courtier means to remain only temporarily, but he's fond and adoring while he's there, and that's O.K. Other times he just wants to conquer what you have – or see if he can, as a test of his ability. He just wants to use up your supplies, then he loses interest, walks off, returns nothing, and can even grow cruel. Sometimes the Courtier wants to settle down and harvest – for the long-run benefits. In this case, he can be shrewd while pretending to care – not so good. Or he can just plain love you and love to stay because part of what you have is you.

Whatever the minor variations, his theme remains: NOW. He wants the ripe fruit, not that due to ripen. Whether the affair is to be short- or long-term, your problem is discarding the pretenders and getting the prince so you benefit as well.

Quite obviously, he goes for a certain sort of woman – older, wealthier, more famous, successful, or simply more skilled than he. He finds women with depth of experience the only ones who intrigue and magnetize him, sexually and otherwise.

Story

Take the story of a woman I met and grew to admire a great deal, Lois. At the age of forty-seven, Lois had been married for twenty-one years and divorced for six. The breakup of her marriage had come as a complete shock to her. Then, six years after she picked up the pieces, she started to date and learned to love again. At first, she had thought she would travel into old age alone and empty. But she had finally passed the panic. She had known that, someday, *something* would work out. But how that something surprised her!

Like most women caught in similar situations, she found very few men of her age and station available. She found herself slowly lowering the age of men she considered as proper suitors. She began to see one man of thirty-nine and ended up wondering who was the loser – he was down and out and obviously used his charms while she took him in. He bedded her a month or two and disappeared.

While still quavering from the experience and determined not to repeat it, she met Alex. Alex was soft and slow, open and lovely. He wanted to live every day as if it were forever, wanted everything there was to have right now or never. And he was only twenty-seven.

Throughout her marriage, Lois had worked part-time as her husband's assistant. She had dealt with many people and had her hand in a lot of happenings; she was active and involved even though all she did officially was raise her children.

Lois missed nothing. She thought about life, devoured every experience, and had a lot of wisdom. People loved her, her friends were long standing. She didn't have much money, but internally she was a very rich woman. And Alex knew it. At first, Lois was uneasy about Alex. She denied any future hope to the affair, claiming he was just a lark. She feared he wasn't bright enough to discuss things with her, that she would find herself stuck with a burden and lose a few more years.

Alex never pretended he was different from what he was. He couldn't guarantee he would stay with Lois forever. He never said he wouldn't enjoy her possessions or connections, didn't feel diminished by taking advantage of something that was none of his own doing. He did find Lois enthralling, with much more to offer in thoughts and insight than his previous young lovers. He knew he wanted to be with her. And for that privilege he was happy to offer anything he could muster. A rarity, he was uncluttered by ambition, unperturbed by guilt, kind, considerate, helpful, even joyous. Sexually, he was warm, huggy, and ever-ready. Lois found herself physically awakened in a way she had thought she could be only within a steady union, but had never achieved in her marriage. What she did know from all her previous practice she taught Alex.

As they grew together, they expected the hard part to come from her children. But strangely enough, after a few upheavals, because Lois and Alex were bluntly honest the children came to the conclusion that what was good for their mother was also good for them. Divorce had strengthened them. They had the capacity to appreciate something novel. When their father objected, they lined up against him until he became a "family friend."

Lois used her experience to open her own insurance firm. Alex both assists her and dabbles in real estate. They share cooking, go camping. He gardens, she relaxes. They have a lot to talk about. It's hard at this point to figure out who's the main adviser. Their ties are loose in some ways, tight in others. They have a solid friendship. There is some jealousy on both parts and some fighting, even an occasional separation. They live for the moment – Alex introduced that. They spend, travel, take what comes. Sometimes, Lois fears the future, but she's decided to deal with later later. But lucky Lois has found the grace to let life ride without reservations and nagging worry. If Alex exploits her; she's willing. Why? Because she likes it.

More than any other kind of man, Courtiers require picking and choosing on your part. Careful picking and choosing. You have to protect yourself. But before you dismiss them completely, it's time to consider that perhaps fewer years and lower position don't put a man at less advantage. For years, older men have considered younger women as personal enhancements. Maybe it's time to turn the tables. Especially if we can avoid the hustle of Baby Chasing and do it right – with love and style.

How Can You Identify This Kind of Man?

Day in and day out, the television asks, "Why wait?" It never says, "Take baby-steps in life's game of Mother-May-I?" No way. Those commercials trumpet that there's no need to grow it, make it, bake it from scratch. Whatever you want is already manufactured. And while the idea refers to products, it easily translates to people. Why else would so many folk wander aimlessly in and out of singles' bars looking for *the one right* person? It's obvious, of course: lately, people expect other people to come already completely packaged, like pizzas and perfume.

The Courtier buys the line. When an item says "partial assembly required," he's off in another direction. The latest model of modern man, he's ready for anything ready. Pop Tarts and Gourmet Delight. He may have grown up that way, or may be a recent convert; it depends partly on his age. At any rate, the Courtier's not patient, even when he's sweet and abetting. He takes his turn now, no matter where his place in line is. When it seems he's dedicated to Number Two (you), in most ways he's still looking out for Number One. You are part of how he takes care of himself. But then, usually, he's part of how you take care of yourself.

So consider the Courtier a user, because he is one (not necessarily in a bad sense). Don't expect him to save money on his clothes, hold off on his sports car, or stash the best liquor for some distant occasion. Don't even freeze last night's dessert. Remember that saying, "Make hay while the sun shines"? It was written for him. He doesn't see life as Mount Everest – no struggles for him. He's here and now. Rarely is he with you to boost himself to the next state. Mostly he just wants to enjoy whatever is available. Usually he's quite willing to reciprocate for his pleasures. If you have achievements to make, he may support you in your climb. Some Courtiers would like career success along with their ladies. Others, usually speedy ones, become front men – they promote or manage for you. Earthier ones prefer to calm you and keep you cozy. If you have no outer-world pressure, but pass your days at home, a Courtier might still keep your house together.

Outer Signs

The Courtier likes quality through and through, which is flattering to you. His mode of dress may be very stylish, easy comfortable, or quite individual, but each piece is hand-picked and particular. He likes good things, rich things. He tends to fancy specialty items, not just regular ones. He's disposed to scarves and jewelry, Borsalinos and cravats. He appreciates beautiful gifts of your choosing. He likes to look a little expensive and unusual. He claims distinction outwardly, even if not in achievement.

He takes pride in his car. Strangely, he selects either a Mercedes or its opposite, a V.W. bus, or a Ferrari or its opposite, a Suzuki Samurai. "In between" sorts of vehicles lack allure for him. He wants one extreme or the other. As far as the Courtier's concerned, material goods are toys and cars are some of the best ones. It's as if they come from Tonka and they only exist for fun. He has, or has had, a motorcycle. And, at least once in his life, he'd like to ride in a limousine.

Houses are less easy for him to have fun with, at least when he's on his own. So when the Courtier lives by himself, he looks as if he's on the move. He simply prefers to live with somebody else. His place is always bare, except for his favorite playthings. It's probably not quite in order or else his things are still in boxes. He selects places that resemble motel rooms and evoke entrance foyers, the better to get out fast. He cares about nice furnishings (and loves later to pick them out with you), comfort, and aesthetics. But part of that means having another tasteful human being present to create the atmosphere, so he moves in with you.

He's more than civil, he's downright polite and amiable. Sometimes he's urbane, but oily-tongued Courtiers are passé. He can be direct and honest. He's usually good-humored and soft-spoken. Odds are high that he's nice looking. No matter what his origins, he seems to have good breeding. Despite what others think when they see how quiet he is in public with you, he's not a passive fellow. He speaks his mind in private. He stipulates how he wants to live, but he compromises to blend with you.

He's a creature of the moment. He lives in active verbs. He finds himself pleasurable. He consumes, imbibes, carries on as he wants to. He prefers to *like*, perhaps like strongly, rather than *love*. To like is to enjoy. To love is often to suffer.

Sex Signals

He thinks of women as a connoisseur thinks of wine. He doesn't want the raw new press. He savors full bouquet, nose, fine head (in any number of ways). Sometimes, he cares about the size and shape of the bottle. Sometimes he doesn't. What's more important to him is your decision that he's worth it.

To approach you, he places himself in your attention, often enough so that you know it's persistence. He waits for you to break through the polite conversation and make a high sign; in true Courtier fashion, he's attentive. You make the first advance or let it happen. Soon you both understand that you're advancing in some unspoken process. He's more and more available as your company until you move from public to private pairing. Then you work out your relationship until you're ready to go public as an item.

Sex comes immediately or sometimes not at all. Occasional women want permanent escorts without physical relations; some Courtiers are gay. If he is sexually inclined, he's ever so subtly persistent. He stands close, picks up and fondles a strand of hair until you ask, "Why not?" If you're hungering to try his body right away, he wants you to. If you're not sure, he waits. It's amazing how far nonaggressiveness gets him. He's hard to shoo away because he's never abrasive. Usually he's a very sexual and enthusiastic, if youthful, lover. He's not into educational programs. He likes the fact that you both know what you are doing. Novices are not his number and nothing virginal appeals. So you indulge in a mutual refinement of old techniques instead of new ones. What he lacks in quality he makes up for in quantity. You're in a sexual peak, and he's up and coming – and coming. It can be a perfect combination, for two people who like to use themselves.

How he treats you once you're a twosome changes little from courtship. You become one another's major interest. Differences sink to the bottom; the courtesy goes on. The Courtier relationship is one of the most delicate – it can't tolerate much abuse – and both parties seem to know this. Its maintenance depends on formal consideration: respect reigns, along with regard and obligations.

Money Markers

Though some Courtiers earn money, generally the major amount comes from your handbag. If you don't provide cash, you probably supply property. He doesn't care where the money comes from. It exists to use, and he's good at it. If you like to spend for pleasure, too, it's all the merrier. An older Courtier, or one who ponders aging, might want an account in his name alone. As your agent or helper, he might ask for (and deserve) a salary. It's not unlike a Courtier to keep some money separate for independent purposes while generally living on yours. Occasionally it bothers the Courtier if he has little or no income, but more so if he has no creations, so he attempts separate endeavors. But his projects have an uncanny tendency to not happen or to simply become follies.

Family Aspects

In most Courtier situations, if anyone has children, it's you. Usually, he wants none or thinks of them as so much in the future that they never happen. Even if your difference is one of wealth and status, instead of age, generally the decision on both your parts is to avoid two-legged, slowly maturing dependents. You two are the primary playthings.

However, older children, in and out of your custody, might be involved. Then the major concern is what they do with the Courtier and what he does with them. He has little choice but to hang on the edge until they like him. He figures his one and only necessary connection is to you, so he's guiltless toward others. His relationship to your family depends on what you demand as bottom-line courtesy. Often, they like him, since he's a likeable fellow. He pals with them, but rarely fathers.

As for his family, they've gotten quite used to him since childhood. He's always had his own pace, his own ways. They've never been able to make him conform. They've given up on bribes. If they grumble in quiet, that's all he expects. He's independent but distantly fond of them. He treats them like just people, not parents. The same goes for brothers and sisters.

He rarely grows close to your circle of friends, though he's polite and agreeable. He probably has, and makes, separate friends from you, both male and female. He may see them independently or he may bring them around; but for you to have two groups of friends is definitely not uncommon.

There's no way you can say he's everything. He's not the man on the white horse, the provider, or the chairman of your board. He's got other pluses and minuses: he's joy and pleasure, someone there, a lover, he's for spontaneity. Mostly he's there because you can't do it, feel it, and be it all on your own. You can't expect him to save for a rainy day or build formidable foundations. He probably won't lavish you with diamonds, although he may use your money from a joint account to get you some – unannounced. He's an easy rider.

What Is in Store for You?

Too many King Arthurs can try any Guinevere to her limit. After all, how much did she see of him? He was always off ruling, warring, and pontificating, while she turned into a dowager. If Arthur had owned a telephone, he'd have been on it day and night. Sooner or later almost any lady is ready for Sir Lancelot – attentive, delighting in your society (although not a bit ambitious). Or, better yet, Sir Galahad – known for his courtesy, humility, and quiet wisdom despite his youth.

If you're ready to spend what you have – money, status, sex, looks – and the Courtier offers what you like – sex, looks, company, congeniality – the ride can be fine. But it's best to know consciously what you're doing. The Courtier is flattering to you. So remember the old maxim: flatterers always live at the expense of the one who listens.

Still, if you want music to your ears, not to mention to the rest of your body, and you don't care about costs – it's nobody's business but yours. The Courtier isn't a first affair. He comes as step two – step one is you. Before he happens, you've reached a new conclusion about what's good for you. The Moguls, Geniuses, and Woman Haters no longer look like prime rib. Rather they look like gristle. You've decided that hard work, good income, glory, and prestige in a man are usually more crunch than munch. Besides, you've got enough of that stuff in your refrigerator and now you want some salad days! All is not easy with the Courtier, but if you are confident enough of your intentions, you *can* overcome the obstacles, for Courtiers really do reciprocate. They make margaritas *and* love.

Right from word one, your having things he hasn't presents problems, and you have to discover how you both feel about that. You go through delicate maneuvers to discover answers to certain questions. What does he want? Has he got what I want? Am I flirting? Is he swindling? Who's on top? Usually, you do this figuring-out undercover.

The first phase is private because it also has another reason: you need time to reprogram your computer, to dig down and decide just how much normality means to you and if you can disregard convention. If you can't fight the conservative streak within you, or feel that you'll always remain embarrassed in public, probably your partnership stops there. But if you can fight your conservative streak, you then incorporate, go public, and take stock of the reactions. Things can quickly become no laughing matter. Potentially you face not only angry elders but nasty children. You need to band together against gossip and derision.

It's usually then that you have your first split. Bad times usually don't bring out the best in *any* couple. It's now you face pitfalls and boredom. Perhaps you really didn't have enough between you. Then there's the dead end that sophistication can bring: to handle your friends you act so jaded, you hurt your lover's feelings. Or you might discover that despite what you thought, you just can't handle the affair. Guilt, shame, or jealousy is wreaking havoc in your brain.

But usually only very independent women go for Courtiers. So for you, fighting other peoples expectations and oversimplifications is routine. What makes or breaks the relationship is what you have between you and whether you continue to mellow, for even the Courtier requires surrender. You may not be willing to lose control. You may not succeed. You might totally triumph. Even so, while you eventually outlive criticism, other adjustments continue to arise. Even friendly children can present a constant problem. They tend to switch you out of parent and into peer, since you're doing what young people do, not what parents ought to. Without your old parental stance, you have to restructure discipline. They might flout convention, get in trouble, and claim it's imitation of you. And your parents can be a problem, too. Most likely they'll put you through at least a few hoops.

You two are faced with all the problems that any couple has, plus a few new ones. Dominance is always an issue. Dependence and fear can nag at you. Even if all else goes well, you've got a worse old-age problem than most. In the worst of Courtier unions, you stick together like master and dog. In the best of Courtier twosomes, sooner or later you equalize who has and who hasn't, who gives and who takes, who domineers and who doesn't. And you go long-term because you're developing, because you're in love.

What Are the Telltale Signs of Trouble?

All that glitters isn't gold: sometimes it's gum wrappers or con games. So watch out. There's a big difference between a Courtier and a thief. Make sure you've got the one and not the other. The best way is to exercise caution.

Recently, a woman wrote a letter to "Dear Abby." A younger man, unknown to her, had shown up at her husband's funeral. He said he had known her husband, and then began coming over to see her. He was charming and genteel. She started to desire his comfortable companionship, but a sixth sense told her to check him out. To her shock and her saving, she found out he'd collected off an armload of widows.

Real Courtiers don't approach you out of the blue. You meet them the way you would anyone else – through work, mutual acquaintances, and social events. They haven't lived off one single woman after another, although you may not be the first. They're just people of the moment, and somehow you hit it off. Usually, when a true Courtier flags you down, he offers a voucher: he may well be a user, but he's rarely a borrower. (Only much later, as his partner, might you lend him money.) The only odd thing about him is that *you* have what *he* should have, according to prevalent custom.

There are some definite indications when you're involved with him if things aren't going as they should be: if he's got a wandering eye, or if you're getting restless, or jealously seeing the green-eyed monster. Even worse is if one of you grows possessive and allows the other no breathing space (generally it's you over him). Of if someone plays games to make the other upset. Any relationship grows crow's feet. But in a Courtier union they should look like laugh lines. No matter what your age, your bank account, or your wisdom, when the wrinkles turn downward, it means you aren't having such a good time. Of all men, the Courtier should offer some sort of ecstasy.

What Are Your Chances and What Should You Do?

Anyone for that $64,000 question? When you ask about chances with the Courtier, there's no simple answer. Is it a good thing to do? Depends on you. Will it last? Sometimes yes, sometimes no. Odds are against it at the moment, but times are changing, and, throughout history, some have always made it. Are the short-term benefits worth it? They might be and they might not be – 60-40 for it.

The Courtier remains hard for most people to handle. Outside of a few super-cities and fast classes, it's still rough to turn tables on what's expected of males and females. But it's *not* impossible. In a small coastal California town I met a woman in her forties living with a twenty-year old man. They were open about it, which is healthy, but so defensive that you could tell their honesty was costly. She was walking the edge of outcast status. And yet *everywhere* you meet forty-year-old men with twenty-year-old women. In most places it still takes courage for cowgirls to tell the world nobody can take away their gusto.

But think about it. Your pleasure merits holding onto even in the face of an adverse community. After all, being pushed around by custom is like acting out of guilt, shame, and fear. Social rules aren't really *real;* they're just ideas. And it's pretty silly indeed when a rule that nobody you know invented comes between you and how you feel.

If you're more comfortable with the socially accepted, admit it to yourself. If the particular stresses in the Courtier combination are more than you care to handle, O.K., look for a man who fits your expectations and with whom you have a better chance. Keep your zest – but keep it in more commonplace ways.

Otherwise, *I'm* all for adventure. If he comes along and looks interesting, try the Courtier. See where it gets you. But only under certain conditions. Both of you have to *know* that with the right attitude you have nothing to lose. And don't forget it! You should foresee the possibility that you or he will end it. You're more likely to cut it short at first. He's more likely to farther on down the line. As in any relationship, to get the best from the Courtier you have to give yourself to it. If you just toy around or try to control him, you're probably Baby Chasing in reverse – it's called Chicken Stalking. I don't think it's any better or less exploitive when women do it than when men do. When the man is very young, it's *very* bad. On the other hand, if you're both of age and both choose a carnal caper, it's your affair. Still, if you aim to get something from him but keep him from getting much from you, neither of you is bound to get much at all.

A permanent Courtier alliance, or a mutually successful temporary one, requires you to give more of yourself than is usual – not only emotionally, but in territory, money, and place in the community. In no union can you keep everything in your own hands, and only one approach is operable here. That is, what you use and what you lose simply don't matter. If you start to fear for your property, you'd better back off.

If you come to hunger for someone whose intellect, ambition, and knowledge are closer to your own, it bodes a bleak future. Individuals don't necessarily need a lot of similarities to establish a solid foundation, but certain correspondences do help. You may drift apart because the pleasure was ephemeral, the first flash fizzled. Or you might still be getting over other types of men. You tried a new idea, but the Courtier proved transitory. Or he might be too devoted, like a child to a teacher, and the adoration held no payoff for you.

In any of these situations you should put the whole business in a file marked "inactive" and start on a new case study. But if all goes well and more interest, richness, and affection develop, buck tradition and fight to keep your Courtier affair alive.

Where Do You Fit In?

So Courtiers are looking luscious. But you're not sure of your own black-widow potential You suspect you might want this man just to use him and toss him. Or else Courtiers have come and gone and left a bitter taste, and you wonder who's at fault.

It's probably harder than you think to do the Courtier right. It's no good if you start out a Courtier relationship in less than the best climate. You need to work for an awareness of what you're in for. Consider some bad reasons: deep down underneath, you may need to show off that you can have or can lure a young, attractive man. Then you discover that while you may desire an exciting mate to prove your value or provide an escort, a man on a leash doesn't make you look better. He makes you look worse. Perhaps instead you're afraid to look as if nobody finds you sexy. Or you fear that, all alone, your erotic desires might shrivel and die – you want to reassure yourself by having a lusty admirer. If so, then you need to realize that sexual confidence is hard to gain. It comes internally, not from alluring partners. And while you may go through periods without a bedmate, that doesn't mean you have lost your fire. If there's any coal that rekindles instantly, it's your remembrance of things past – and how to do them!

If you're separated, divorced, or widowed, and the months stretch on an on, don't jump on the Courtier to avoid the mourning process. If he's the man who comes along when you're ready, that's fine, but he's no shortcut. Wait, no matter how long, until you're resilient and ready. And don't give up hope of love.

Often, women go into a Courtier affair as if on a spending spree. Then the spendthrift instinct dwindles and results in a double bind. They want to keep the relationship but want to put a lid on financial and psychological expenses. If that happens to you, consider this: monetary and sharing problems with the Courtier are not that dissimilar to those in any union. If you feel you must change things, you'd better discuss it honestly with him. All too often women fear they'll lose a lover if they change any rules. But if you don't clarify your concerns, your worry is bound to surface in unpleasant ways – you'll belittle your man in public, or in private get sour. Rather than do that, better to announce your anxiety and hope for the best. It's hard enough for a man with less and a woman with more to maintain mutual respect. Don't worsen the situation with corrosive tendencies. Take the chance of loss and keep your policies open. You can find joy almost anywhere. Don't dispel the happiness that comes from seemingly upside-down, unexpected situations. Every time you worry about convention and what people will think, remind yourself that it doesn't *matter*. Your value comes from *you*. And so do your values.

A Courtier can be an Idle Lord, doing nothing, never working, and that's bad. He can also be a loving, Many-Faceted Man, and that's the best.

Only rarely would he be the Kid. But if he is the Kid, who is the subject of the next chapter, don't do him. The Courtier should be for pleasure, and the Kid is too much work. The Kid can be fine for some women, but only very special women. So, before you get too involved with the man who's a perennial child – for that's what the Kid is – you should find out if you're one of the special women. Because chances are, you're not. Few women are.

The Kid

The Proverbial Boy-Man
Who Never Grows Up

A time machine came along and froze the Kid just at the moment when he stood between youth and maturity. It transfixed him forever in that awkward age. Then, despite all efforts to prevent it (letters from his doctor, Coke-bottle eyeglasses, color blindness, and *selective* deafness), he was drafted into adulthood.

It was a mistake. He should have been 4F. But now that he's in the army of aging humanity, he's found one way to fit. He plays perpetual recruit. He locates a sergeant, a mess hall and barracks, and becomes Beetle Bailey. Under the charge of his superior officer he bungles most chores and errands. He never had to figure out what orders to give. He may end up with menial tasks and occasional K.P. duty, but he runs no risk of promotion. He's such a duck that most people let him alone, which is, of course, just what he wants.

The Kid will never grow up all the way. He's real nice; everybody likes him. He's good-humored and tells jokes, although they don't always work. But he certainly doesn't pull his weight in his daily duties. It's enough that he keeps a job. He usually manages that.

He is, however, a steadfast husband and daddy for the kids and often he's one thing more – an almost genius who displays a streak of brilliance that becomes his saving grace. The world acclaims him and you get off on it. Perhaps he's one of the only people in the world who knows the formula and properties of Nucleicgastropotiasis-13. Or can run the LXMN-532 computer, translate Middle Minoan, or tune ZYT Typhoon racing cars. He read when he was two and did fractions at four. He took his mother's washing machine apart and put it back together again (with two more experimental gears, it never washed again) at five.

Everybody knows he's a former whiz kid. As he grew bigger, they let him turn his whiz into a sweet, passive knack for getting everyone else (especially women) to do everything for him, to care for him like a child and not get angry about it.

When it comes to ladies, he's negatively selective: he lets women pick him. Sometimes they directly go after him, sometimes he hangs around so incessantly they pick him because he's so there. Either way, it cuts his effort in half. That means he ends up with shy, but resolute women. She's decisive, has ability, efficacy and tenacity. Her fortitude offers him a Linus blanket. She's everything an admiral should be. And to him that's paradise. He can bumble away in peace and tranquility and leave her to run his life.

Story

Sonia, whom I've known since elementary school, didn't really start out the Kid's sort of woman. She became that way by adapting. And that's just how she coupled with Ollie.

Sonia was shy, but too proud to let it show. So she set up making herself as undetectable, undelectable, and nondescript as possible. The good-old-reliable-in-the-background-good-sport, friend-to-everyone-will-do-all-the-jobs-nobody-else-wants-to-do type girl. She got all the way through high school and beyond pretty successfully, but pretty much un-dated. She never appeared lonely, though, just not . . . noticed. Then all of a sudden she decided she didn't want the unattached act to continue.

Behind her screen she had always been a hard driver and a high achiever. When she wanted something, she got it. She had excellent grades and was a fine pianist. She worked on committees, helped put out the school newspapers, and could bake a better chocolate cake than anyone else. True, she had never known how to be or get what the so-called "popular" women could. But then she'd never tried.

About that time she noticed Ollie. Not that Ollie was new. He tripped into the crowd somewhere along the line (nobody remembered when). In fact, except for when he was fussing with electrons, protons, and neutrons, he was virtually always underfoot. Nobody ever shooed him away, yet nobody ever took him seriously either. He was *tolerated* more than anything else. He fumbled everything he tried to do. But he was funny and canny. Ollie didn't appear aware of women at all. It seemed the only figures he cared about were algebraic, and the only mass that mattered to him was relative. Yet he preferred female company and hung out with women more than men. Women rarely played basketball, at which he was hopeless. Women put up with him with more resignation. Once convinced of his total ineptitude, they simply ceased expecting him to do anything. They did it themselves. Besides, Ollie really was interested in women and in sex, he just didn't know how to go about it.

Sonia started thinking. While the others had jealousies, heartbreaks, and disasters, she saw something unique, albeit odd, right in her own backyard – Ollie. She didn't want to play the field and go through a lot of men, nor did she want to become a bench-sitter and have none. In Ollie she saw a man who would be all hers, with permanence practically guaranteed. Her only competition was a cyclotron. To Sonia that was worth a lot of other prices: drinks spilled in her lap, broken dishes, pink laundry, and so on.

So she asked Ollie to dinner – candles and everything. She took him on a picnic, to the zoo, to a concert. Then she led him to bed. Neither one of them knew much about sex firsthand, although Ollie was certainly avid and eager. But both had *read* a lot. They developed a simple sort of devouring style that suited them both. Besides, their sex life, if not elaborate, had a special quality: no one else had ever shared it. Eventually it led to the nuclear fusion of a family.

Maybe you could call their life restrictive. To this day Sonia never lets anything, including friends, work, and outside interests, interfere with her purpose. She deals in daily activities while Ollie dwells in some microcosm. He's charming, aggravating, gentle, awkward, apologetic, and irredeemably forgetful. He looks twelve; Sonia looks older. He doesn't seem to know Sonia is around. You couldn't say she gets much attention. But if his mind isn't at home, it's only with some atom or other. He doesn't provide an explosive life – sex is no big deal to Sonia. But it's enough to keep them happy.

What would happen if she ever needed more fun from him? That's the unbroached question. So far she's got the hatches battened down. But lately a crack has appeared. Sonia has voiced some complaints. She didn't really think Ollie would stay so irresponsible, nor did she foresee that her work would expand so rapidly while his participation remained so totally unchanged. She thought perhaps, as the chores grew, he'd at least take to helping with them, if not handling one area of their lives, but he hasn't. She has to deal with everything – kids, schools, transportation, house, banking, insurance, purchases, trips, social life, relatives, health, pets. She also didn't realize Ollie would take her for granted quite so much. But the attention he pays her has become increasingly haphazard. He loves her, but he treats her like a "good old chair" that's always there. Nor did Sonia realize that in so fiercely wrapping herself around her Ollie, she would end up walling herself off a good deal from the outside world. She leads a completely relationship- and family-oriented life despite her work. At first she was proud. Now she finds herself making sure never to tell or show any outsider her true feelings. She always presents a cheery, no-problems, couldn't be happier wife-mother-matron front. One of Sonia's friends left her marriage to Ollie's buddy because she could no longer stand the work, antics, and neglect, unintentional as they were. Sonia also knows that some people find amusement in her and Ollie's isolated devotion and the way she has to be a mother hen.

Not many women are like Sonia. Most want more emotion and attention. Sonia rarely "bothers" Ollie for anything. Not many women would like the tremendous load of responsibilities, or the exasperation of dealing with a continuously scatterbrained, preoc-cupied, or comic partner. Sonia gets to run her ship and be Ollie's first and only mate, but she doesn't get to make the kind of waves that bring change and variety into life. Still, Sonia is generally happy with the bargain she struck. While Ollie, the Kid, isn't right for many, he's been pretty good for her and she's determined they'll succeed.

The Kid is a matter of weights and balances. He's got his virtues but has plenty of drawbacks as well. At least he's easy to recognize. Just think of Harpo Marx, Lou Costello, Jerry Lewis, Stan Laurel, and Einstein – rolled into one likable klutz. What's hard to see is that he aims to stay the way he is – and how much you can take.

How Can You Identify This Kind of Man?

You can't say the Kid walks into your life. He stumbles. He doesn't exactly court you – he shows up hungry. He *still* scarfs a bowl of granola before he takes you out to dinner. And he'll always think hamburgers, hot dogs, Coke, and instant oatmeal are a gourmet's delight.

The Kid, what can you say? He's so boyish, so *seemingly* without guile, so wide-eyed and charming... plunk, you're sunk. Even those who won't go out with him let him hang around. Each Kid provides a new meaning for incompetence. He's not outwardly lazy; indeed, he tackles everything. He just manages not to be able to *do* anything. And in the most amazing ways: he can't boil an egg, can't change a tire, can't write a check. And worst of all, he can't pick up a dropped towel or dropped jockey shorts. He never sees anything below his knees.

He even looks like an eternal adolescent. The parts of his body seem to belong to different people, some full grown, some not. His arms hang too low or too high, never at his hip line. His feet were meant for someone bigger. He hasn't quite filled out yet. His beard is still trying to thicken, or else he can't quite keep up with it and at-tacks it only randomly. He suffers from chronic colic and cowlick.

He either lacks hand-eye coordination, or else he merely absents his mind from his errand. If it's the particular job at which he's expert, however, suddenly he's dexterous and precise as can be. One of the few ways he connects his brain to his daily survival is his humor. He gets a lot of mileage out of his boyish grin and wit. He turns clumsy into comic. He creates a perfect evasionary tactic. He fails at little things so amusingly that few recognize the truant that dwells within.

Behind his bumbling facade, he's honest and true. He can't tell a lie. He has no way to hide one. When shirking work, he just keeps quiet or finds some sudden reason to do something else, and hopes no one will notice. If caught, he feigns surprise, immediately jumps in, and promptly knocks over the pot he's asked to stir.

Basically he's a happy person even though he lives almost exclusively in his own world. To him life is always like a day that Mother Earth bakes cookies. He's as spaced out and delirious as a child in an enchanted forest, always engrossed in his own mind. But like a dreamy child, he misses many things in his blissful wandering. He pays little heed to people's coming and goings, so naturally he commits multiple faux pas. You never know when he'll embarrass you, like a boy who yells, "But I'm twelve," when you get him an eleven-and-under ticket. You also don't know how or when he'll hurt your feelings. He'll hardly notice your crying, much less a new dress. One of his drawbacks is that he never learns. He makes the same mistake time and again. He wants to make amends, but he doesn't know how.

Outer Signs

The Kid's clothes never fit right. Just how badly depends on who bought them. When he shops alone he always gets the wrong size. What's more, he picks such unlikely colors and styles that people cross the street when they see him coming. The more you don't like his garments, the more he wears them. Soon people try to take over and give him proper outfits, thinking they are helping him. He puts their selections deep in his closet. Then one day he goes on a safari through his belongings and puts together an outfit of gift items in a way no one else would be able to conceive. As a result, he does have his own definite style. You could call it contemporary-historical conglomeration in the casual mode. Often he ends up in T-shirts and jeans on which he spilled acid. His tennis shoes lace to the shin bone. (He thinks he has weak ankles.) Whatever his shoe size, you're tempted to bronze them. No one else could mold footwear into such a formation.

His skin is a disaster, part of his continued adolescence. His fingernails are down to the quick and not necessarily clean. He doesn't like the sun in his face, so he collects baseball caps, which is a good thing with his cowlick. His features don't matter to him. He never looks at them.

The only way he could possibly make the whole thing work is to become the Kid.

Most often he owns a bus, a van, or a big old car or wagon. He needs room for a lot of objects in his vehicle: old tires, greasy machines, microphones, amplifiers. Usually the Kid has an affection for his car as if it were his pal. He *wipes* it a lot instead of cleaning it. He might put on decals, but otherwise he won't decorate it. Or he might keep the outside exactly as it came but strip down the inside and add a mobile tool warehouse, small laboratory, or some other madness. He might also be a bus and subway taker who can whiz across any route.

His living space is just as you would guess – like the wreck of the Hesperus. When you meet him, he lives in a room in someone's basement, often his parents'. Or perhaps he hibernates in a converted garage. Or he might share an old frame house with five other Kids, where nobody does the dishes. Disarray somehow makes him comfortable.

When it comes to decoration, he thinks of paint (he reaches the same conclusion when it comes to covering dirt). He has a facility of picking the most garish colors imaginable, like a combination of canary yellow, avocado, and electric blue. He might have a few posters that, once up, he never takes down. Soon they look as if they were left by the former tenants – or the tenants before that. Or perhaps you can't see them behind the enormous T.V. antennae anyway. If you're the decorator and you ask him to hang a picture, he'll require four helpers. He *thinks* he's the fix-it type. But it's not worth asking him. It just doubles the labor. Of course, some Kids always seem busy at something. In fact, he appears tireless. He keeps the world's oddest schedule and needs the least sleep. He works from two to six A.M., then sleeps from seven to eleven after two bowls of Cheerios. Then he's up at his employment, prowling garage sales, or looking at old books. Then he shows up at someone's home just in time for supper. He eats seven meals a day – anytime and anyplace. Or he eats no *formal* meal but snacks without stop.

Actually he treats himself quite well, just in an idiosyncratic manner. He certainly sees to it that he's left unbothered. He gets himself relieved of all petty time-consuming duties or thought-consuming decisions.

Sex Signals

The Kid doesn't treat women as mothers, he just brings out the mothering in them. Few women can compensate for his incompetence any other way. He develops a client-manager contract with a woman – he the client, you forever his manager. He grows so dependent it's hard to say if he loves you or grows increasingly fond of you.

It's also hard to say whether he's sexual or not. Some Kids don't seem much to notice whether sex happens or not. Others are as avid about sex as they are their other compulsions.

The Kid who isn't very sexual waits for you to approach him. He pairs up a little or a lot later than other men. He slows down his rate of lovemaking fairly rapidly after your first days of pairing. You have to remind him.

The Kid that likes sex also doesn't exactly approach you romantically either. Rather, he waits on your runway. He comes over or hangs around so incessantly, any other suitor who comes to your door has to pass him – your personal court jester. Or he calls and calls, harder to shake off than a Siamese twin. He plays a waiting game. He'll try and try again. As a result, this kind of Kid pairs up surprisingly early. He find his caretaker, settles in and settles down by his late teens and early twenties.

Either way, in his first approach with you the Kid disguises any strong sexual motivation. When something sexual finally happens – a kiss or an embrace – it happens as if unexpected, almost accidental. He seemingly bumps into you and it turns into a kiss. He drops something and as you pick it up, he accidentally falls on top of you. Once kissing and touching are broached, he's affectionate, but often so eager he leapfrogs right for sex and skips the warm-up. He needs instruction and often never quite discovers what you want. He's energetic more than erotic. He sticks to simple basics and some of the milder variations. Then he falls asleep – *instantly*. He'd rather make love lots of times in one night than once every day. Very sexually charged Kids aren't longer lovers – just frequent.

Both kinds of Kids are often premature ejaculators.

Some young Kids, and some divorced ones as well, can become Hustlers under their beguiling cover. They streak away at one-night stands. But not so strangely, as they get older and older, the perennial Kid finds fewer and fewer women to sleep with.

Money Markers

The Kid doesn't use much of *anybody's* money. Some make big bucks – from their electronics or whatever. Many are lawyers or accountants. Others never make much money. If his genius brings monetary rewards, that's fine, but he'd rather fiddle than work hard for money. He doesn't keep track of finances. You do.

Since he doesn't ever know exactly how much money you have (he assumes you know), he's a moderate spender. He takes great delight in saving and using old, used things. He finds funny bargains and gleefully feels he tricked the merchant. He buys leftover paint cans, clocks that work except for one part, or wrapped mystery packages that were lost in the mail. Often he ends up losing money. He often has no cunning about what he's doing, so he winds up with items that were no bargain at all. He does short-form taxes even when he shouldn't. He doesn't read the fine print in contracts and makes verbal agreements and gets sued. His needs aren't elaborate. You and he probably don't go out much either. At best you attend third-run movies or go to places where unknown bands try out.

Family Aspects

When it comes to fatherhood he says, "Sure, that'd be nice," as if that's all there is to it. He rarely thinks of what's involved, even later, when you're snowed under a mountain of diapers right before his very eyes. He thinks kids are playmates and, besides, *you're* there to feed them. He's totally unmindful of their schedule.

Yet in most ways he's really a great father. Since he's just like his children, they think he's a pal, not a parent. And they're always sure of his love. Half the time he's with them you never know where they are, what they're doing, or when they'll show up again. But while you may not think they rest in safe hands, somehow they always come back whole.

The Kid's parents tend to shake their head a lot. There's nothing else they *can* do. They don't understand what *didn't* happen to him. But they really can't fault him, because he's nice and he's smart. He hardly hears what they're saying, but he smiles fondly at them. He loves them but thinks of them as misguided peers. You'll have to be the one who takes their calls, advice, and admonitions. He can never be found. They're grateful to you.

As for your family, he'll pull your fathers and brothers right back to puberty with him, leaving all the women cooking and cleaning in the kitchen, when he can. Your mother and sisters will disgustedly lose patience, but in his presence will remain totally disarmed.

The Kid collects a parcel of friends who all look like odds and ends. He makes pals of everyone as he goes along. Some are short-term, some long-term, some clear from elementary school. He's not at all good at making enemies, which is too bad, because he tends to get cheated. Due to his indiscriminate nature, all too often he opens himself, you, and the children up for unnecessary blows from the world. But he's better off gullible than *completely* cut off.

Despite how friendly he is and how many buddies he has, he manages a funny separation from his pals. He always remains autonomous enough to do his own thing. Since much of his life is mental, nobody *can* enter it.

When people refer to him, they use the phrase "put up with." Or they ask, "How do you do it?" but don't expect an answer. Nobody shuns him. Nobody screams at him. The worst he receives is nagging after he's been really detached. He rarely gets angry though he can certainly whine. He hardly ever changes. In fact, no one expects or encourages him to alter. That's his major problem: he's gotten everyone to consider him his own justification. Whenever he breaks a lamp, falls down the stairs, or pours lemonade down a bodice, everyone says, "Oh, it's just him." As if just being the Kid explains – and excuses – everything.

What Is in Store for You?

He bumbles into your women's committee meeting one more time to ask where the screwdriver is. He just *has* to know what's happening, and any excuse will do. Then he addles the ladies so much that when he finally goes they start talking about men instead of grass-roots congressional bills. And you know you'll have to do all the campaigning yourself because the meeting accomplished nothing. That sort of day epitomizes life with the Kid to a T.

Two things lie in store for you with the Kid. One is that what he *doesn't* do is what's in your future. (And if you are blinded by his brilliant part and counting on the rest of him to catch up, better count again.) The other is that rather than being completely a waif, you have to realize he's more of an *enfant terrible*. The Kid may look insignificant but he's the world's greatest scene stealer. He always finagles the center of attention. So no matter what you do, your role with him is in the orchestra pit. Simplicity of character doesn't mean he lacks guile. The Kid likes attention and he has his genius to attract it. After all, he's good enough to manage a lifelong portrayal of someone on the brink of adolescence. (Obviously he's realized that his freedom is invested in it's maintenance.) And he's good enough to take star billing no matter how much you do and how little he does.

But let's go back to number one, that what he *doesn't* do is what lies in your future, and what this means. The Kid successfully learned what we'd all like to know: how *not* to do what you don't want to do. How does he do it? When some people leave gaps in conversations, you know how you feel compelled to fill them? You find yourself chattering away out of compulsion or embarrassment. *Anything* to avoid a heavy, awkward silence. The Kid is one of those people – only with him it's actions, not words. The more he leaves, the more you do for him, filling in the gaps of what he doesn't accomplish. And the more you do, the more he leaves for you. His appetite for irresponsibility is almost infinite. He not only silently encourages you to overdo, he somehow pushes you to do it.

Your role has a way of growing ever bigger and bigger. You become like the lady in the commercial who stands by the back door of her home, arms extended. Children, dogs, and husband heap dirty clothes on her as they exit. When the camera moves outside, you see that she lives in a box of laundry detergent.

In time, because of all you do for him, your life gets completely wrapped up with him, and you eventually begin to feel boxed in. Constant duty tends to make people feel that way. Maybe something comes along that breaks your (the camel's) back, and you protest, but more often something else happens. You alter yourself in such a way that no load becomes too heavy for you. You turn into a Valkyrie, or perhaps a battle-axe. Mind you, you don't necessarily receive more adoration for your increased ministrations. Though in some corner of his mind the Kid thinks lovingly of you, mostly he takes the ease you give him to drift off all the more into his own preoccupation. In fact, he practically *vaporizes*. He becomes the invisible man. Soon you find yourself clinging to the idea that he loves you more than to any demonstration of his love, because the demonstrations grow rarer.

On the other hand, the Kid does offer you a straight and steady road. The twists and curves are few. He's unlikely to leave you. He rarely has amorous adventures. He comes home to eat, but he may be unwilling to go out at night or take any holidays. His idea of a vacation is to be in a mobile home where you are still in the same situation you have at home. Only on wheels. Eating out means pizza. Chop suey ranks as fancy. When you insist on relaxation, he thinks in terms of playgrounds and campgrounds. He may not only forget birthdays, he won't even know it's Sunday.

Also very much on the bright side, you get one advantage from the Kid that few men provide. You take no guff from him. He doesn't care how things are done, banked, or bought. Anything you do is O.K. He never appraises or criticizes you. He's a guaranteed opportunity to run your own country, your way. You may have to provide the labor, of course, but you're also the boss.

In the end of a long, long run with the Kid, you tend to grow into one of those couples who are so interdependent they need no one else. Sometimes they're sweet, sometimes they're grumpy. You could be either way.

What Are the Telltale Signs of Trouble?

If a creature like one of Walt Disney's unwieldy dragons starts licking your fingers, stop and think about it. Consider the cost of his Purina – and if you're willing to pay it. Remember, his rapid heartbeat means he has to eat and eat – and eat. And just count how often he's caught in awkward situations or how many times he breaks the china.

In quite a different twist from other kinds of men, the Kid turns out to be exactly what he seems. It's your first warning when he keeps on *not* getting any older or any more graceful.

It's a second and more serious warning if he doesn't notice your moods and feelings. But it's worse if *you* don't. You can tell things are bad when you're angry, sad, elated, miserable, or about to crack into crumb cake, but keep acting like a robot. If you exist simply to *operate*, you're heading for problems.

If your Kid is so oblivious and inattentive that he can't come through for you when the chips are down, heed this. You can't need someone who isn't there to need. In that case you'll have to send him away and hire help. If he returns nothing you should cut the leash and turn your attention to those who pay back – namely you.

And if he does come through for you, consider yourself vindicated. Despite the trials and tribulations, you were right to be there all along.

What Are Your Chances and What Should You Do?

What do you do about the Kid?

Of course, typical of life's problems, there's no one right answer. You could stay with him, leave him, stay and try to change him, or *leave* and try to change him. You could also stay with him only a while and then leave him. Or you could do *all* of the above in any order you choose. But what's best? Well, here's the hint. Staying with him but attempting changes probably outweighs the other choices. Leaving him (or threatening to) in order to enact change, then going back to him, is highly common and ranks as second choice. But if you're fed up to the gills and think that changing him is an impossibility, your only choice is to head for the hills.

The Kid can change only in measured degrees. I wouldn't expect miracles. He's always going to be what he is. But after all, he doesn't carry a hard line of unalterable male superiority. He doesn't even play the game of "If you really loved me, you'd clean my tub for me." He just plays deaf and blind. And he's probably never heard an ultimatum or had his shades knocked off. You simply have to bring what you consider intolerable to his attention, but only do so if you really mean to change him. There's a common word for half-hearted notification. It's called "nagging." Any child knows that when you say, "If you don't straighten out . . ." that you don't really mean it. In fact, you're stating that you expect repetition. Watch those "If you don't"s and stick to "I am" (followed by action) statements. Move things steadily by insistent steps to bring matters to a head. And remember he'll always need plenty of time to himself.

It may turn out that you simply misread your capacity, that you need more attention, more help, and much less work. He may never come up to the responsible companion of your desires. In this case, contemplate a friendly, loving leaving. You don't have to carry on. Backing out is one kind of winning: it offers the relief of one less person who requires your constant service. With the Kid it's better to go with sad resignation than with anger. He's such a resilient and entrenched character that if you can't take him, leave him, and don't waste time on blame.

On the other hand, he may be your cup of tea even if he never budges an inch and you have to make all the crumpets. So if you elect to stay with him, try to accept the situation. Don't fault him, and avoid becoming claustrophobic. Deep down you may prefer to read Agatha Christie rather than handle the push and pull of a more attentive relationship. There's nothing wrong with that. A lot can be said for having someone around *not* to talk to. As for the work and responsibility, just consider that you're getting executive training. Not everyone gets to be both labor and management. Maybe you can use your experience later. You can open a hangout for wayward juveniles. Or you may want to think of yourself as a single parent. Read all you can about unitary parenthood. Your stress, your fatigue, your problems, will be very similar. When the buck stops with you all the time, it's never easy. But at least your big Kid returns to your bunk in a way that little ones don't.

Where Do You Fit In?

You may need distance but avoid recognizing the fact. You may want intimacy but so divert it into mothering that you defeat yourself. Two very different propositions, it's true. But either one can lead to a stint with the Kid. For that matter, you might have both tendencies, mixed up. You might seek removal or so want command that when you do draw close you only do so behind a maternal shield. An adult-to-adult love affair can be just *too* close. In either case, the Kid suits you. While staying relatively apart from him and/or providing for his care, you can remain the boss, and it's all right with him.

If you have either tendency, but don't care because things are fine and dandy with the Kid, great. But if you have a fatal weakness for the Kid, and are finding it less than satisfying, the time is nigh to determine if you have one or both of the above predilections. How much does distance really mean to you, you might ask yourself; and how much do you want to make sure you stay in command of a relationship? And, how much might you perhaps unconsciously equate nurturing with loving?

It isn't strange that with either trait you would still seek out a relationship. In the first place, women often have trouble admitting their fear of too much closeness or loss of control in a union. After all, according to popular credo, you're supposed to want a man and even be love crazy. It's hard for any woman to own up to contrary tendencies. If you prefer remoteness or no relationship at all, people ask, "What's wrong with you?" As for the second factor, you may have also *learned* to equate mothering with romance, so that you now do it quite unwittingly. All women in our society are taught to nurse and nurture to some degree. One can easily confuse romantic concern with maternal concern. It could be that you learned no other version of love. Care simply meant "taking care of." But if that's so, it's sad. To view loving only as care-taking is limiting. It narrows the huge emotional potential of love, and can often involve self-suffocation and self-denial.

If you discover you have either or both of the above tendencies, what can you do? Well, first you need to realize there's nothing wrong with finding that you're most comfortable without too much intimacy. You might not want the constant interaction of a close relationship. And that's fine. The only times it's bad are when the joy you take in solitude and having command is secret, when you think something is wrong with you, or when you use devious devices, such as mothering and overloading, to give you the distance you desire. Much better to declare forthrightly that too much closeness, or giving up command, isn't for you.

If you want to run the ship, however, there may be better alternatives than a Kid. Ones that mean less work, more attention, and more equality in your union. Check out the Loving Traditional Man, the Loving Many-Faceted Man, or the Loving Limited Partner unions, instead of getting attached to a perennial child.

You might also want to open yourself up to the discovery that adult love can have a far wider range of feeling than parental love. Perhaps you should sample some of the varieties of adult to adult love. Why get trapped in a colorless love by treating a man like a child, or in a nothing existence by being too tired to feel, when you could experience more? Certainly feelings can be frightening, and yes, they can mean some loss of control (a loss that is avoided by having maternal feelings only), but look at it this way – starting to explore your feelings doesn't mean you can't retreat. You can learn to . . . well, operate a swinging door. You could let in intimacy and sensation when you want them, and put up a Closed for Business sign when you need solitude. Chances are you can build such a swinging door better as an adult than as a mother.

You might discover mothering is not enough. If so, you might want to grow your Kid up, leave him, or avoid the ones that come by you. Then again, the Kid is a good man (if not for everyone), and as I said before, if both you and the Kid are happy with your relative removal from one another, and who takes care of whom, recognizing that you like and want it the way you have it can make life with the eternal boy easier.

You find a lot of Kids in urban centers where not growing up or being a comic are a way to survive. You also find a lot of Kids in men who go through painful divorces. They become so afraid of involvement, pain, or being interfered with by a woman, they turn into a combination of the Kid and the Short Affair and Quick Escape Artist.

Meanwhile, we've been slowly building up to the three kinds of wonderful men, and while the Kid is not yet there and not for everyone, he's well meaning, responsible, and yes, even caring.

Next is a man who is also good, but has one insidious drawback. And it's a major drawback. He's the Secret Manipulator. Trouble is, while the Kid is somewhat rare, the Manipulator is *very common*. In fact, he's probably the most common sort of man. Sweet, wonderful, caring, committed, he seems so concordant, yet somehow things always go his way. Chances are you've met him, been with him, or are with him. He's hard to spot, but he's willing to change once you catch him in his trickery. He's last on the list of men who might not be the best for you. But as with other men, what's bad for some women may be good for others. And he's close to the best

The Secret Manipulator

The Man Who Seems Wonderful and Everybody Loves, But Somehow He Always Gets His Own Way

Concealed in a haze of sunshine, as if there couldn't be anything devious about such a nice guy. Speaking in a code of direct honesty, as if he never says anything he doesn't mean. Listening through an attentive filter, as if he's heeding everything you say. He's the Secret Manipulator. He's so used to acting as if he's true blue, he even thinks he's being completely straight with you.

The Secret Manipulator hides his real intentions so well, he often doesn't even know he has them. You know he does, however, because somehow your plans and ideas always turn into puffs of thin air. No matter how *you* want to do something, it never happens. No matter how often he says he has no preference, he always gets it. He tells you to go ahead, handle things the way you want, but little do you know that when he gives you the wheel, he snaps on the automatic pilot. Happily you steer away, never knowing you're following the plan he already laid out.

The Secret Manipulator never thought much of himself when he was growing up. Dates, popularity, and sex were a long time coming. Jealously eyeing the jocks and class valedictorians, he learned to cultivate women, to find out how to be their friend and, more importantly, to make them friendly to *him*. But listening as if he really cared, and becoming a really nice guy, even *liking* women, didn't mean he didn't want to have control. Oh no. Underneath his loving front, he's refined manipulation to a high art. On the surface he's cooperative, kind, supportive, fair. Underneath he makes sure he always gets his own way.

He goes for women. Almost any women. But he likes earnest ones a little more than the others, because the more practical, straightforward and discussion-prone you are, the easier for him. And if you have the simple goal of just loving a nice guy with whom you feel pretty equal and can be best friends, he hits the jackpot. But he can mold himself to almost any variety of woman who comes along: tall, short, lively, sedate, career minded, domestic, snappish, or even-tempered.

Story

I've collected many, many stories about the Secret Manipulator. I'll tell you about Jill. She may seem an unlikely victim to you, but believe me, she's pretty typical.

Jill was a normal, sensible, capable woman who suddenly turned into a sputtering maniac. No one could see any reason for her metamorphosis. *Imagine* packing up and walking out on a nice man like David! The incidents mentioned certainly seemed trivial. She was just having a fit. Maybe it was her thyroid or pituitary? Had she seen a doctor lately?

David claimed total befuddlement. One day all was fine. The next day Jill started screaming and stalked out. (Of course there had been warnings; he just hadn't heeded them.)

Jill grew up as what used to be called a tomboy – in other words, healthy, independent, and full of strength. She went from tricycle to bicycle to car with glee. She loved making things, doing things, and using all her capabilities. When the idea of women's equal rights came along, it suited her nature. Without being political or fashionable, she set about finding a union that contained both love and symmetry.

She had met David long before and considered him just a friend. Then one day she took a whole new look at him. He adored women, espoused equality, and wanted a long-term partnership and maybe, later, a family. Jill, with all her common sense, decided David was a good bet. A long, cautious courtship ensued. Finally she moved in with him. But even that was no impulse. Being Jill, she wanted a good tryout before final commitment.

David was caring and devoted. He shared the household chores. He shared the business matters. They openly discussed all plans and finances. They never quarreled – they "hashed things out." Jill decided they had compatibility on almost every level. "A good working relationship," she called it. Besides, she really grew to love him, so the tryout became permanent.

But what Jill didn't see was that while talking about cooperative responsibility, David never let go of any of his. Instead, he merely transformed Jill into a secret pet. He let her talk about and decide all she wanted; meanwhile he did *everything the way he* thought best.

For example, it was Jill's assignment to pick their insurance. She made numerous inquiries, then made her decision. When she told David, he announced that just that morning he had purchased all the necessary policies. It seems he had independently called the various companies and reached his own conclusions.

David would ask Jill to choose the evening's entertainment. He didn't care, he said. He'd like whatever she chose. After Jill happily picked a play, they'd end up at the movies – bad American comedy, not even foreign drama! Jill would survey the pantry and make a grocery list. David would go to the store (it was his turn) but come back with everything different from what she asked for. When Jill went to purchase the car she wanted (a sports model), David said "wouldn't you rather?" so many times she found herself buying a hatchback wagon. She wanted a Lamaze birth, but as soon as things began to get difficult, he had her put under. How could she complain when the baby emerged healthy?

But if anything vexed her the most, it was sex. David had a problem with maintenance – he just came too fast. In fact, instantly. Being modern and open, they not only discussed it, they worked on it. But despite Jill's foreplay, afterplay, tricks, and bizarre devices, which did bring some satisfaction, David remained unchanged.

It was David's persistent sexual standstill that gave Jill the first insight into what was happening. When she realized that no matter what she did or said to David she never got through to him, she saw something remarkable. By getting in and out quickly, David could keep total command over himself. She realized that their sex life merely exaggerated everything else in their relationship. Deep down, David never delegated anything to anyone else's command. All her work, in bed and otherwise, was futile.

She began to view David as a sneaky opponent. She tried to fight, but she couldn't argue with him. He always listened, then he'd ask her to explain and reconstruct. In so doing, he trapped her into the old pattern. He skirted around her by agreeing with her and went on as before. When she tried to pin down how she always lost, she couldn't. Decisions just slipped through her fingers so insidiously, before she could say "Hey," it was too late.

One day she found herself alone at home. They were going somewhere that night she didn't want to go. She had agreed to "just this once" once again. The house was full of furniture she couldn't stand. Suddenly, it all became intolerable. As he came home and said, "Hi, honey," something snapped. She pulled down a suitcase, threw in some clothes, grabbed the baby, and said, "It's all yours. I've had enough."

David was flabbergasted. Over the next few weeks everyone lined up on his side as he played poor beleaguered victim. Jill wouldn't even speak to him, and became more furious and entrenched every time friends and family questioned her. Finally a friend suggested they seek counseling, at least in order to start talking.

Counseling was like a breath of fresh air. The counselor had seen and worked with Manipulators before, and knew what was happening with Jill. It was David that was the problem. For a long time he couldn't admit that he manipulated. He just tried agreeing with the counselor and Jill, meanwhile going along as before. But Jill meant business. She learned techniques to deal with him. She didn't let him "discuss" his way around things. She stopped him every time he said "wouldn't you rather?" and pointed out that no, it was he who "rathered" that way, not she. If he messed with her plans or arrangements she refused to go along with his "don't you think this is better?" claim. She also learned to change herself, to say clearly what she wanted, and not give way.

They are back together now, and the surprising thing is, not only is Jill happier, so is David. He didn't realize that by letting go of his tight, but secret, control, he could relax more. They're expecting another child soon.

He's a hard one to spot, the old Secret Manipulator. After all, manipulators are as manipulation is: indirect, inarticulate, and undercover. If things keep happening (or not happening) to you as if by magic, you have your first clue. The second one is equally indirect: if you're fuming and blathering, feeling like you're frittering your life away, you've probably got a Manipulator near. Nobody makes you angrier than a Secret Manipulator.

How Can You Identify This Kind of Man?

When it comes to prevalence, the Secret Manipulator is way up there. Almost every man has a little of him in there somewhere. But whether a man has a little or a lot, the manipulation boils down to one thing: *liking* women does not mean *trusting* them. While the Secret Manipulator *seemingly* accepts female persons as on a par with himself, secretly he's sure he's. . . if not superior, certainly more capable.

He was raised a boy, after all. And unconsciously he assumes males – or at least this male – are just a touch smarter, better, and more able than females. Often he grew up alone or with a brother, and no sister to tell him off. Besides, like anybody else, he wants what's best for, and what pleases, *him*. So when he combines his belief in his higher ability with his hidden self-indulgent streak, he comes out with a shiny key to a smooth existence: he relies only on himself. He knows, however, that only trusting himself strikes others as decidedly anti-social. People who won't release any decision to others appear too brittle for friendship. And repelling others, especially ladies, definitely acts against his best interest. So he curbs his egocentricity and covers it, only to pull it out at the last minute.

He seeks the company of women because they make his life more comfortable. It's not that he doesn't like men. He does. It's simply that he's not as sure he can get his way with men. When he believes he can hold on to the deciding factor – as he can with women – he feels more secure.

Outer Signs

He dresses for comfort. He's not a high-style man. He likes to look like the boy next door, your brother, and/or a milk drinker – somebody who's sincerely unpretentious. Look for him in cozy clothes, ever so slightly wrinkled, washed in Tide (by himself). He wears the same shoes (brown) till they look like Kentucky Fried Chicken legs.

He doesn't smell perfumed, but he doesn't smell sweaty either. He wafts . . . *humanity*. A very huggable odor. If he's tall, he tries to look shorter (more your size). If he's short, he jokes about it, as if he's sublimely synchronized for females.

He likes his car, and he keeps it quite a while. He's a long-time clinger. He prefers use and familiarity. His steering wheel has smooth spots; he holds it from the back side with the palm of his hand (it gives him the feeling he's heftier). There's an old blanket to wrap cold shoulders or a pillow that never leaves the vehicle. He drives a normal car. Part of his approach is never to be surprising. Look for him in almost any old car. Maybe a Honda Accord, a Toyota Corolla, a Ford Escort, a Chevy van, Volkswagen bus, or Datsun (before it became Nissan). He's also inclined to drive to the bus or train, then take public transportation while tying up the car for the day.

Often he's a do-it-yourselfer. His surroundings might show bits of carpentry or photography. The basement or garage become workrooms or darkrooms containing fix-it benches. Other than that, he's not much of a decorator. He surrounds himself with items made or picked by people he knows, rather than anything store bought. The objects he hangs on the wall are always in odd places. He needs help in the arrangement department. It takes him ten years to change anything.

His home or apartment is not in an especially nice or convenient area. It's maybe ten blocks farther out, up, or down than it should be. It's not that he's hanging back. It's because he just got tired of looking. Once situated, he hangs onto his spot. He's not much for leaving. He likes suburbs.

He's outwardly amiable. His conversation always contains a lot of questions. His walk is never too driven-looking, and he makes frequent stops. He always gives you three choices of where to go and what to do there. Sometimes you wonder if his personality resulted from Parent Effectiveness Training.

All in all, he treats himself quite well, except for one major failing – he's unable to furnish himself or you with complete honesty. Unconsciously or not, he lightly connives, slightly contrives, and even lies. He double talks, not telling you and maybe not telling himself what he really has in mind. He's thinking and scheming constantly and busily to make sure he stays in control, for which he pays an awful price: he doesn't *dare* let in diverting stimuli, including love. He can't recognize what's really going on around him. And he doesn't hear what you tell him.

Sex Signals

It's not unlikely that the Secret Manipulator finally pairs up with someone who *grows* to love him, rather than falling head over heels for him. That's his secret hope. Using his friendliness, his ease and harmony, and *all those questions*, he can talk to (and win) almost any woman. His desire to befriend women and his insightful perceptions about your life lead him to become almost everything he says he is as a man, and almost everything you could want. *Almost* is the key word here. He certainly seems as concerned with a woman's inner qualities as much as beauty. He grows close, knows and appreciates your mind. He can be a very appealing man when you see how much he seems to truly like women.

But his fear of giving himself over to anyone else often shows up abruptly during sexual intimacy. He's always a little nervous about sex. He just can't hand over that much of himself. Many Secret Manipulators do sex quick as a rabbit. They give you all kinds of prior leeway – touching, kissing, but mostly hugging. To make up for fear of things too deeply giving, they focus on surfaces, until they get inside you, then it's over very fast. Again, not every Secret Manipulator has a quick ejaculation problem – the details for any man may not be exact. Maybe your Manipulator cultivated a long sexual performance as part of his attentiveness to women. But I'll bet there is something controlling about the way he handles sex.

As reluctant as the Manipulator is to let go of his body, he's the opposite with his mind. He loves to talk about sex and any sexual problems you have. He's also an intimate sleeper. The sex may not be too avid, but he's a close snuggler in the night and he'll wake up to talk to you.

Sexually he's committed, though. He keeps his promise. He's a faithful spouse. And he doesn't humiliate you or hand out criticism.

Money Markers

He's not tight with money, but he is exacting. Neither parsimonious nor a spendthrift, he simply examines every expenditure. In order to make any purchase, he goes through an inquisition. He checks brands and prices, asks every possible question, fiddles with every model, gets at least seven opinions, and reads *Consumer Reports*. In short, he *uses* his money eventually, but he has trouble spending spontaneously.

He doesn't care if you don't make the money he does. He prefers to contribute all, or at least more, of the funds. Even-steven finances threaten his assumption that he's the more qualified. Whatever funds he has he generally applies to both of you. But whenever you buy anything, he goes along. Having access to his money doesn't imply you can use it freely. He wants to be there to see what you're doing and where it goes.

Family Aspects

The Secret Manipulator wants to have a family. But if he frustrates you, he nearly *suffocates* children. In his adoration of them, he goes overboard. With them as with you, he pretends to be fair, but he always keeps the final decision. He finagles them until they get quite snippy (they have to ward him off *some* way). He has his fingers in their every pie until they yell, "Stop it." He *means* well, as usual. But he has a hard time giving anyone independence. Unlike the Father Knows Best, however, he pretends he gives them independence. Only they know the truth. But he does love his children (and basically they love him), and he spends a lot of time with them.

He's close and kind to his parents. So kind, in fact, he's never gone through an open rebellion. He didn't have to. He learned how to be furtive and to hide what he was doing, perhaps manipulating them. Usually they think of him as sweet, compliant, and good. He's liable to be their "best son." It turn, he thinks of them as harmless. In their eyes there's no way you can quite come up to him. You're good, but never as good as he is.

He maintains a "blood is thicker than water" – i.e., blind – approach to his brothers. They assist one another anywhere, anytime, if one calls upon the other. If he has a sister, he's very protective towards her. After all, he "knows better" than she does, and needs care. She's the only one who gives him guff, but secretly she, too, relies on him. He has a pal or two from way back in childhood. Often they are similar, unpopular types. He picks up other close male friends, one every five or ten years. Each, amazingly, resembles him in one way or another – in inertia or broken love affairs. He also has long-term women friends, ones whose relationships with him have always been platonic.

The Secret Manipulator has heaps of potential. His riches are like an oil well's. They can gush, or flow and last a long time. But you have to crack through lots of layers – subtle deception, chicanery, and self-blindness – to get to them. And even then you have problems: you have to pump what he's hiding to the surface.

What Is in Store for You?

In almost every story there's a hero and a heavy. One character is villainous, the other draws your sympathy. But then the cunning author twists the plot to make it more enthralling. He makes the bad guy shine with an angelic streak while the good guy looks evil.

That's the way it goes with the Secret Manipulator, like a twisted plot. Only it's the Manipulator, not an author, who throws the monkey wrench. What's in store for you is – like Bugs Bunny and Porky Pig – he's the one who acts rascally, you're the one who winds up looking like a villain.

And in the end you often actually become a villain.

The Secret Manipulator makes your every decision appear like a caprice, your every desire appear like a mere whim, and your every way of doing things look like mere fancy. When there's nothing about you that's treated seriously, you get your essence plucked away. And in the long run it can give you very big problems, because the most difficult thing in the world to get over is being taken lightly.

All too often with the Secret Manipulator, when you don't know what's happening and you can't fight back, you simply join in. It seems you have no gravity, so you might as well begin to float. After all, nothing happens the way it's supposed to. Everything you do turns to meaningless thumb twiddling, so you might as well just disconnect. You get giddy and silly or, worse, you get paranoid.

Perhaps at some point you make a few stabs at defending how you want to do things, perhaps you get angry with him. But the Secret Manipulator, in all his furtive glory, can throw cold water on your anger so fast. He turns your rage into whining. He says, "Are you sure . . . ?" as you yell at him, and "I didn't really mean . . . I was just . . . " He washes over your accusations with semi-sweet, beguiling phrases that he knows you have little on-the-spot defense against, because those phrases are just the sort that women sometimes use to make men think *they* made the decision. He comes on so sweet it's you that begins to appear as either a meany or a fuss pot, and that keeps you silent. You don't yell very often when you discover all your friends and family blame you. He so discusses around you, when you try to explain to him what he's doing to you, you begin to think he has *reason* to complain. Of course, you just misunderstood him. You got mixed up, misinterpreted, saw it wrong. So you store up all your anger until it's bazooka size. Or else you start to perpetually nag.

Over the long haul, if this process isn't halted, what happens becomes far from comical. If you can't figure out why you lose all the decisions, and you don't get your own self-determination back, you simply slip into acting as if you've received a frontal lobotomy. You carry on as if your brain were disconnected, thoughts are totally disassociated from any serious meaning, and your gestures are unrelated to any goal. You act senile or ineffectual. Or you waver in and out of depression.

Perhaps, if you're lucky, some incident happens with your Secret Manipulator that brings what he's up to into focus. Maybe you really wanted to go to a certain party and he managed to lose the invitation, schedule a business meeting, or leave the car at the mechanic's. You suddenly see how he's been undermining you, and all your vexation comes to a culmination. Maybe, instead, your instincts tell you something's not right and you start to try ways to get some sort of power back. Not knowing why, you begin to see counselors, join women's groups, or take some sort of personal action. Whether she sees it all at once or slowly, sometimes when a woman realizes how manipulated she's been, she starts immediate hard core retaliation. She gets very tough and stern. She turns her home into a battle zone. Some try to correct the situation more gently. Others, like Jill, torpedo their domicile and leave. Be prepared that whatever you do, now you really look like the bad guy.

Often when and if you break up with a Secret Manipulator, you go through a strange reaction. Once free, you discover the joy of becoming as utterly non-sensible as you were previously made to feel. Out of the blue, you live up to the dingy image that was never you before. You act out your version of free living and of having total decision in your hands, much to his dismay. You wear bracelets and bangles. You take on a string of short-term lovers. You put the children into alternative schools. You move to the country and live in a van. There's nothing as thrilling as a "Look Ma, no hands" reentry into life. He chases after you trying to make you be "sensible". Again he plays poor sweet man, you the crazed woman.

Sometimes you even begin to act zany if you stay with him, but are no longer taking his manipulation. And sometimes, staying with him or returning to him, if he's promised to mend his ways, you get carried away. You go too far the other way and demand to have your way in everything.

Most of the time a woman "normalizes" – becomes her old self and "nice" again whether she's left him or stayed on to change him. In either case, you're a new and more assertive you. You have to get used to a new approach to things. And he, or anyone new you meet, will have to get used to the new you.

What Are the Telltale Signs of Trouble?

With the Secret Manipulator, trouble doesn't burst upon the scene. It gathers. Like little puffy clouds, one almost inconsequential annoyance after another rolls by, one time after another things don't go your way, and they accumulate into a mighty storm. So, when every vexation is a minor one, but there's a steady stream of them, take notice. And remember, sometimes little things need big attention.

You reach a critical point as soon as you discover that you're meandering. You go from assignment to assignment, chore to chore, task to task, none of which accomplishes anything at all, none of which happens the way you planned it. If it occurs to you that the only reason a man would give you all kinds of little tasks that end up meaning nothing is to keep all the decisions for himself, you're on the right track.

It's another big warning when you think you have no reason to be angry with your man, but you're *really* angry anyway. You snap at him and he says, "What did I do?" and you'll be damned if you know. But you know it was something. If it starts happening often – you're angry for apparently no reason – you're heading for a major blow up, and it may be so big it leaves irreparable damage.

Still, better to be angry and better to end your relationship than to feel as if the nuts and bolts that hold your brain together have come unscrewed. If you feel "floaty," useless, or like a pet puppy, don't flip off your switches. Blow the whistle instead.

What Are Your Chances and What Should You Do?

This may sound crazy, but when it comes to the Secret Manipulator, I say – fight before fleeing.

It depends on how fed up you are and how deep your affection is for him. If you're up to the gills and no longer feeling any fondness, then it's best to head for the nearest exit. But if you've still got a glimmer of patience and love, then hang on a little longer. There's no way to find out if he's a hopeless case unless you try to reclaim him. You may or may not have success. If your efforts fail, you can always walk out later!

Consider what you have in hand to start with. He's already supportive, loving, and good – up to a point. Chances are he is as he is and does as he does *unconsciously*. And though that doesn't make him blameless, it does give you a chance. If he prefers to stay blind to what he's doing and keep his underhand power, consider it *his* loss and responsibility. But if he wants to face what he's doing, you have a big start – namely, the fact that he really does like women.

The thing to do is call him on it. He starts out thinking and claiming he likes women, so he can hardly say no when you show him he's not following through. Since he says he considers you an equal, all you have to do is catch him every time he overrides you. He really doesn't see that he believes himself superior until you point it out. So, when you point it out again and again, he'll have to heed you. Most Manipulators mean well. When they get caught not being as nice as they claim to be, they lose face with themselves. So unravel his actions to see if he really *does* like women before thinking that maybe he doesn't.

Calling him on his superiority complex entails two quite different problems. The first one is yours: you have to become both quick and blunt. You can't stop decisions from slipping through your fingers if you're not on top of them. Looking back and remembering how it happened is already too late. You have to know what you want and see that you get it as it happens. It takes work to stay on the button, but you have to do it.

The second is his: he has to give up tried-and-true methods of winning and start to heed you. And that takes *incredible* effort. He has a lot staked on his old system, and he'll find the new one threatening. He may or may not be able to change. He may always have a problem with trust, and you may always have to struggle against his manipulative ways.

Even with success, you'll have another dilemma – not going overboard. You have to recognize when things have reached a balance so you can stop pushing and trust him again. Half the power is all you should ask. Remember to leave him his share. You can easily over-demand your own way once you've started, but that's just another way to ruin a relationship.

There are bound to be false starts, backsliding, and hopeless moments. I suggest a good strong commitment. Lots of time is needed, so is vision. Without thinking you still have a rainbow together, why try? Jill fought to change David and it took quite a while. But after her first flight she was determined she would succeed.

If you are currently with a Secret Manipulator or expect to meet one (don't laugh, it's highly likely!), keep in mind a simple equation that will help in your decision to fight or flee. Before making the effort to save or establish a good union, size up how much you like him as opposed to how much you love him. Believe me, they're different. If the "like" equals or tops the "love," the odds are in your favor. But if you don't like him all that much, you're better off to cut the cord. Try to stay fond of him and friendly, but don't let him hang around your door – or bed. The Secret Manipulator tends to switch roles once rejected. He, not you, becomes the soulful pet. If you left because he wouldn't change or you wanted something else, avoid this situation. You'd be surprised how easily the wind can blow him in again. You'll begin again. And end again.

Where Do You Fit In?

How does the Secret Manipulator get away with it, you may well ask yourself? Well, he does it with the help of another party – you.

Consider the possibility that you've got a foot in two worlds. On the one hand you're strong-minded and know your worth. On the other, resulting from the way you grew up, you're still a bit of a willow. A Manipulator can't work without an edge. How you fit in is by giving that edge to him. He can gain a foothold on domination only if, when push comes to shove, you act like a *lady*.

It's not that I'm against ladies. Quite the contrary. I'm warning against learned, so-called *"ladylike" behavior*. That's what gets you in trouble.

When you lose by default, the fault is still yours. It means you didn't show up, you backed out, or you tossed the game. Unfortunately, women all too commonly do just that. Women learn how to give up and give in, while growing up. It's one of the best things to learn how to stop. But first you have to become aware of the habit. Consider that you may still be following that old, buried pattern, no matter how liberated your outward philosophy.

For example, you may be too flexible, because "a woman is always gracious." Or you're too ready to give up your convictions – especially when they come up against a man's. You may hold a belief that men are or *should* be more right. You might acquiesce when you don't feel like it, because it's "feminine" to give in and it earns you brownie points.

Sure, you might still want to achieve your ends "nicely," that is, without fights or hostility. But if you always back off in the end in order to *please*, you can bet that the Secret Manipulator knows it. He can bargain that you will bend before you'll open fire.

You also need to check your language for feminine cover phrases. If his lines are persuasive, most likely yours are submissive. Women, from early on, learn language that gives men the final decision. We have a style of speech and phrasing that men don't share. Males use direct statements to show their command, like "Get me this" and

"We're going now." We women learn little linguistic ways to win approval and to make sure we're not alone. For example, "I like this, don't you?" as opposed to "I want this one," and "Don't you think it's time to leave?" instead of "Let's go!" But when you speak this way, you hand over the vote. You mean for him to agree with you but give him the chance to oppose. When women make delicate decisions they often make soft requests for confirmation. When you say, "aren't you?," "would you?," and "could you?," you seem feminine and open to discussion. But when someone uses your rhetorical queries to disagree instead of to concur, it can make you very angry. And you can't fight back because, after all, you asked!

The best way to save yourself is to stop using such futile ploys. Say what you mean directly and forget the need for consensus. As your speech and gestures become less ambiguous, you become more assertive, and being assertive, no matter what some say, is in *no* way unfeminine. There are a hundred ways to combine femininity, softness, and romance with being clear about your desires and meaningful in your actions. When you coordinate your speech, motions, and preferences, you gain spectacular freedom. Once there, you can be any kind of lady you want. The choice is yours.

Among other ways that men act in relationships with women, the Secret Manipulator is most like the Sugar Pie Honey and the Father Knows Best. In fact he can be *very* like the Father Knows Best, only in a slyer manner. But again, secret manipulation can be part of many men's behavior vocabulary towards women. We are the ones often characterized as manipulators, but we're not alone by a long shot.

At last we come to the final chapters, the three best men and relationships. Each is an intimate man, caring, loving, and wonderful. But the three are surprisingly different. What's more, not every one of them is good for every one of us. For example, while the Loving Traditional Man is a devoted, loyal, sharing spouse, some women shun him. His conventional ways are simply not right for them. The Loving Many-Faceted Man is what most of us seem to want in a man, pal, partner, and especially in a mate, nowadays. Yet many women find him almost too involving, too intimate, and a little too unpredictable. The Loving Limited Partner is good for very independent women, but not necessarily for others. Once again, although any one of these men can make a fine companion and you should check them all out, it's a matter of finding who is right – and who is wrong – for you. Even among the Intimate Men, you have to determine what you want, what you can and can't live with, and in whom you can see and achieve what you need.

I begin with the Intimate One – the Loving Traditional Man.

Intimate One – The Loving Traditional Man

The Best of the Old Fashioned Husband, Father, Breadwinner

Man as the earner, woman as the homemaker. Any number of men perpetuate or prefer the old ancestral arrangement for men and women – man out working, woman in the home. But of all of them, only one has it truly right – the Loving Traditional Man. So, if your angle is old-fangled and you care to get the very best of the "man the breadwinner, woman the wife and mother" arrangement, get Loving Traditional Man. He's the tops of the way it used to be, and the way it very often still is.

What makes the Loving Traditional Man special? Here's what: he doesn't think men are superior to women. He also doesn't believe your household is less important than his job. Quite the opposite. He thinks it's *more* important. He wants a good home and family more than anything, including his career. It's the reason he believes in the old formula. He thinks a division, but happy coordination, of labor works best for a good home and family. A home and family take a lot of care as well as work. It takes two people to handle everything, and divided work and different areas of authority make for the smoothest partnership and strongest home center. So he does one thing, you another, but toward the same purpose – the formation, care, and keeping of a single family unit.

Together you make a little corporation, and your little corporation is the center of his universe. You mow the lawn and paint the walls to keep it nice. You do your separate daily chores, but once they're finished you spend almost all your time together. He returns home to run the Lionel train or watch a good game of baseball. You fry eggs, patch skinned knees, and visit Fabric City. But then you sit with him, plan with him, camp with him. He loves you. You love him. In perpetuity. And you are both monogamous.

You see, the Loving Traditional Man figures it's equal. You don't cheat on him and he doesn't cheat on you. It's part of the deal. Man has no special right to philander that a woman doesn't have as well. So if he wants you only to have one man, then by rights he can only have one woman.

Naturally, the Loving Traditional Man union works only if a woman is in agreement. So Loving Traditional Men tend to head for the old-fashioned flavors in women, a blend of wholesome ingredients and down-home intentions. He goes through all the steps, never missing a procedure – falling in love, courtship, going steady, proposal, and marriage. Five layers, slow oven. Hopefully you have time to test the batter before you add the frosting.

It all sounds pretty ideal. But in truth, as with all the Intimate Men, the relationship is hard work to establish and even harder to keep – and the most painful when it fails, because it relies so much on faith. But if tradition is your comfort zone, there's nothing to lose and much to gain from a Loving Traditional Man. If you find him, that is, for Traditional *Not* Loving Men are all too prevalent!

Story

My sister's friend Donna luxuriates in family life as if she were a Queen of Sheba – for her, dishpan hands don't matter. But then she's hooked up with Hank. And for Donna, Hank is a humdinger. Nothing makes either of them happier than to meet at the table at the stroke of six, even when they have to eat their daughter's Stir and Serve.

Strangely enough, Donna's own mother was either home acting fragile and inept, or she was out fitfully pursuing a concert career. Donna's upbringing was almost devoid of indoctrination in the domestic arts. While many women who come from a line of strong homesteaders seem to want to try their chance in the outer world because they know the inner, Donna followed the opposite tack. She valued every afghan and brooch from her grandmother. She took to sewing and knitting before she could whistle or pop her Double-Bubble.

Not that Donna didn't finish her education. She did. But even then she found herself leaning toward a customary role – she trained as a schoolteacher. Then she took a job in an elementary school, in a distant, medium-sized town. It was there, at a basketball game, that she met Hank.

Hank was a bit younger that Donna, a college dropout and a natural laborer. You couldn't keep Hank inside, much less behind a desk or on a chair, for long. But none of that mattered. Donna and Hank were like pippins meeting pastry dough. All Hank really wanted in life was a home and a wife plus a kid or two, then to install them where he could love them to death. As for work, he just wanted a job with enough interest and progress to support them, not kill him, and maybe to buy a camper.

There was no question that he meant it to be forever. So did Donna. In fact, through thick and thin (for things weren't always blissful), what held them together wasn't their love for each other; it was their *commitment* to the idea of one, lasting marriage.

After a short courtship, they got hitched. Although Donna got cold feet at the last minute – she wasn't quite sure Hank was the right man for her – luckily her instincts said "go." The first baby came pretty quickly – nine months. Clearly it wasn't a shotgun wedding.

The first seven years were the hardest. Hank had his work, and since they both agreed that Donna would stay home, she had her house. It took them quite a while to work out the balance of their different realms. Hank tried to preempt the household management and overdo the "head of the family" role. Donna sometimes stepped on Hank's toes and undermined his discipline. They had to get used to each other's habits, good dust-raising quarrels, labor layoffs, different driving speeds, and sets of in-laws. They also had more babies who ate a lot and kept things dilapidated. But Donna and Hank knuckled down to raise the kids and grow old together.

Donna never feels sorry for herself because she stays home and doesn't have a career. She *likes* what she's doing and says so. She doesn't have to lie or feel guilty. Hank never rambles on about having the final word or being boss. He doesn't feel less masculine because he quits work on the button and goes straight home. Their decisions are so intermingled it drives their kids crazy. Hank always says, "I'll go along with what your mother says," then Donna sends them back to Hank.

Their sex life – they have to hang a "do not disturb" sign on the door – started fast and awkwardly but grew better. It never got very wild, just substantial. A lot of the time, they simply snuggle. When the day fades, they're pretty tired. But then they discovered that, for them, cuddling was almost more important than sex.

There have been some rough times, but never have they been near breakup. Sometimes Hank gets a little distant and uncommunicative. Donna occasionally feels isolated and fed up. Age, boredom, and monetary problems have touched them, like they touch any adults. And like all adults, they have to solve such issues for themselves. But they never questioned that it's better to build on what they have than to end things and start over with someone else.

Lately they're learning the trick of thinking up new ideas to keep interest alive. They've discussed early retirement, desert retreats, and trips to the Amazon. They change their minds a lot and half their ideas will probably never reach fruition, they just have fun thinking about them. It's pretty obvious that Donna and Hank will stay together to the end. They have a good chance. Donna claims she intends to stay with Hank. Hank says he couldn't go on without Donna. And they tell each other so every day.

True, they limit their entertainments and explorations in life. Their goals are simple compared to many people's. But they know that, have chosen it, and make no bones about it.

The tradition of man the breadwinner, woman the homemaker, is, of course, largely incorrect. From prehistoric times to the present, women have brought home much of the food. They gathered or tilled away from home until fairly recent times, as they now do again. Still, correct or not, what we *think* of as the old-fashioned recipe – oatmeal cookies with no chocolate chips – is many people's idea of heaven. Sometimes the recipe succeeds, sometimes, with all the stress of modern times, it doesn't. Nonetheless, the Loving Traditional relationship has all the ingredients necessary – especially the most important one, mutual respect – that can help you win the gold medal.

How Can You Identify This Kind of Man?

Churning around in the Loving Traditional Man's head are a bunch of theories. He doesn't always know he's got them, nor does he check his principles for correctness, he just assumes they're right and staunchly upholds them. Strangely enough for a conservative man, his beliefs are rather liberal. He believes the family is the atom of society. He sees your alliance as the old division of labor. He believes in justice and democracy, plus equal rights for all. If he has a slight shortcoming in his policies, it's in his notion of liberty. He isn't sure just what personal freedom is, but he's sure it has limits.

He's a social scientist's delight. He believes in ideal rules that he doesn't derive from any form of logic. He leaves a pristine legacy. What's been good enough for others throughout time is good enough for him, with some minor alterations he thinks of as his own.

Certainly he's a positive man. Since so much is settled and simple for him, he has time left to get *happy*. He more than expects you to be an equal boss with him – he wants it. Why should he make decisions in departments that aren't his responsibility? Isn't that what pairing is for, to divide half the weight?

He may expect you to bend to major curves in his life. But that's not because his employment is all important. Rather it's because the money he earns is simply a necessity. Still a Loving Traditional Man will often refuse to go along with a work transfer or change if it means a disruption of family, friends, and harmony.

Outer Signs

A Loving Traditional Man is not traditional only in principles. He generally dons customary dress. He subscribes to the civilities of etiquette. The Loving Traditional Man is anything but rude or flashy. He likes clothing middling, modest, and passable. Grey, blue, and brown with buttons, proper zippers, and no plunging necklines. He always wears a belt. Usually he picks a never-changing style, such as collegiate, cowboy, carpenter, or C.P.A., and stays with it forever. Indeed, most Loving Traditional Men keep two sets of dress, formal and informal. He's a properly dressed businessman, storekeeper, or laborer in the outer world, then he comes home, showers it all off, and out comes Man of the House – tidy, casual, usually dressed in the style of his school days. He's simply not clothes-conscious enough to shift with the winds of fashion.

He is, however, decidedly clean. From his Arrow cotton-and-polyester collar down to his black (or white) socks, he's scrubbed. His hair is shortish and shiny. He's often afraid he has dandruff. Even if he doesn't, he chemically wards off any errant flake before it dares approach him. He shaves a lot, though he may try a beard or moustache every now and again. He's not exactly meticulous and spotless. He just takes joy in eliminating the presence of whatever he was doing last, and in drying out his skin. (He's also afraid he's greasy). He goes through tons of Dial and Irish Spring. He doesn't drop his towel afterward. He hangs it up! He doesn't want to make more work for you – no extra folding, no soggy trail.

He likes order and he knows where things are supposed to go. Most of the time he'll put items back where they belong. He considers himself responsible for what he uses but not for how supplies get on the shelves or what happens when they get used up. He'll take out the trash and drive in the nails, but he has to be told when and where. He thinks it's proper for you to take his last name and for him to sign first on documents, insurance forms, and loans, but you sign right there with him and the benefits are for all. Often he denies himself goodies so that you and the kids can have more.

He doesn't like his car too new or too old. If it doesn't last a proper time span, he feels highly cheated. He chooses square and practical autos. The car he drives, instead of being a little bigger than yours, as with the Man Who Would Be Mogul, is a bit smaller. He figures you need the seats and space. He has a second-hand Maverick, while you have the wagon or bus. Or you both have wagons. He drives your bigger car for family expeditions, after checking the water, oil, and air, of course.

Since he thinks all machines are in his department, he washes both cars, sees to their maintenance, and makes the kids help wax. He makes everybody do some of the labor. After all, he's an economical man. He thinks up work assignments for different ages and abilities. That goes for the cooking of waffles, the purchase of flea collars, and the dishing up of Alpo.

By the time he gets a place with you, he likes to have it surrounded by a little lawn. Before, he shared an apartment. He doesn't buy a house till he has his "other half." He'll go for living in a condominium or apartment when he must, but he usually shuns the center of town. He wants a little space, and he likes it to be his – an exclusive shelter for his group. Usually he prefers to buy rather than rent. He'd pay in cash if he could. Being moderate, he relaxes more in a place of sensible size; he's not the mansion type.

He doesn't pay much heed to walls and furniture. He might expect to come along with his checkbook for purchases, but he defers to you in the aesthetics of choice. If asked his preference, he'll opt for big and heavy items, often plaid or maple. Probably only French Provincial, doilies, and little tea tables will make him voice a veto.

In mannerisms, he tends towards pleasantries and chivalry. He says "please" and "thank you" and expects to hear some back. Gestures of respect please his fancy, and obligation is his major driving force. He works to provide sustenance even when he doesn't particularly care for his position. And deep down he harbors an instinct to guard his loved ones without exploiting others. He aims to get his family schooled, his old age secured, and his woman's wishes met, and to accomplish this with love, attention, and responsibility. As much as he may seem antiquated, somehow he's not out of date. He's just doing what he thinks was meant to be and hoping it still operates. When it doesn't, he suffers.

Like the other Intimate Kinds of Men he treats himself with care and honesty. He pays attention to his health and welfare, but some of his care will depend on you – he relies on your help. After all, upkeep is interdependence with the Loving Traditional arrangement. Without aid, he can be blind to nutrition and not inclined to lose weight (you have to bet that he can't). He often practices a sport or activity, frequently with other men or kids. Most likely his game removes him to the nearby park, school, or gym. He roams a wider range than you. And he may be gone more than you like. He may coach a soccer team and get involved in Boy Scouting. But his adventures are tethered. He's roped to his work half the time and his home most of the rest.

Sex Signals

He heads for moderate women, nice rather than sweet, good rather than gushy. He avoids shy ladies who don't announce their likes. He thrives on a little simple, sometimes snappy, commentary. He's more comfortable when he knows what you've got to say. After all, he bases his system on interchange, not submission, though women with determined career ambitions don't suit him. Since he tends to women of substance, he often finds himself most drawn to women who have always had a home and family as a main goal but who have tried a few years out in the world.

His idea of courtship is pretty predictable. He takes you out, drives you about, and spends some, but not a lot of, money. He gleams with delight when you cook him a meal or invite him on a field day. He likes to put his arm around you almost more than kissing. Tucking you into his elbow makes him feel you aspire to a union in the future.

Sex comes at a simmer, not a boil. He's not much of a hustler, and he doesn't take sex lightly. He'll go long spells with none rather than seek sex with no relationship. He doesn't demand virginity from you or himself – that's more the Male Supremacist's double standard. Each of you may have had one or two serious involvements before. More than that on your part might give him pause. Once you're together, he caters to your requests and gives exclusive sexual access. No others for himself or for you. He sees fidelity not so much as possessiveness but as a major gesture of love.

At first, he may not be completely without sexual problems. More than likely he comes a little quickly or he lacks a little grace. Perhaps he doesn't show his best until he's good and comfortable. He needs time to find his pacing before good sex between you emerges. It comes from learning which versions are just right for one another.

Your sexual interaction stays behind closed doors. His moderate streak turns to modesty when things get erotic. To outside appearances, there's little amorous innuendo between you. Whatever wonderful things go on, no one knows. Later, your kids say about you, "I can't imagine them ever doing it." But you *do*, and often, too.

Money Markers

The Loving Traditional Man's money never belongs to specific persons. It belongs to particular *purposes*. Some goes for upkeep, some for the future, for a vacation, education, or a new car. He divides dollars up and directs them toward certain objectives for his little kinship unit. All cash is corporate stock to him. He might have a 51 to 49 vote over you, or he might have 49 to your 51. Sometimes the kids win them all.

He is less than loose with money. He's not petty, but he's guarded and inflexible. Even wealthy Loving Traditional Men spend moderately, think in terms of good investments, and buy conservative items that don't depreciate.

Your money or earnings give the Loving Traditional Man a ticklish problem. More and more families require two incomes to survive, and he knows it. Your *needing* to work can punch a hole in his self-image, but he adjusts if the income serves a good purpose, whereas the Male Supremacist doesn't. The Loving Traditional Man solves the problem of pride with a clever trick. He keeps the finances separate. You file yours away for the kid's college or retirement and use his daily bread.

Family Aspects

Loving Traditional Men always want children, preferably their own. But they'll adopt, too. The Loving Traditional Man doesn't do much of day to day child raising, unlike the Loving Many-Faceted Man. Children are still by and large your job. After all, he isn't home when many of their troubles arise. He leaves their general management to your expertise. Yet he values his fatherhood and forms his own view of fatherly interaction and discipline. He treats his sons and daughters equally but differently. He wants his girls to have the same education and rights, but he expects more, often *too* much, from his boys, just as he does himself.

The Loving Traditional Man maintains some good male pals from his work or past, but mostly he likes to keep company with you and other couples. His active friends come from among neighbors or colleagues who live in much the same style. Occasionally he and the other men play sports, cards, go fishing or the like, without the accompaniment of women, which means that every now and then your Loving Traditional Man will be off for a night or weekend.

He rarely has women friends other than his one and only lady. He even feels strange getting close to his chum's mates, though he may like them a lot, aid them in a crisis, or offer them support. The same goes for your friends. He enjoys them, looks forward to seeing them, helps them if they need it, but doesn't seek their company.

Being familial as he is, he sees relatives as friends. He loves your sisters, cousins, and nieces (if you do) and defers to your parents. He's not sure about your brother. He treats his own parents with respect and his siblings with fondness. He thinks holidays and relatives go together. Such occasions usually become big family affairs. Not that there isn't some quarreling. Not all Loving Traditional Men come from happy families. Often a man becomes more familial and traditional *because* his own parents were troubled.

Certainly he has some drawbacks. He's not the world's most exciting man. He can be stubborn and resist new ideas, get stodgy. He can close you off from a lot. But mostly he has assets. He's yours. He shares. He cares. He's respectful and supportive. He's a bread-and-butter lover. He deserves three stars.

What Is in Store for You?

So the workaday world was never your aspiration. And you're just as happy to read Mother Goose as Proust. What you want is a pal, a partner, and a chicken in the pot (with you doing the cooking). Well, that's what you get with the Loving Traditional Man.

You start off with all kinds of pluses when you enter a Loving Traditional relationship. He's not saccharine, stealthy, or sly. He keeps his career interest in balance with his intimate life. His respect doesn't depend on a person's sex or occupation. Sure, he's a bit possessive. Yes, he's a touch jealous. Not because you're his property or because he's a maniac, but because he has a sense of tenure and he feels all the complexities of love and attachment.

But remember this: his idea of sharing – to divide and assign according to gender – is permanently fixed. He doesn't overlap, alternate, or assimilate roles as the Loving Many-Faceted Man might. Prepare for the fact that your lives will always remain somewhat apart. You spend *many* hours in different places, doing *very* different tasks. And while the Loving Traditional Man is a honey, he's no great shakes at tripping the light fantastic. If you're looking to step lively and have a lot of fancy flying good times, find another Nureyev. Certainly a Loving Traditional Man can come from any walk and lead any sort of life, street corner to ivory tower. But his conservative ways and less-than- spontaneous pace always incline him to schedule his thrills and limit his delights, no matter what his station. You're heading for a *planned* life course. He doesn't expect alteration in his feelings, circumstances, or goals. His future vision is tunneled toward narrow, rosy, and cosy ends. Through lengthy stretches of years you establish your relationship, build your establishment, and collect your rewards. Even the ups and downs, as heartfelt as they are, tend to come as protracted pendulum swings, not sharp, fast peaks and lows. The aspect that makes most Loving Traditional couples happy is that you spend most of your beginning years *preparing* your life, then in the end you're left with exactly what you worked for.

Making a lasting relationship stay alive, and not just together, invariably requires effort. No two people's moods, sensitivities, trust, or motives remain even all the time. And major weak spots occur.

One is when you wait for all the payoffs to come in the end and don't enjoy your life *as* you go along, only to find that the fates deprive you. A second is loneliness. It's not just in the beginning and middle stages that you spend much of your time apart, but also in the end. A third is that often, just as your way together is getting paved, along comes a surprisingly hard period. When either he or you turns forty or so, gets bored with work, or faces the death of parents and friends, the waters sometimes get troubled. And at that point the Loving Traditional Man can sometimes change for the worse, not the better. Usually he gets back on keel, but sometimes he doesn't. He can lose energy and slowly decline into stodginess. He can even desert his principles and transform himself into a not-so-intimate man. Indeed, over the years, he can go through a number of times when he's simply not happy, when he has crises or depressions. He may question why he's working and his reasons for devotion. Retirement can also he hard for him, especially if he's left without a realm of his own. His sexual interest can decidedly dwindle. This is a real problem if your libido stays lively and his doesn't. Also, most Loving Traditional couples don't tend to deal easily with unexpected changes, particularly if their children don't come out as expected, and that is something that happens more often than you'd expect.

Still, most Loving Traditional Men make it through these storms. That's why they're Loving Traditionals. They even laugh at themselves. After all, both he and you *work* on your relationship. He doesn't expect a union to perpetuate itself without care and stick-to-it-iveness. Both of you keep your perspective about the past, present, and future.

Anyway, there's always one constant advantage with the Loving Traditional Man, no matter what happens. Once he loves you, he always loves you. That's why the romantic part is short with him. He wants the loving part to last as long as possible.

What Are the Telltale Signs of Trouble?

Loving Traditional Men are usually great, and usually you can easily make it together for life. But of all the Intimate Men, the Loving Traditional Man is the one who can occasionally, and bafflingly, turn sour. The others, the Loving Many-Faceted Man and the Loving Limited Partner, have a less utopian vision of the future. They foresee that life's miracles and miseries can cause unexpected happenings. The Loving Traditional Man so simplistically predicts his by-and-by, he forgets about the possibility that unexpected circumstances can drastically change one's life.

There are various signals that indicate a Loving Traditional relationship has lost its crucial balance. He stops valuing your work; he denigrates your role and upgrades his own; he withholds his pay;

or he gives lip service to principles and morals, but doesn't act on them.

Very often, when a Loving Traditional Man goes astray, he begins to lie a little. First he tells himself that what he's doing or contemplating doing with his time or money isn't *really* what it is, then he goes on to cover up his tracks. Most Loving Traditional Men who break promises feel very guilty, so if he starts acting like a Sugar Pie Honey, you might wonder what rule he's no longer keeping. Usually he gets disgusted with himself and 'fesses up to some entanglement. But when he doesn't, you might be heading toward a nasty shock. Before that happens, consider the above signals as omens.

With age, an occasional Loving Traditional Man grows into a Father Knows Best. Or, with success, some edge their way into the Male Supremacist, the Man Who Would Be Mogul, or even a Mr. Genius. Matters get serious if he starts to think he's superior. If he turns helping into unmitigated bossing, it means he's sliding backwards into purported tradition more than you should tolerate. If such occurrences happen to you, above all don't slip into becoming an anxious pleaser—hold onto your equal-partner status while you try to straighten things out.

What's worse is if he starts to feel that his contacts at work have left you a dullard in the suburb. In this case, he probably hid status desires and pretensions about himself all along. Such late revelations are hard to swallow, but if he isn't the man you thought he was, he isn't the man for you. A real Loving Traditional Man isn't concerned with whether you match him like a sweater set. He doesn't expect you to follow his commands like a lackey. He only cares that you provide the other half of his life.

There's a final critical issue, rare but conceivable, with the Loving Traditional Man. Sometimes people stay together (even remain faithful) in hatred, not in love. They develop an unending bond of dislike that holds them together better than epoxy. Their perpetual quarrel becomes their very food for life. If this happens to you, no matter that money, long years, or children have kept you hanging on, you should get your walking papers. To grow inward and bitter is not just anti-life, it's not living at all.

All in all, few Loving Traditional relationships have abrupt and terminal crises. The prevalent problem is a slow descent into flavorlessness. So watch for it. When you start to develop the blahs, don't depend on your partner for the solution. Get yourself together and stir up some action. Go square dancing, roller skating, or join your local Save the Whale Society. Then bring him along. Just because he's old-fashioned doesn't mean you get to sit on your duff. Up and at 'em. It's life and life only! Don't live it with cobwebs.

What Are Your Chances and What Should You Do?

With the Loving Traditional Man, you have the opportunity not only to be in a snapshot but to become a daguerreotype -- you seated in a velvet chair, he standing behind with his hand on your shoulder. The tone might be a little dated, the pose a little formal, but you just might grow into a septuagenarian couple. In terms of potential permanence, the Loving Traditional Man is a winner.

No good things are easy. As much as the relationship relies on him, it also relies on you. Some special areas need constant attention. But don't throw this baby out with the bath water during troubled times — keep scrubbing. Fight before fleeing. And don't flee at all if the situation is in any way viable.

Don't forget these tips: prize, don't spoil the balance, keep in mind your original commitment to pairing, and know the depth of responsibilities not only to your mate but to yourself. If anything starts to go amiss, add time, surveillance, and forgiveness if necessary.

With the Loving Traditional Man, you start with the *idea* of permanent partnership as much as your mate does. But obviously you also need to love and admire your partner to achieve success. Surely if you lose your love, if you enter the match with no feeling, or even if you misconceived the degree of your emotion, you doom your efforts to a large chance of failure.

When you give both affection and assurance, you have a tremendous advantage. Both of you have already implied that you're responsible for your own participation and that you're pledged to overcome what befalls you. So if life shifts the glass in your kaleidoscope into a new pattern, just remember the pieces are the same. All you have is a new perspective. Go with it. You have nothing to fear. With a Loving Traditional Man, never delve into backbiting, revenge tactics, or sleeping around. A breach of principle can break the Loving Traditional foundation irreparably. Better to lose the fight than lose what you were fighting for.

No relationship is guaranteed anymore. A changed Loving Traditional Man or a new you could decide to back out of the original declaration of duality. But when you both remain pledged, your contract helps you win a long-term future together. Of course, it doesn't come without sacrifice. When you stick with one sort of experience, you give up the chance to try others. But it's worth the chance with this man -- you could come out with something great.

Remember to enjoy yourself, whatever you've got. In life you don't get a trial run -- so take what you get. Don't waste time on the paradoxes. Don't question what you lose for what you gain. Do what seems best for you and do it thoroughly.

Where Do You Fit In?

Never give up a right: that's the best piece of advice my father ever gave me. That maxim, which applies to many situations, forms the keystone to the Loving Traditional association. Does that seem contradictory to a traditional male-female arrangement? Not a bit. Not if you want a healthy partnership.

It's your right to live as you want. If you want to stay home, mind a house, raise children, do crafts in your basement, or whatever, do so. It's your privilege to make the match that suits you. If you prefer a traditional man, then no matter *what* your women friends and trendy magazines say, tarry with one. But keep in mind the one thing that more than anything else keeps the union wholesome -- the knowledge that you're doing what you *want* to do.

Never giving up a right can not only help you choose a Loving Traditional Man but also provide you with the best formula for *keeping* the partnership functioning. The Loving Traditional union works best when you think of yourselves not as male and female but as equal partners and peers. If you want a voice in all decisions, search out the mate who confers. The Loving Traditional association doesn't stem from deference and submission but from joint ventures and goals. If you renounce your desires and demands, you end up with something less worthy.

You're ready to fit with a Loving Traditional Man when you decide that you wish to follow the conventional female lifestyle and that you need a man who matches your qualifications. You don't fall in with any old breadwinner and hope he treats you like an equal. You know what you are, and you look for a man who's equal to you. Only when you respect and admire yourself can you select the right mate and keep your union steady. You're on the beam when you value your work and worth to the highest, even if your favorite chore is canning with your pressure cooker. The Loving Traditional mate never underestimates herself. Nor does she assume she's any more dependent on her pal and partner than he is on her.

As with the other Intimate Men, with the Loving Traditional Man it's very important that you stay in touch with yourself and your man. You need lots of lines of communication and a great deal of honesty. You have many bargains to work out: who handles which responsibility, under whose command is which decision, how each of you feels about proposed changes. He may want to quit a job and you feel threatened. You may tire of home and want to go to school while he thinks *work* should come first. Remember, you're a corporation. Make appointments with one another. Have conferences. Schedule times to talk. Even write letters.

You can go wrong with a Loving Traditional Man if you expect him to solve all your problems. Just because he brings home the bacon and puts his body in your bed nightly doesn't mean he's father, brother, uncle, or repairman to you. You're still on your own in life, no matter what your domestic combination. Daily disasters ranging from broken dishwashers to depression remain yours to handle. Don't lose your capabilities and turn into a weeping willow just because you're coupled and have a shoulder to lean on.

His role as household supporter, husband, and father is where he holds self-esteem. Keep your hands off it. Get your rewards from what *you* do and not from being his sidekick. Yours is *not* a Loving, Limited Partner contract. You're a *full* partner who does half the work. You should know his business, what he's doing, and how things are going.

It's most important in the Loving Traditional relationship that you enter and stay with no nagging doubts. Don't become a mate and mother because it's expected of you, forced upon you, or considered *normal*. It's not an easy relationship. You literally have to stick through thick and thin, good and bad, sickness and health. So you'd better be sure it's worth it -- for you.

The Loving Traditional Man is related to both the other Intimate types of men and can overlap with both. He can have aspects of the Loving Many-Faceted Man or aspects of the Loving Limited Partner.

Next is the second of the three super relationships, perhaps today's most desired one, the Loving Many-Faceted Man.

21

Intimate Two – The Loving Many-Faceted Man

The Modern Man Who Has Many Sides to Him and Shares With You on Every Level

After thinking it over, the Loving Many-Faceted Man comes to a marvelous conclusion. Life is a huge toy store of a very special sort in which you don't just get to look at the games and dolls. Instead, you get to live them and *be* them. He then proceeds to emerge from creation's shopping mall not as a single item, but as a whole *parcel* of things. He's a mate, a father, a fisherman, businessman, baseball player, teacher, scout leader, bookworm, carpenter, dress designer, and homemaker. Maybe he'll become a lawyer, maybe he'll give up lawyering and be a photographer. Maybe he'll quit work and raise the kids for a year. Maybe he'll learn to fly an airplane. He's a worker and a man of leisure. He's everything he can think of.

Actually, more than facets, what he has is many identities. And that's how he wants to live, as all of them, or switching them around as he lives. He scorns the idea of having to be one way or do one thing throughout his existence. He prefers to exist as a multiple creature. Whatever combination of roles or tasks he ends up assuming, he is all of them. He doesn't just play act them, or try them out, or try to *look* great. He finds within himself any number of desires and any number of things he wants to be and do. He feels each one is vital. And he gives every facet equal importance and care.

He wants to enjoy life, the Loving Many-Faceted Man does, so he heads for pleasure. He also wants to make what he does pleasureful. He aims to adore his lover, relish his work, and delight in his play – or else he'll try another sort. He's inclined to change and vacillate, especially in his vocation and interests. Still, he strives for proportion in his existential goulash. He wants a modicum of success, of romance, and maybe of kids, dogs, volleyball games, and trips up the Ganges. Before he gets overrun with greenbacks, he spends on enjoyment. But his love is deep and so are his involvements.

He tends to be the most easy and harmonious of men. He willingly explores and shares the avenues his lady takes as well as his own. If any man can thrive with a woman who lives her life in a varied fashion, the Loving Many-Faceted Man can. He sometimes goes for straight-line career women, or sometimes a domestic sort, but generally he likes the woman who's a bit of a mélange. The Loving Many-Faceted Man goes for the woman who leads life with a very light touch. She displays a spectrum of many facets herself. Stepping through any prisms society declares, she allows herself free range to be everything she wants to be: industrial designer, mother, fashion follower, P.T.A. member, computer specialist, tear wiper, cook and gardener. Anything, all things. And she knows that behind all her refractions lies a single beam – herself.

Story

My friend Gabe showed every glint of budding Loving Many-Facetism early. An amazing number of people had dismissed him as having no singular distinction. But every now and then some lady realized she was talking to a Pied Piper who would lead her on adventures and treat her well. Liza was one. In no time flat she knew she had met a man remarkably in harmony with himself and yet very adaptable. He would not only share his life but would step right in and join hers.

And she was right. Gabe was the sort who threw himself into every aspect of life with unpretentious abandon. He was always active and yet relaxed. He was purposeful and yet flexible and accepting. Rules about who is supposed to do what didn't faze him. He'd handle whatever was necessary. He was by no means humble but was just so human he didn't have any affectations. He was good to people, good to himself, and just plain lovely company.

Gabe tried business school and hated it. He studied sociology and carpentry and then ended up in public health. Once he thought he wanted to have a store of his own. Despite an indecisiveness with his calling, he never shirked friends or responsibilities. Quite the opposite. He figured that concern for other people was the natural way to get the best results. So Gabe was rarely found without someone whom he cared for and who cared about him. He always had a dog or pet. He kept his own place. He did the laundry, shopping, and mopping. He had open and affectionate relationships with women, and with each one he loved, he sought a rich and full alliance. But that didn't mean that things always worked out.

When Liza met Gabe, he was not without a past. But then, neither was she. Both had loved before, and while those episodes ended in sorrow, neither was afraid to take a chance again. Loving and risking were part of life to Liza and Gabe.

Liza met Gabe in a most haphazard way: she bumped into him in a used-book store as he was leaning on a rack reading *Captain Marvel* and *Conan*. To cover her embarrassment, Liza asked his advice in getting a comic for her four-year-old son. He asked her to lunch. And she went.

The Orange Julius and corn dog could have been champagne and lobster thermidor and they wouldn't have noticed. They were too busy hitting it off. Liza still claims his lunch choice was in retaliation for knocking into him. He says the Doggie Diner provided the only suitable repast to go with the *Bugs Bunny* comic they purchased. At any rate, lunch led to supper, supper led to a double feature, and *The Pink Panther* led to bed. They left in the middle. Why watch United Artists when you can go home and be them?

Their sex life, says Liza, was and is still wonderful. Gabe is all warmth and intimacy; he gives himself completely to her pleasure and his own. He melts her like butter, and he adores the times she takes over. He can be silly; he can be hot. He can just hug and not make love.

Liza and Gabe are still together. Slowly but steadily after that first day, they just merged. Gabe introduced Liza to his pals and his whole world. Liza made it clear that she, her kid, her friends, her work, and her funny habits came in a single wrapper. Liza knows that as an occupational therapist, artist, dance teacher, mother, and lover, her life will never be simple. Adding Gabe makes it harder yet. In order to follow his tangents and participate in his ways, she gives up and adjusts some of her own. But she gets something else – he also helps her, shares her burdens, and allows for her crazy notions.

After two years together, they had a child; Liza had wanted another. Since she had just gotten her first gallery show and Gabe had wearied of his work, he quit to manage the home and the baby. Three years later, Liza cut back, plunked down all her funds, and they opened Gabe's bookstore.

They know the future will always be quixotic. But they never know which one is Don Quixote and which is Sancho Panza: clearly one or the other is always preparing to do battle with some windmill while the other assists. They've had some rough times. They went through two retreats into separate space during which time they shared the children equally. They don't give eternal promises that they'll be together forever, only that they'll try. They are loyal to one another. They don't have affairs. They know that if they had one it could possibly break them up, and they don't want to take the chance. Still, if one happened by some odd circumstance, perhaps it wouldn't break them up, not by itself. Their relationship takes a lot of work. But it's worth it to them. They have the gifts of remaining true to themselves while being totally involved.

Women have long found themselves with many diverse duties in their laps, now more than ever before. You find yourself keeping house and managing one as well (and we all know that the management is a whole separate chore). You go to work, you quit, you try one kind of job and them maybe another, or you follow one straight through; you toss a splendid spaghetti, you fix a shelf, you throw a five-year-old's birthday party, you volunteer for charity. You drain the dirty Pennzoil, you buy three shares of Polaroid, you knit a pattern from *McCall's*. And you know you're not only one of the above, but *all* of them. You thrive on going from one role to another. Happiness is switching from funky to fancy at fifty-five miles per hour.

The Loving Many-Faceted Man is much the same. He has come upon a philosophy of life, by desire, that many modern women have come upon by necessity. He wants to do it all and be it all, and he's never been so free to try before. When you look for the Loving Many-Faceted Man get ready for the liberated man.

How Can You Identify This Kind of Man?

The Loving Many-Faceted Man holds a special key that many men never discover: he can say no, but more importantly, he can say yes. He contradicts the single-identity male syndrome. He breaks out of being just truck driver or judge or any one title. He thinks of himself as the world's greatest lover, soccer instructor, vacuumer, and baby tender also. He cooperates. At a party when someone asks him what he does, he's left at quite a loss. He says, "Well, let's see. I clean, wire, write, doctor, lob, job, use Aramis, drink J & B, have a great mind, and roast a terrific turkey."

He likes change. He may not know he does, but he seeks it just the same. He balances his act on a ball, not a box. He can't predict his future in absolutes. Sometimes he realizes he must do something else, so his promises are only 99 and 44/100 percent pure. He'd be a dummy to close down that other, tiny .56 percent and he knows it.

The Loving Many-Faceted Man comes with no permanent warranties. Balls roll along in life, but occasionally they also bounce. He *does* offer the best of intentions. And the *almost* promises from a Loving Many-Faceted Man usually work out better than total promises from a less intimate man.

Since he means his vows but accepts his quirks more than any of the other types of men, the Loving Many-Faceted Man is honest, blunt, and as real as real can be. He's also a bit loony and impulsive. When he shows up with a fish aquarium bought with your last ten dollars – because he just *had* to raise a *koi* – you know you just got a vote of confidence. He wants a relationship where he and you can say, do, feel, and share almost anything. And he does it. He's out to like you *permanently*. Better yet, he's not afraid to like himself.

Outer Signs

The Loving Many-Faceted Man's look is stubbornly himself. His exercise is on and off. His discipline fights his lazy streak. He lets his body go in some spot, but by no means everywhere. He tends to grow a little thick and shaggy rather than scrawny. He loves desserts.

He sticks to the attire he prefers – mainly comfortable clothes. When he wears what he wants, he makes whatever he has put on look as if he's worn it for years. Even when he has to go before the boss, the devil, or the Secretary General in a brand new tuxedo, which he'd do and enjoy, somehow he manages to mold the material to all his personal creases before the appointed hour.

The ease with which he wears his clothes often covers the fact that his parts overlap here and there. His total arrangement almost always shows a slight mix-up in details. In his switch from dad or pal to man of the world and back, he wears the wrong shoes, or a cuff link shirt with chinos, sews on two kinds of buttons, nicks himself using your razor, tries to trim his own hair, or uses his belt as a leash so his Cardin pants hang from tooth-marked leather. But his order is only disheveled at the edges and looks like the "I meant to return to it and didn't get to it" kind.

Some Loving Many-Faceted Men keep their cars clean, but never scrupulously so. Many let their cars take total care of themselves and hope for an occasional rain. However he keeps it, his car is more than a car to him; it's a room. If he's going to spend so much time in it, he's going to feel comfortable there! At any one time his auto carries a list, a ticket, half a map, papers, a pack of gum, an old tennis ball that rolls around the floor. It smells like him. (So do his clothes. But then, a lot of his clothes ride around in his car.) He generally selects a not-too-big, not-too-small kind of car in which he can feel the ride. He cares little about razzle-dazzle. He can go for vans or more sporty cars, Daytonas, Camaros, Mazda 626's, plain outdoorsy sorts like

Blazers or Nissan 4x4's, regular cars like Novas, Saabs and Subarus, a classic '53 Chevy truck, or a messy old Mercedes. Even when he possesses wealth, he rarely pays heed to glory and size. Despite the homey atmosphere in his personal vehicle, he often likes to switch and drive yours for a while. Indeed, he drives whichever one is handy. When you go out together, half the time he'd just as soon you drove anyway. His ego doesn't ride on who steers.

Since people interest the Loving Many-Faceted Man more than anything else, he finds himself drawn to people-oriented occupations, often services, and people-occupied places, usually towns. He mixes in with his community. Even when he dwells in rural areas, he knows and is known by his fellows. In the city, he often prefers areas that bear sectional names, neighborhoods that fight freeways, plant trees, and have some sense of politics.

His desire to huddle and participate sometimes leads him to seek even closer quarters than neighborhoods. He might head for apartments and co-ops. When he gets a flat or house, he shies away from the gigantic.

He more than uses his home, he *nests*. His place is cozy, a little zany. He does a lot of living on the floor. His desk, library, and television most likely are alongside his bed. He likes plenty of access to indoors and outdoors. He finds barbecues, sandboxes, and fish ponds appealing. He's intrigued by lots of little rooms, and loves drawers, nooks, and crannies.

The main difference between when he's mated and when he isn't is that one way all his stuff is mixed up with yours, the other way not. Whether he's with you or alone, the Loving Many-Faceted abode is never completely fixed up or decorated. With the Loving Many-Faceted Man, when friends, family, or funny business come to play, *anything* can wait for another day.

Since he really likes to play with toys (grown-up ones, that is), he tends to acquire things not for status, but because he'd like to try them. Once used, however, the items slip away from his attention and into the garage. Every now and then he puts everything in the trash and goes on to the next stage in his life.

He's a user. His most valued possessions have a "lived in" look. Sometimes you do, too. His volleyball is properly pumped but scuffed from being shot through baskets – he couldn't find his basketball. And if he owned a Gutenberg Bible and Shakespeare Folios, they, along with his other books, would be on the floor stacked in order of reading. As for his tools – he keeps them in three different places. But which one they're in at the moment is always up for grabs.

If his external space is in disorder, his internal one rarely is. Despite his variations, the Loving Many-Faceted Man has an unwavering view of life and of what a good person is. And he lives up to it. Values are important to him. He takes care to keep them. He has a sense of complete mutuality. To him, compromise is a perfectly pragmatic way to live. He knows when giving up and giving in win him the things he wants – love, trust, and respect.

Sex Signals

Since he wants to be so many things, the Loving Many-Faceted Man seeks a woman with whom he can feel most free. He looks for an assured maturity that means joy in life, a self-reliance that implies a willingness to flow. The woman he likes has the basic ingredients for flexibility. She's both curious and easily satisfied. He treats a woman as a complete equal, as an across-the-board partner, right from the first moment. He thinks the best companion makes her own decisions, but also consults him – and vice versa. He's prepared for and gives a wide range of emotions, but he doesn't go for tricks. He wants you to be you, not to just agree with him. He knows whom he's coupled with.

The Loving Many-Faceted Man likes nakedness – everything about bodies – as much as he likes honesty. He feels that you look best when you have no make-up on. He *loves* sex. He's very sensual. He loves his lovemaking rich, down to earth, cuddly, unashamed, not theatrical. He likes lots of foreplay and frequently prefers the bottom position or enters from behind in the double spoon shape. He wants his lady to have enough control that she really gets satisfied. He's nonplussed when you don't feel inclined or he doesn't feel active. Even when he's not making love he looks at your face and touches your skin. He exudes an easy ecstasy. He's warm and radiant. The most difficult part about bedding down with him is getting him not to creep all over your side of the bed.

Money Markers

Money isn't *money* to the Loving Many-Faceted Man, it's a Creative Plaything. While you may have plans and goals together, he doesn't think you should *deny* yourselves just to stockpile cash. Dollars are for down sleeping bags, nights out, an old jalopy, or a child! To play with and live with.

Usually his money is your money and yours is his. You give each other support and you split all the work, no matter who brings home the paycheck. Sometimes you may trade off roles of earner and homemaker. Most of the time you both do both. Occasionally one or both of you may decide to quit and fritter around a bit. It really doesn't matter who makes the bucks and who mops up.

Family Aspects

A Loving Many-Faceted Man almost always wants to jump into the generational flow and have children. He may want offspring of his own or he may be perfectly happy with someone else's. He figures children are part of life no matter whom they belong to. He wants to try out his father side as well as be pal, coach, and adviser. He concerns himself wholeheartedly with child raising and comes up with a very Many-Faceted solution – he treats kids as regular human beings. He listens to and plays with them. He gives his kids lots of time and involvement, taking care of them as much as he can and often as much as you do.

Usually, at some point, the Loving Many-Faceted Man reaches some understanding with his family that frees him truly to like his parents, brothers, and sisters. After that he thinks of them more as friends than relatives. He likes his links to other generations. His father and mother become pals and confidants. He bypasses rivalry with siblings and aims for teamwork. He discovers there's a common set of interests and a common history with his family – and with yours. No matter how different they are from him, they have a lot to offer.

But, strangely enough, while the Loving Many-Faceted Man makes friends with many people, both men and women, he's sort of a loner when it comes to close chums. He gets along with people and finds them the best of playthings, but doesn't especially depend on relationships with buddies. He sees friends for pure pleasure rather than support. Most of his time goes toward his many roles and the intensity with which he leads them, so while he enjoys social occasions and sports, he engages with his fellows less than you would expect.

The Loving Many-Faceted Man is unpredictable. Sometimes he takes silly chances. Maybe he never gains great heights. He goes against lots of traditional expectations – but meets more contemporary ones. Sometimes he seems to lack drive and direction, dropping things in the middle and never returning to them. He doesn't give you warning to prepare for new brainstorms. You have to be right on top of things with him. He's sort of diffuse and unsettled. And you might be right to worry about where his restlessness might lead.

But he also offers great assets. He sure knows who he is and how to take care of himself. He's one of the best of playmates and companions you could ever get and often comes closer to a women's point of view than any other man. He certainly tries to. And he's a show you can watch over the years – the Loving Many-Faceted Man's serendipity makes for a live version of *That's Entertainment*.

What Is in Store for You?

So you've come to the oracle to ask the age-old riddle: is there a way to love one and still have fun? A way to love two and still be true? How about a way to love three and have a certain he? Or a way to love four and maybe still more? The answer is – it's not impossible if they're all rolled into one.

You've got a good chance with the Loving Many-Faceted Man. And yet life with him is not always easy. Since the Loving Many-Faceted Man is a mixed bag, he may arrive at any time as a mechanic, a chef, a loner, or as Casanova. You have to be on your toes and ready to say, "Oh, it's *you!*" He may be one part predictable with maybe one element in his package that especially pleases him, or he may have no traditional traits or special predilections at all. In any case, life with him requires that you shed many ideas and categories (if you still have them and he doesn't). That includes preconceived notions about who does what for whom and also about whether life entails working toward ends, staying consistent, or always staying settled in a single town. You have to be secure in yourself and in a relationship that has few absolute ground rules to hold you together and not many customary habits to fall back upon. The more you can get future-free, role-free, guilt-free, and game-free, the more you can achieve a real relationship with this man.

With the Loving Many-Faceted Man, you can expect intimacy on just about every plane. Each twosome varies on how much they collaborate, but in general the Loving Many-Faceted Man holds back very little. Most aspects of his life are open, if not to your control, then at least to your awareness and consideration. He lacks closed realms that exclude his mate, unlike the Loving Limited Partner. Nor does he predicate the union on division and domain, as does the Loving Traditional Man. What you have in store is real cooperation. You get independence and yet interdependent support. There's hardly a change from courtship to committed life. He bends to your obligations, endeavors, and hankerings and releases you for your pursuits as much as you do him.

But in some ways you have the subtlest and trickiest of all twosomes. In no other relationship do you so constantly have to calculate the different advantages of surrender and demand as you do with the Loving Many-Faceted Man. Since almost every autonomous action on either of your parts entails, if not sacrifice, at least some adjustment, you always have to judge not simply what you want, but whether what you want is worth more than what you have. You also have to size up whether you are due your desire more than your mate is due his. It's true that with the Loving Many-

Faceted Man you can be many shapes and do many things. But you can't have all you want all of the time and still have a relationship.

Some of the other conditions that come with the Loving Many-Faceted Man are also quite strenuous. When two people steadily generate new propositions for their existence, problem-solving becomes a constant process. Almost every day starts with a definition of what has to be done, moves to decision (when, how, and by whom?) and evaluation (will it work for all concerned?), and then goes to implementation. And just because you reach an agreement with a Loving Many-Faceted Man once doesn't mean the matter is resolved. Almost every matter you settle reappears on a recurrent cycle.

With a Loving Many-Faceted Man you usually proceed ahead in a moderate way. You rarely come into spectacular fame or abundant wealth. Sometimes you do, however, and other times a wealthy man turns into a Loving Many-Faceted Man. Usually the Loving Many-Faceted Man is simply not that driven, is too diverse to reach ambitious pinnacles. Generally you settle for a certain modesty in your lifestyle. You slide by with some debts and scuffs. You go on trips to motels but not to the Ritz.

The character of the Loving Many-Faceted Man has some weak spots that might make him go amiss as you move to mid-life. His balance between compromise and insistence can go haywire, and he can start to exclude you. With his deep-seated mutability, a Loving Many-Faceted Man is prone to upheavals and sometimes the desire to shift away from life and wife.

Still, the challenge is terrific. The shape of things to come with him is a parallelogram. You trust life and you trust your mate. If you've discovered that there is no such thing as external security, but that you have security inside yourself, you're in the right place with the Loving Many-Faceted Man.

What Are the Telltale Signs of Trouble?

Suddenly the air is clear. You haven't heard a threat (like the Woman Hater's) or excuse (Short Affair and Quick Escape Artist's), heavy panting (like the Hustler's), cloying clucking (like the Sugar Pie Honey's), or a soul-searching cry for succor (like the Compelling Intense But Crazy Man's). Instead the man goes off to his labor happily and still calls you up to say hello. He finds it easy to come home to play and leave his work behind.

He and you presumably expect an alliance to grow. The Loving Many-Faceted couple is usually aware of up and down cycles, love and hate spells, and periods of alternating boredom and interest. Time shifts the perspective in any couple's picture, and sometimes the Loving Many-Faceted Man gets out of focus. The first sign of

Loving Many-Faceted trouble is almost always physical. He stops touching and hugging both in public and private. While he might be angry, most likely he's merely weary. He's not sure what to change next. Usually it's best to give him some distance and time. But if a natural resurgence doesn't soon move him close again, it's time to confer. It may be up to you to offer a plan that will revitalize your alliance.

Occasionally one party or the other starts to desire too much and compromise too little. Then the association takes on an air of dominance and submission. Someone starts to win and the other one to lose. If this situation builds too far, you're heading for real problems. The injured party starts to count "turns" and insists on rotation. You take your turn for the sake of the turn itself, not because you need it. Then you neglect the real essence of giving and getting. For the Loving Many-Faceted relationship, keeping tabs instead of meeting needs spells a bad downward spiral.

Some Loving Many-Faceted Men start sliding into the Secret Manipulator, sometimes even worse – they go toward the Sugar Pie Honey. If your man slyly begins to get his way always or complies overly with you while secretly keeping track of his sacrifices, the intimacy between you just took a dead-end turn. Occasionally a Many-Faceted Man turns into an Idle Lord and stops doing anything. Or one gets so enamored of change he either immediately becomes a Disaster Broker or he distances and reemerges as a Short Affair and Quick Escape Artist. Obviously, any of these alterations seriously changes the nature of your alliance.

You *can* overcome much with the Loving Many-Faceted Man. You can work, wait, call for compromise, or accept. But occasionally one mate decides on a policy that the other simply finds intolerable. You might come to lock horns over lovers, a separation, a move to Uganda, life in the wilds on fruits and berries, or a lack in cooperation. If the changes truly go against your desires, it's better to take a divided road. You can't keep the loving part of this relationship when you foolishly swallow an unbearable condition. You might stalemate for now and try for concordance later, but since ending a stalemate means one party has to bend, you're usually faced with checkmate sooner or later.

What Are Your Chances and What Should You Do?

A Loving Many-Faceted union means *committed intimates*. As mates, you aim to keep on keeping on. So long-term teaming is possible, and in fact, it's highly probable. But while all the relationships with the three Intimate Men are rich and full, none of them springs full grown from the sea on a half shell. Nor do they stay rosy without effort. The Loving Many-Faceted union requires more sustenance than any other.

Two crucial weak spots plague the Loving Many-Faceted relationship. One is the presumption that what is best for you is best for your mate. The theory is that your fulfillment and your happiness enables your lover and others to derive more from you. And that's true. But there's a hitch: when one of the important points of your fulfillment is the relationship itself, you always have to consider that what is best for you *may* be what your mate wants and not what you desire.

When you eliminate boundaries between roles and responsibilities, sometimes you end up with more fences to mend than ever. With the Loving Many-Faceted Man you can experience "upkeep fatigue." Working on relating well requires lots of energy, and people are inclined to get lazy, or they just get tired of paying constant attention. The Loving Many-Faceted alliance is too intricate to leave alone. To lie back all too often means to lay waste.

However, this is a countermeasure: work on *yourself*. From there you can work on how you relate to your mate. The happier you keep yourself, the more centered you are, the better you can live with whatever comes your way and accept change, yet maintain sharing. The more philosophically you lead your life, the less important particulars become.

With the Loving Many-Faceted Man, I suggest you sidestep jealousy as much as you can. By that I mean not just the carnal kind – in case of an affair – but the kind that surrounds what you did or didn't get to do. Basically the Loving Many-Faceted Man is a monogamous, mutual man. He gives fidelity and openly shares his life. At some point he expects the same in return, as a statement of commitment. Just remember the key to your pairing is your pledge of trust and troth despite peculiar events.

Stay mindful of repression and restrictions. Remember that curiosity and freedom are vital to the Loving Many-Faceted Man. Limit your no's and be generous with your yes's. What the hell? Go on and get silly! Drink Chablis straight from the bottle in a rowboat on an off-limits canal. Take up disco dancing. Get a hot tub. Shed your inhibitions and don't resist fun. But stay true to yourself. Your cooperation should by no means mean obedience. If you turn your Many-Faceted Man into an unwilling dominant party over a submissive you – or vice versa – you head for a rough spell, if not total ruin.

A parting from a Loving Many-Faceted Man is both sad and painful. All too often, separating Many-Faceted mates try to keep close while untying their emotions, so the mourning lasts a long time and so does the disentanglement. If this happens to you, muster all the conviction you have, cut yourself off completely, and reopen channels only after a lengthy period. Usually there is a bond of affection and mutual admiration; in time you can become friends and helpers. But the detachment must come first. If you have to have an ex-lover, at least you have one who cares in the Loving Many-Faceted Man.

I must add one last piece of advice. If you're thinking of doing or staying with a Loving Many-Faceted Man because the man is *so* good but not because you love him . . . Don't. As a great all-around character and a backer-upper, he can look like the best way to be good to yourself whether you adore him or not. But you don't do yourself a favor in allying yourself with *anyone* for whom you don't have that special spark. Denying yourself love is always a mistake. And it always catches up, in the form of remorse, disappointment, or bitterness, despite what pluses you gain in the meantime. Furthermore, he'll resent your lack of candor and sooner or later he'll retaliate – he may grow selfish, or he may walk out the door.

But if you fall for the Loving Many-Faceted Man, I heartily advise that you close your eyes and jump on in for better or worse. If he lacks guarantees and gives imperfect promises, remember he doesn't know what may cause him to change or transport him to somewhere else; he just knows the possibility lurks inside him as long as he's alive. If he shakes up your expectations, and will never be exactly normal, don't forget he will stay where the rewards are good and he'll compromise to keep them flowing.

You could hardly ask more of yourself.

Where Do You Fit In?

The ad hypes that "you've come a long way, baby." Well maybe you have. Certainly you have it in you to do, think, and be all the things you want. And that's a giant step for humankind whatever your sex may be. The resolution to be all you are lies right in your mind. Striving for your full potential goes hand in hand with reaching intimacy. Some people call it self-actualization. Some call it being centered, or being your own best friend. Others rightly tag it as having nothing to lose. But whatever you call it, when you're ready to do or be a Loving Many-Faceted person, you have to reach a step that's beyond plain self-knowledge. You have to become full of yourself. It means moving beyond myths of how you're supposed to live and just *being*. That's not to say that you might not then *choose* to live in a customary way, but whatever path you pick, you do so for fulfillment.

Almost every woman I know feels she needs love. And so she searches for it. And almost every woman also questions whether or not she's like other people; not only if she fits in, but if something might be innately *wrong* with her. Some individuals get their feet caught in these mires and never progress. They spend a major part of their lives in a quest for affection and approval. As a result, no matter what they do, they suffer distress. They worry if their dress is wrong, their bearing unseemly, their verbiage derived from Dick and Jane. They're sure others will dislike them if they don't come off just right.

Unfortunately, when you wallow in such a bog, most likely you fritter away all chance for intimacy right when it's in the palm of your hand. The Intimate Man, especially the Loving Many-Faceted Man, requires a personal evolution on your part beyond the need for love and approval. When you discover that wanting love is a strong desire and an easily fulfilled one, then you can take life the way it comes. When you don't care whether you fit in or not, you find situations more curious than threatening. Presto change-o, a great thing happens. You find pleasure however and wherever you are!

Once you've reached this plateau, you derive something even *more* significant, a special secret. You discover that it's challenge itself that keeps you vibrant. You're ready to take on anything new and different. You become the Marco Polo, Columbus, Admiral Byrd, Einstein, and Madame Curie of your own world. You turn your energy from potential to kinetic. You activate yourself. You learn that tackling new problems is as vital to you as food and water.

But watch out for two common pitfalls. If you take actualization to mean you should take on a plethora of activities, you turn energy into just another distance mechanism, and you probably still need outside recognition. The woman who becomes superwoman, super mom, and wonder worker eliminates intimacy and substitutes frenzy. And if you think that having once achieved heights of balancing yourself means you will always stay perfectly balanced, then you fool yourself. Real feelings don't always match up to consciousness. People go up and they also come down. If you deny your feelings you also deny your cycles, and you can go down a long, long way before you come back up.

If you're willing to let your mate both change and vacillate, and also move on to new challenges and fulfillment . . . why not allow yourself? It's good, and good for you!

All three Intimate Men are similar to one another in their patterns and behaviors. Sometimes they are combinations, being mainly one kind of man but having some traits of the others. A Loving Many-Faceted Man, for example, might prefer to be the major breadwinner and can harbor some traditional ideas like the Loving

Traditional Man. He can also be quite devoted to one particular interest, a hobby, sport, or his work, so that although he's more well-rounded and sharing, he can be a little like the Loving Limited Partner.

The Loving Limited Partner is the last man I describe. He's an intimate, adoring man, but he differs from the other two in one way or aspect. You see, where a relationship with a woman comes first and foremost with the other two Intimate Men, with the Loving Limited Partner it doesn't. Something else comes first, and his relationship comes second. *High*, but second. How can I call him Intimate then? Because even though he has another devotion, he still *is* an intimate man. Loving Limited Partners have always existed and have always been good men, but in the past they didn't suit us very well. Women wanted and needed more. We didn't recognize him. Now we have changed. We often have major compelling work or devotions of our own, and suddenly the Loving Limited Partner has begun to shine for us in all his glory. He's perfect for many of us nowadays. Maybe for you.

22

Intimate Three – The Loving Limited Partner

His Work Comes First – Maybe Yours Does Too – But After That He's the Best of Romantic, Caring, Committed Men

He's a cream-of-the-crop lover. He's willing to be your one and only partner. But there's a condition. You've got some competition, and that competition will always come first. Still, he loves and adores you. He likes nothing better than talking to you, seeing you, romancing you, after hours and on the weekends. He's the Loving Limited Partner.

The Loving Many-Faceted man is a potpourri of everything he can be. The Loving Traditional Man brings home the bacon to his lady in the castle. But the Loving Limited Partner is a little different. He has a compulsion that takes up the lion's share of his devotions. But beyond that, he's a primo pal and confidant.

The Loving Limited Partner wants a close love and union. But his vocation, interest, hobby, *something*, is the most important thing in his life and he knows it. As much as he might love a woman, he is simply unwilling to subordinate his compelling devotion to the demands of a full scale union. Usually, it is his work that transcends all else. Yet, his work doesn't completely consume him. He's not hell bent for power, position, or duty to the point of spending every hour with five phones, ten pens, and a drawing board in hand, like the Man Who Would Be Mogul. Yes, he wants achievement, but beyond it he wants camaraderie and commitment from a special someone.

He loves. He enjoys things. He knows intimacy and wants it. He takes pleasure in his lover. He wants a partnership. But his relationship simply comes second. If forced, he would part with a woman before he'd part with his primary devotion.

Still, as a partner, despite that one condition, he's pretty close to perfect. Indeed, he's almost storybook. He tends to be a romantic mate, dashing at times, always devoted, interested. He's the best of roses in boxes. Gallant, delicious, and he'll hire somebody else to do the dishes.

Because of his dedication to some interest, what suits him best is a woman who's his match. If you have some major drive that competes with your love life, a career or calling that means more to you than anything, a major interest, or if you simply thrive on a great deal of autonomy and plenty of time to yourself, yet you also desire an intimate sidekick – get yourself a Loving Limited Partner.

In fact, the lady who displays such individualism and absorption is just what the Loving Limited Partner is looking for. When he picks a consort he proceeds with caution. Usually he errs once or twice in picking mates until he realizes clearly and painfully just how much his work means to him, and how it comes before his alliance. Once he discovers that fact, he seeks a woman who also requires a certain detachment. He likes self-reliant women, women who know their minds. A combination of composure and drive carries him away. If you state your stance and keep your equilibrium, if you relish both romance and some other calling, you could make a Loving Limited Partner as happy as a clam. And he you.

Story

Probably the most go-getting, persevering, self-confident person I have ever met in all my years of interviewing is a woman named Nadine. Nadine was determined to become a doctor – and not just a pediatrician. With a hemostat in hand and a green surgical mask on her face, she threw her class and professors into total turmoil when she told them she aimed to be a neurosurgeon and cut brains.

Nadine never had a doubt about her destined profession since the day she was four, a fateful birthday when, despite grandparental disapproval, she insisted on a doctor's kit and refused a nurse's. She was determined and driven, but Nadine was no bulldozer or ice maiden. And no one could dismiss her as "masculine." She preferred Chanel to PhisoHex any day. Just because she was set on her career didn't mean she desired to forfeit a love life. Nadine wanted and needed love as much as anyone. But early on she knew she would relegate a *stressful* passion into the wastebasket if it interfered with her wielding a scalpel.

She got involved, too involved, in a heavy emotional romance with a classmate early in her medical training. It nearly unstrung her – the ups and down, his fits and demands, her agonies and wasted nights. After that she kept her alliances casual and short-lived the rest of the way through medical school. She had little energy for personal drama as an intern and resident. Nonetheless, casual attachments left her feeling hollow, as if something were missing. Besides, many of her devoted suitors seemed to be dependent persons who needed her in ways that chilled her. She knew, she hoped, that a relationship without the strain of too little emotion, or too much, existed somewhere. But she didn't know where, and she didn't know how to arrange it.

Then she met Colin. In many ways he seemed totally different from her. His parents were divorced. He himself was divorced. He was devoted to the arts, not the sciences. But one similarity stood out. Nothing but nothing was as important to Colin as his obsession and work – architecture. The main thing Colin wanted in life was an empty space, a pencil sharpener, paper, and no telephone. The second thing he sought, but only after the first, was a person. He wanted somebody to love. For a long time he'd been looking for a special, emancipated partner with whom to live.

There are two kinds of Loving Limited Partner: those who develop a deep *like* (rather than love) and seek a warm, but mutually "convenient" relationship of living together, and those who are more erotic and romantic, who continue a kind of live-in courtship. In Colin, Nadine found a lucky combination of both. Eroticism plays a big part in their relationship. They get ever lustier the more they grow committed. Yet they rely on one another like business associates and no-nonsense negotiators about who does what. They are clearly and publicly a couple, yet they don't go everywhere together. When they do go to some event, they often arrive at different times and in separate cars. They delight in the soirees they give. They call each other without fail when apart, late, or unable to appear, although it's hard to say if they miss each other even when one or the other is gone on a trip. They figure that consideration and civility are the keys that allow them to maintain their alliance while doing as they please. When they're alone together, they love to go to restaurants, go away for the weekend, or just spend hours saying nothing while reading in their king-sized bed. They steadfastly refuse to acquire any knowledge whatsoever about the other's profession, and put up with only some of each other's professional pals. But they find all kinds of other common interests – the symphony, or movies on their VCR. Their main controversy at first, when funds were low, was the division of labor: who handled the bills, maintenance, shopping. They almost split up over the issue several times. Now they hire help even when funds are down, and they keep to a rigid assignment of who oversees what work. They keep separate accounts while putting equal shares toward the house and trips. Nadine earns more money, more steadily; Colin's income is on and off.

Frequently they discuss, objectively, whether they will remain together permanently. If conditions change and Nadine goes to Pago Pago to open a clinic, Colin would not follow, although he'd fly in occasionally. When Colin gets obsessed and irascible, Nadine withdraws to her office and the company of fellow doctors. Nadine and Colin *intend* to stay together forever. But their deal reads that if their separate desires lead them apart, they will arrange a more part-time affiliation or part with a fond good-bye.

They discuss the issue of children about once every three years or so. They continue to decide against them. They agree that with so few moments together, they would rather greedily hoard them to themselves. They love their restaurants, travel, and other delights where children would present an obstacle. And since they still turn each other on, without children they have the time and privacy to add wine and candles.

The Loving Limited Partner takes more restraint, but also more vows (words of honor, declarations) than either of the other Intimate Men. Still, one of his difficulties is that he prefers to avoid heavy discussions, and the bottom line is always that you have to rely on yourself. It takes determination and, at the same time, expansion, to overcome matters that would knock many other people apart – solitude, separation, self-direction. But the rewards can be tremendous. At the very least you get security, care, comfort, and sharing. At the top – elegance, independence, and sexiness. More Loving Limited Partner males than females used to exist. Now there are nearly equal numbers of such men and women. Both recognize the fact that life with *controlled* intimacy is a levelheaded possibility.

How Can You Identify This Kind of Man?

The storms of total entanglement? He'd rather not weather them All-encompassing intensity? He says no, thank you. He doesn't want to come out and play, like a Many-Faceted Man. And being a provider is not his favorite role. He's a singular person who finds satisfaction and the richest experiences with a mate. So although he knows love could bring him trouble and a rocky road, he risks the possible bad for the potential good. He just sets limits first.

The Loving Limited Partner is a very composed man, often rather quiet. He's usually determined, linear in his approach to his devotion and to other things, and of course, he's strongly one-themed.

But that doesn't mean it's his *only* theme. He adds other interests like counterpoints. They add richness to his life, new and different tones. He likes them, gets involved in them, learns about them, but only as sidelines. He may, for example, love music in addition to his major interest. He might like some sports (to practice more than watch), or he may enjoy the outdoors. He might get quite interested in art, food and wine, or electronics. But again, these are only added colors to his main tone.

He also tends to think of himself as a rational man. In fact, he thinks of himself as *the* Rational Man. He believes logic, plans, and outlines solve anything. But he has a good sense of humor (that is most do, some are too devoted to laugh much), and you can usually tease him about his logic. At any rate, the way you run things, even if he calls you irrational, isn't his business and he willingly says so.

He tends to go about his life good-temperedly. He plunks down time and attention in measured and concentrated sequences. He has a schedule. He rises and meets it. He thinks ahead. He's responsible and obligated. He's liable to fret a bit.

Outer Signs

In personal habits, the Loving Limited Partner tends to be clean, clipped, and cool. He's generally a statement in efficiency. His hair just licks the tops of his ears. His beard never, never looks like whiskers. His bathroom routine is set, and it always takes exactly the same amount of time.

His clothes and trappings resemble a walking résumé. He states what he is in his dress, and he states it briefly and swiftly. He's bus-iness-y if his devotion is business. He's design-y if it's design. He's woodsy if he is an ecologist, science-y if it's science, sportsy if it's race cars. He doesn't like complications in attire. Whatever it is, he's not the kind to wear patches, tatters, or patterns. (Strangely enough though, he likes his food complicated and highly flavored, whether it's city French or country chili.)

His speech bears a certain reticence. He pauses before vocalizing; his smile only goes halfway. Instead of laughing, he shows pleasure by crinkling up his crow's-feet. He's not so much a *happy* man as one who has dealt with *unhappiness* and learned the joy of contentment.

His aura of control seeps into his environment. He keeps his papers straight and clipped, or he lives in a marvelous mess you could call "perfected chaos" in which he knows where everything is. He listens to Haydn, Bach, and Mozart because the themes repeat beautifully, or else he switches to Coltrane.

He sees things holistically. Just a snap and focus and he's got the picture. He's inclined to generalize and reluctant to spell out details. He may not know how he reaches his conclusions. Often Loving

Limited Partners claim introspection is a waste. Sometimes his quick conclusions make him seem insensitive to others. He isn't. He just doesn't how how to solve problems for anyone but himself.

He prefers his tools to be an extension of himself, not an obstruction. He selects a smooth car, if not automatic then something that fits him like a part of his body. A Porsche is not unlikely, nor an Alfa Romeo or Corvette. Or it's a perfect Jeep or pickup, or a well- kept Thunderbird, even an Acura or Honda. Whatever it its, it's perfect for his work or his style. He takes care of his vehicle. The Loving Limited Partner usually keeps it well-oiled, well-tuned, and well-polished. It may be his only baby. He doesn't like to lend it to anyone, not even his mate.

Rather than just having a place to flop, he cares to provide himself with a *home*. Even prior to partnering, he makes his apartment homelike or else buys his own house. He becomes attached to his nest, which is surprising considering his other detachments. (Often you have to move in with him. He won't give up his place for yours.) He tends to opt for massiveness and expanse although he doesn't choose size for the impression it makes, like the Man Who Would Be Mogul. He likes lots of room for a sense of *quiet*. He always picks somewhere private. He often creates a Spartan atmosphere. When he does fill up the walls, it's with books or some special collection. The idea of *use* always concerns the Loving Limited Partner – even in parapets and mantels. So as well as having art, his collections consist of objects that work or once worked, such as old cameras, utensils, or tools. When his vocation is such that he can work alone, his residence becomes an office as well as a domicile. His bedroom functions as his work room and his bed doubles as his desk.

After pairing up, he requires privacy as much as ever. Although he has a place of business elsewhere, he establishes a household nook for himself that no other living soul gets to dust – a den, a study, a space in the basement or garage. He encourages you to keep a place of *your* own and to have a separate desk. When he's at work or in his hideaway, he may cut himself off for hours. He puts the phone on hold (or in the refrigerator). He has his secretary fend off the world or else he pulls the shades and puts the unopened mail under the kitty litter.

When he comes out of his compulsion and into the warmth of communication, he does it fast. He heads for the kitchen, which may well be part of his turf. Cooking is often his household job. Loving Limited Partners very frequently take a fancy to food preparation: they go for haute cuisine such as North Italian, or good Chinese or Kansas Provincial.

Sex Signals

When he meets a woman, he takes the time to peruse. He's very selective. He seeks an affectionate, sexual co-conspirator, wishes to avoid a champion or keeper. He's definitely not the Kid. Sometimes it seems as if he doesn't even really need a friend. Indeed, as the relationship develops, he has little to say that wasn't all said in the first few months.

Love is important to him. He wants his permanence and commitment with his lady to have a reason. And he likes the tie to be both mental and physical. When he's with you, he's with you all the way. Your conversations more often center on things (such as crock pots, rose bushes, and exhibits at the museum) than on feelings. Still, he's the kind of companion you don't *have* to talk to. His silences are eloquent.

Certainly he converses sexually, usually loudly and clearly. He likes sex to be private, very special, erotic as opposed to giddy, a touch traditional. He gets quite artful. He makes love as if he were Rembrandt painting a masterpiece. He studies your lines, your contours and corners. He builds you up layer after layer, until you burst into color. He has an air of control. He may like to make love often for a while – and then have long quiet spells. But even the quick morning sketches he sometimes performs are *very* deftly stroked! Despite his reserve, he's quite a sexual man. Once you're paired, that sexuality envelops you both.

The Loving Limited Partner commits himself to his partner. Once mated, no matter how much he moves about on his own, he never carries on as if he's single. He doesn't pretend he's unattached in order to maneuver better, like The Man Who Would Be Mogul. The Loving Limited Partner values his romance and his honesty. His attachment is real and has no secrecy to it.

Money Markers

The Loving Limited Partner usually likes money matters separately managed. He gets almost square about financial arrangements. The subject of money always makes him tense and touchy, touchy enough to make him unhappy if all his money is combined with someone else's. He doesn't like supporting you or him. Most likely he has his account and he likes you to keep yours. And just the way you don't switch cars, you don't use each other's checks.

You do have a mutual fund that goes for expenses you run up in common. Generally you summon up equal amounts, or perhaps it goes 60/40 or 70/30, according to salary. But you always keep records, rebalance, and actually write out loans. The drawback in this arrangement is all the decisions. Do electricity, Nyquil, and olive oil go down as mutual expenditures? If so, are driving gloves, high heels, and secretarial services separate?

You may become formal business partners in various ventures. He may invest with you and for you (he prefers real estate). The Loving Limited Partner is cautious with money. He likes it to grow slowly and carefully. But whether or not he turns out a wealthy man, he rarely lets either you or himself flounder into ruin.

Family Aspects

Most Loving Limited Partners look askance on children. They hesitate over, or simply decline, the notion. It's not the *responsibility* of children that deters them, it's the interference. After all, the Loving Limited Partner is a self-interested man, and he well recognizes his inclinations. He prefers to spend his limited leisure and money on grown-up pleasures. He knows that a child could threaten and encumber his highly prized work. Occasionally, as he gets somewhat older and his career, money, and relationships are more solid, or if his mate expresses a strong desire, he becomes inclined to try fatherhood. But even then he tends to limit the number. He allows for one well-cared-for child.

He not only backs off from descendants, he backs off from ascendants and collaterals as well, namely parents, siblings, and cousins. He may well be an only child or the child of divorced parents, who learned to love his solitude early. The Loving Limited Partner keeps his ties to his family as trimmed, formal, and symbolic as possible. He notes Christmas, Mother's Day, and other days with cards, calls, and perhaps a gift. He may pay the necessary two-day visit. Because of the distance he feels from them, he worries about how he will handle the future care of his parents. He views your family as yours. He rarely makes anything other than a friendly tie with them.

The Loving Limited Partner usually maintains longstanding friendships with one or two men from his same field of endeavor. He sees them in the office, at home, for lunch and sports – in other words, often. He might jog with his pal. Despite how bookish or isolated he seems, the Loving Limited Partner is surprisingly athletic. Sometimes he and his two friends go bowling or play squash. But mostly they visit and chat; their conversations are so continuous they never seem to start or terminate. He and his pals seem commonly to fear aging. They figure they'll all go together if they stay tightly knit.

More than likely the Loving Limited Partner has one or two good woman friends, too. Probably they had an affair and managed to become platonic chums. Usually they are from the same profession. Rather than lose one another, they shift into friendly consultants.

Beyond his regular circle, however, the Loving Limited Partner says no. He easily turns down invitations. Mostly he prefers the one person he doesn't have to chat with – you. You two make up a closed community of just each other.

He's not good at changing. He resists experiments. The way he makes independent decisions without consulting you can be irksome, and sometimes he acts businesslike about emotions. But he's a great partner and an intimate lover. He's rich in wonderful qualities. His own determination makes him a constant source of interest. His energy never dwindles. He's loving and sharing, honest and trustworthy. And you don't have to take care of him. He can take care of himself.

What Is in Store for You?

Here's a whole new recipe for cooking up a twosome. The ingredients are the same – combine one man and one woman – only you don't completely blend them. Sometimes this method makes for a successful concoction. Sometimes the attempt fails and the sauce curdles. But if you follow the instructions carefully, one thing is for certain. Nobody gets diluted, or creamed.

No, *The Joy of Cooking* is not the reference book for the Loving Limited Partner repast. The book you need is a text of basic law. The term "Limited Partner" comes straight from legal practice. It concerns contractual agreements between business partners. While among most of the types of men the relationships are the more "marital" sort, this particular alliance in many ways, instead, parallels a business association – albeit a romantic one.

In short, you can enter into an association in one of two ways. You can go for a general partnership of the "one for all and all for one" sort. Or you can set specific limits and name specific terms. Naturally, these two methods differ in significant respects – particularly in how much the parties involved have to lose or gain with each other's ups and downs, and how much say-so they get in each other's decisions. In the general partnership, you completely share all obligations, belongings, and duties, no matter whose they are. Ostensibly *no* separate decisions exist. They are all mutual decisions, whether they were actually made together or not. And all expenses and profits are shared, no matter who contracts the costs or makes the gain. In a limited partnership, on the other hand, you are obligated only for the amount of money, work, and obligation that you declare. You share in and are responsible for only those conditions that you agree to. But those conditions are also the only ones in which you get to add your say-so. You get no vote in matters beyond your stated participation. Beyond the shared area, all your decisions, purchases, costs, losses and profits are your own. Your partner doesn't join in them. The same goes for your partner. His separate decisions are his own, as are his possessions, his debts and gains. You don't necessarily partake. All told, you take fewer risks with a limited partnership than you do with a general partnership, for which you derive a narrower range of benefits. You have less control over your partner, his actions, possessions, choices. But you retain more control over your own and yourself.

Among both the more "convenience" sort of Loving Limited Partnership and the more romantic type, the particular agreements differ vastly. The contract between you and your lover can be narrow, covering only limited occasions and specific items, with no shared items. Or, it can be broad, covering all your monies, work, space, fidelity, care, property, objects, pastimes, passports, and patents. In any case a Loving Limited Partner is more your "associate" than your caretaker. He only hears your tribulations as a listener and sounding board. He doesn't solve your problems. And while you consider his requests, you don't have to meet them. You can both declare your desires, but it's up to each of you to seek fulfillment for yourselves.

You simmer, more than boil, if you're in the "convenience" kind of Loving Limited Partnership. You want and have a partner for comfort, for a shared life and lifestyle, for companionship, not for passion. In the other sort of Loving Limited Partnerships, more romance and eroticism are involved. You're nuts about each other, deeply, lustily in love. You simply happen to have a greater devotion. You feel strong emotion, but you keep the lid on it, enough so that your passion never interferes with your interest.

In the first sort, though it sounds less romantic, you still get a powerful potion. When you're interested in each other, feel great affection, and have cultivated many common pleasures, despite your independence, you can develop a very special kind of love. Rather than pitched, it's deep, steady, amiable. It's like having a best friend – one you don't have to see constantly but you always know is there – forever. In the other kind of Loving Limited Partnership you can acquire another type of special love, again another rare sort. You can get a love that's almost like constant courtship. It's thrilling, invigorating. Your separations work to keep you quietly anticipating, waiting to see one another. And anticipation is one of the world's most enjoyable feelings.

The best part of both sorts of Loving Limited Partner pairings is that they involve tremendous, adult acceptance of one another. And that's the tops in love. The bad side, if there is one, is that you must constantly and cautiously keep an equilibrium between your independence and dependence, your autonomy and your sharing. The balance involved is very, very tricky. In some respects you must become dependent on your partner in order to stay together, as any couple does. You must bow to compromise. Yet in other ways, you absolutely have to stay independent. If you don't follow your own life, you alter the basic premise of your relationship, and you ruin it. That means, on a daily basis, you have to know just how much to share, and how much to keep your distance. You have to watch the ebb and flow of your needs, like a weatherman watches the clouds.

Other aspects of the Loving Limited Partnership can also prove problematic. While the Loving Limited Partner is a very honest man (as are all the Intimate Men), he in particular has trouble telling you exactly how he feels. He can give you a blanket statement, such as "I love you," but he's not very good at describing just how and why. Or he can bring you roses and diamond clips, but never tell you he cares. With a Loving Limited Partner, you have to accept what he says and what he does as enough.

He also means the limitations he sets. They don't alter. He'll tell you what his rules are, what he likes and doesn't like, can and can't take, will and won't handle. Perhaps he'll tell you too much. He's inclined to over-set his boundaries as a precautionary measure. He figures it's safer to have too many limits than too few. So if you ever want to change any of his limits, you'll have to proceed carefully and not expect many changes. Often he also gets stuck in his own self-definition and over-restricts himself. That can cut into the time and things you do together. Anything he says he won't do, but which you still desire (whether it's taking out the trash or going to see *Fidelio* in Vienna), you'll have to do yourself.

Your dance of separation, then moments of lovely togetherness, could last for life. You could grow closer and do more together with age and retirement. (Remember, he may never be able to leave his central obsession for long, so trips may be limited. But then maybe you can't leave yours either.) On the other hand your independence and your desire to do things your own way could last forever too. You might have to travel together sometimes and separately others, explore life both on your own and with your pal, even when you're old. With a Loving Limited Partner, you can.

What Are the Telltale Signs of Trouble?

When a man grades you as excellent but not at the top of his list, you have an immediate decision to make. If you really want to be a man's major subject and number one concern, you should change to another man posthaste. But if second place (since the competition isn't another woman) is O.K. with you, in fact it's the place you *want*, you could well have met the man that could be your second place devotion for life.

Generally things go well, but if they begin to get unbalanced you'll hear your Loving Limited Partner using three little words a lot. These words are money, time, and work. The more frequently he brings up one or more of these topics, the more he's signalling internal disturbance, anger, resentment, disappointment, or frustration. Sometimes he's simply feeling his independence threatened. After using these words, he'll start to distance himself, letting you know in gesture what he was saying in words. He feels something – you, or whatever – encroaching on his main concern. The funny thing is, of course, the same set of signals operates for you. When you feel he's intruding on your cash, concerns, or time, you retreat. You can emerge from these troubles in one of three ways: heed the warnings, get to the bottom, and work out the problem; find another outlet where you can discharge your needs and emotions without disturbing your partner; or pop up and declare that the Loving Limited Partner setup isn't working out for you – for whatever reason, you need more.

Occasionally a resentful or jealous Loving Limited Partner starts to act like a Woman Hater. He finds himself embroiled in difficult feelings and he decides to cite you as the cause. He attacks you as being at fault instead of revamping himself. He grows cold and critical. At other times, the Loving Limited Partner can get over-rational. Constantly calling on logic, he eliminates all closeness. Call him on it. It's depressing when someone claims people have sex only because they "need" it. Or he says love is only a trumped up emotion to cover dependency. If he persists in woman hating or over-rationalizing, it may be time for a separation – or time to look for another Loving Limited Partner.

What Are Your Chances and What Should You Do?

The point of commitment is to go the distance. The Loving Limited Partner has every intention of doing so. Working it out and staying together is, as with the other Intimate Men, the highest of possibilities.

Loving Limited Partnering, however, can come in several variations that can affect the chances of your future success. Most commonly, the two partners in the union have diverse preoccupations, say, tinker and tailor. Sometimes both members have the same profession but go separately – two doctors, two senators, two journalists or two caterers. Sometimes they are partners in some establishment – a store, office, or shop. Occasionally the career of one mate involves the occupation of the other. He sings, she manages his singing. She dances, he promotes her. In all cases, Loving

Limited Partnerships succeed only when the parties coordinate their individual ambitions and labor with their personal relations. I am loath to wave the finger of prophecy. But it seems the more entangled a couple's business and bedding are, the more difficult the balance. When partners mix it up by night and day, in work and play, the more cause for adversity arises and the more iffy their chances become. In other words, the more separate your callings and the more you work apart, the better the odds are you'll stay together.

Still, with the Loving Limited Partner, the trying is good in any case. All kinds of Loving Limited Partner pairs make fine, long hauls of varying lengths, up to and through old age. Some intend to go for forever right from the start. Some never try to second-guess the fates, go one day at a time, but make it all the way just the same.

In order to thrive along with constant divergences in taste, opinion, scheduling, will, and location, you need particular fortitude. You can make or break your relationship depending upon your ability to keep your equanimity. Since it's such a tightrope act to balance him and balance you, juggle your work and love life, weigh your togetherness and solitude, I suggest you keep your burdens limited. If you have a mind to add any other problems, such as children or extra commitments, judge carefully: your two lives may add up to enough without added extras. You may or may not stipulate sexual fidelity. It seems most Loving Limited Partnerships are either monogamous or very discreet. Jealousy is anybody's Pandora's box. You may demand certain times off, separate vacations where anything goes, or at least where you're away from each other for a while. You might prefer to live in different cities, even on separate coasts, and have a commuter union. But you'd better get subjects like sex and socializing out in the open and some policy decided.

Loving Limited Partners have more weapons available to hurt one another than do many other couples. They can use distance, lack of response, competition, autonomy, rule-breaking as means of humiliation. Just because you diverge from your mate doesn't mean you should get two-faced. Be careful not to turn your delicate balance into a sparring match.

You have so little time for intimacy, remember to fight for it. The key to the treasure chest means keeping the love alive. If you like the idea of the Loving Limited Partner and you like your man, I advise not only caring for the companion, but caring for the companionship. You *can* avoid touchy subjects and stick to common interests – until you have nothing left but hollow company. Your joys and sorrows are what keep the life blood flowing.

Because of all these complexities, breakups do occur, and despite all the preparations, dissolutions are often more painful than you would expect. Sometimes your careers take you separate ways. I suggest that you fight for your union, but if all else fails, part as friends and don't look back. What you learn from one Loving Limited Partner you can apply to another. The Loving Limited Partner alliance is worth trying again.

Where Do You Fit In?

Some women prefer enclosed spaces and well-known ground; although they go out a certain amount, they really like to be at home. Others love to be out thrashing about the world. Home is where they are least, although they want at least some semblance of a nesting place.

The main trick to the Loving Limited Partner relationship is simply recognizing who you are. If indeed you don't want your autonomy tampered with, prefer a certain amount of distance, back off from over-abundant intimacy, or have an ambition decidedly removed from a romantic relationship, your nature is bound to become apparent.

The problem is when you *don't* recognize your penchant but still *act it out*. Your career goes right, but your love life goes downhill. You *think* you want a permanent alliance but enter unions you know are bound for the same fate as the *Andrea Doria*. You talk about the right man, but somehow he never comes along. You keep picking losers and then ask why. You start to explore a number of good unions but find reasons why they won't work out, and you run. You find a nice situation and get so impossible you push your lover out. You say good unions no longer exist, and you sit in your living room and watch the days pass. You do Short Affair and Quick Escaping ("I'm not ready yet") or you Hustle ("One-night stands are so free of constraint").

The point is, there's nothing *wrong* with wanting solitude or self-determination. When a man hangs around too long in the morning, and you say, "A diller, a dollar, a ten o'clock scholar," and send him on his way, you haven't committed a sin. If he thinks you have, he *is* the wrong man. There's nothing wrong with not wanting a male or a mate at all.

It's only after you establish in what ways you do and don't want an in-depth consortium that you can decide if you want at least a partial one. Only when you no longer envision attachment as imprisonment can you determine how you want to link up. Then alone does controlled intimacy become a levelheaded possibility.

Once you discover that you do want a mate and maybe a long-term mating, but only under certain conditions, you've got work to do. Rather than acting out, you need awareness of your wants. Rather than making assumptions, you have to *express* yourself. And be ethical about your own rules. If you want autonomy, ask for a pact in which you maintain *yourself*. When it comes to the Loving Limited Partner, better think your statements through before you make them. It's up to you to keep them. But when you can and you do, linking up with a Loving Limited Partner can be a perfect solution. Exciting, loving, romantic, caring, sexy, still giving you all the room you need, and worth it.

Sometimes a Loving Limited Partner is willing to take on more roles and share on more levels, like a Loving Many-Faceted Man. Sometimes he'll be the breadwinner exclusively and partner up with a woman who earns no living. He'll do so particularly if his mate still has a very strong other calling, like doing charity, being an artist or musician. He's close to the other types of Intimate Men, for all the men who have truly broken into intimacy are like one another – they understand closeness, love, and sharing. But even though all three are Intimate, it doesn't mean each one matches with any woman. A Loving Traditional Woman would have trouble dealing with a Many-Faceted Man, worse trouble with a Loving Limited Partner. A woman who would suit a Many-Faceted Man perfectly would probably rankle under the bounds of a Loving Traditional Man, no matter how intimate he was. Likewise, and surprisingly, a Loving Limited Partner woman would have trouble living not only with a Loving Traditional Man, but also with a Loving Many-Faceted Man. Oh, she might be able to manage it. He's a good and loving man. But his need for involvement would drive her crazy, and her need for no-questions-asked independence would probably drive him equally angry.

Is there a conclusion to all this information on different men? Yes, and I'll go on to it. Once again, it comes down to the fact that each kind of man tells us something about love, and each tells us something about ourselves.

23

Now That You Can Tell the Difference – Choosing

Now that you have read *Men Who Are Good For You and Men Who Are Bad* I hope it will help you.

The details I give don't cover everything. No book can. We aren't going to notice every aspect about a man. Nor will we always care to pay attention even when we do notice. Still, my hope is that with this book – whether we have just met a man, have been courting him for months or years, or hope to find the right man some day in the future – we will stop entering and staying in our relationships without examining them.

We can begin to decide what a man's character is like and determine where an involvement with him will lead. We can assess what we ourselves want and with whom we can best achieve it. We can determine when we are getting love but recognize that the man is *still* wrong for us. We can learn that although a union is less than wonderful, the man is still right.

We can begin to distinguish between a man who is good for us and a man who is bad.

And we learn there are alternatives.

I also hope we learn about ourselves. We begin to recognize those men who particularly beguile us, and why. We decipher what attracts certain men to us and how we contribute to our alliances with them. If we want a long union, yet constantly choose short affair men, we pinpoint our behavior. If we want security, we avoid disaster lovers. If we hunger for companionship, we say adieu to moguls. We turn our minds, our decisions, and our actions to what we want.

I don't mean to eliminate a woman's desire to experience any kind of man herself. Not at all. Even with prior knowledge of a man's assets and drawbacks, any one of us can still choose to discover any of the men or follow any of the paths on our own. But we no longer have to do so *unknowingly*. If we decide to dally with a man who has major liabilities, we can know what's in store. We can make relationships with similar kinds of men over and over again, a choice not a trap. If we want to fall with the same sort of man again, fine. But we don't have to.

We can also assure ourselves that we are not idiots. If we don't head for or stay with one of the "final" three most intimate men, or even the "middlingly" beneficial men, that's fine, too. Maybe we have another purpose in mind. Maybe we're just having a fling. Maybe we're the *only one* who knows what's best for us.

Part of the message of this book is that what is best for one woman is not necessarily best for another. Some of us thrive in less than great circumstances. Not all of us are devastated by less than terrific unions. Others of us don't want full blown partnerships. We want short ones, purely sexual ones, or we only want an occasional friend or escort. That even includes our involvements with the three most Intimate Men. Some of them are right for some of us and not for others.

We also don't have to "settle." A number of books recently have admonished us that good men aren't as thrilling as bad ones, and we should heed that. But we don't have to heed it, if that's what being with a "good" man means to us. We can go for the excitement. We just have to know what we are doing. We just have to know the men who are good for us and the men who are bad, and learn to tell the difference.

However, now that I've reassured you that it's all right to tarry with a man who isn't the best, I want to strongly urge you to take to heart the advice in this book and head for the men who are the best for women. The reasons should be clear in the chapters, but I'll add some others.

First, why abide with someone who will mistreat, abuse, or ignore you? Why put yourself through risks or domination? Even in a short or purely sexual affair, we can choose the best of men. Surely we should for a permanent union.

Secondly, there's a pitfall involved when we decide to dally with a man who is not the best. It's an insidious one we are all too often prey to. Men who are difficult, distant, controlling, or abusive draw us like magnets. We are highly attracted to them. We find it surprisingly easy to think we are "in love" with them, that they are "right" for us. We know the drawbacks and we want them anyway. But in truth we aren't "in love" with them. We're in love with the *challenge* of them. If they don't love us as much as we love them, there's winning involved in our attraction to them. If they don't behave toward us as we would like, we want and begin to seek how significant we are to them. We struggle to make them – just once – act towards us as we would like them to. We can't let go until we've gotten them to acknowledge how important we are. There's nothing, you see, like not having approval to make us vie to win it, and nothing like not having control to make us hope to get it.

Meanwhile, such men offer us something else. They give us constant crises. With them we always have the next trouble to muddle through and obstacle to overcome. We have an endless excuse for not getting on with our own lives.

I suggest that before any woman decides to abide by a man who is not the best sort, or is bad for her, she separate her love for him from her desire to win something from him. She should distinguish her care for him from merely desiring a response from him. If you are presently considering or staying with a man who isn't good for you, consider getting counseling. Make sure you really know where you fit in and what you are doing. You could seek the advice of friends or join a women's group. Being engaged in a perpetual struggle with a man who isn't good for you isn't love, it's obsession. It's true that even a healthy union takes work, but the work should be rewarding, not detracting. The union should build, not diminish. The work should be refreshing work. The union should be comfortable. It should nurture you and your development. It should be serene.

There is yet another pitfall. We women have a strong tendency to stay with a man in the hope he'll change. He will see the light. He'll make a transformation. Yet not only do some men never change, often they have no reason to. They see nothing wrong with themselves or the relationship. They may like things the way they are. Yet we stay and stay. To our detriment, we remain with the man, cozying the wish that he will come to his senses and see how wonderful we are. We also readily adopt a version of change that isn't change at all. In particular, women who are with a Woman Hater or Mr. Genius go into tailspins thinking they can change their man if only they alter this or that about themselves. Once they overcome his latest criticism, the man will miraculously start to love and care for them. But this rarely happens. For every correction a woman makes, the man finds something new that is wrong. When we adopt this version of change, we don't fix our unions. We reinforce them. We don't stop our victimization, we fall into it.

To remain in a relationship in the hope of change, a woman must first become aware of what truly constitutes change. We should also determine the potential for change in a particular union. We must know what part we play in the syndrome.

Yes, part of what this book says, trite as it may seem, is that you cannot get or expect everything. Instead, determine what you want and learn the consequences. If the price is too high in a certain alliance, don't make it. If you still want a union and can live with the drawbacks, dandy.

Don't forget that difficult men and unfortunate relationships aren't all your fault. You cannot fix everything. Men are often the cause of our bad unions. You are not solely or always to blame for the choices you've made. Often a woman doesn't know what she is getting into. Other times we are chosen, pursued, or pressed into relationships. And if you make a mistake, don't scold yourself. Recognize it and try again. Bear in mind though, that just because you recognize the signals of a bad partner or alliance, doesn't mean you won't make an error. I saw what sort of man I wed well before marrying him. I knew he was not the sort to nurture me or provide the most fruitful union. Yet I still fell into the union. I had two children. I now try better to coordinate my insights with my actions. I've been involved for several years with a wonderful, intimate man. It's because of him I know that things aren't always smooth, but always good.

It may seem after reading all about the various kinds of men that the only way to protect yourself from a disastrous relationship is to avoid them altogether. Good men are few and far between. They are hard to find and even when you find them, relationships with them take work. Maybe you cannot change a man you are attracted to or who is attracted to you. Maybe it's no use trying to change a man and union you're already in. Best to close yourself up in a shell and say no to all comers.

But I don't think so. If you're debating whether to attempt a union, or change one you're in, my advice is to do it.

Of course, there are men you should definitely leave or avoid. Don't stay with an Amoral Passion Monger or a Woman Hitter. Shun the psychologically damaging men, the Woman Haters, Idle Lords, Mr. Geniuses and Hustlers. But if you aren't sure what a man is like, or whether a union might improve, try.

Try until you are sure. Remember, some men only blossom after they are with a woman a while. They need the security of love to unfold. Some unions take a while to reach their glory. It's O.K. to take some time to see.

Don't judge too quickly unless the signs are very clear. For while loving sometimes costs, not loving costs a lot more.